WHAT READ

"Ali Botein-Furrevig is both courageous and empathetic as she provides a vivid portrait of Lakewood's Orthodox Jewish Community. In *Heart of the Stranger*, she crosses the boundary by demystifying stereotypes of the other and calling for compassion, inclusion, and respect. In our diverse and increasingly interdependent communities, state, nation, and world, it behooves all of us to use our voice and touch, as Dr. Botein has done, to reach out to the other. Ultimately, isn't the heart of the stranger the heart of a friend? Our heart?"

Saliba Sarsar, Ph.D.
Associate VP Monmouth University, NJ
Professor of Political Science and author of articles on Middle Eastern relations

"In her book, Dr. Botein-Furrevig describes a horrific event from the Holocaust when a Nazi soldier throws a three year old boy into an open grave containing the bodies of Jews who had been shot; he then fills in the grave with this little child still in it. The boy looks up and innocently asks, "Why are you putting sand in my eyes?" In a read that is sometimes joyous, sometimes painful, but always interesting, Dr. Botein-Furrevig removes the sands of misunderstanding and prejudice from the eyes of non-Jews and non-Orthodox Jews alike, and paints a clear and concise picture of the history, beliefs, rituals, and customs of Jewish Orthodoxy. As a Roman Catholic priest and teacher for 48 years, I believe that this book can do more to improve Christian-Jewish relations than much of what I have previously read."

Msgr. Joseph C. Ansaldi, Principal Emeritus
St. Joseph-by-the-Sea H.S., Episcopal Vicar Emeritus Staten Island, NY

"The author is well versed in Judaism...her conversations with different people in the community serve as a backdrop and lightens the tremendous scholarship evident in her work...a must read for the uninitiated!"

American Jewish Times

"With her trademark good humor and lively writing, Dr. Botein fights the slander of Lakewood's Orthodox community. The book is an easy to read primer on all aspects of Judaism and Orthodox practices as well as a well researched history of Lakewood."

Ami Magazine

HEART OF THE STRANGER
A Portrait of Lakewood's Orthodox Community

Ali Botein-Furrevig, Ph.D.

MARGATE, NEW JERSEY

Copyright © 2011 by Ali Botein-Furrevig

All rights reserved. No part of this book may be used or reproduced in any manner, electronic or mechanical, including photocopying, recording or by any information storage and retrieval system, or otherwise, without written permission from the publisher.

A portion of the royalties from the sales of this book will benefit Lakewood's Kosher *Meals on Wheels,* which, under the auspices of Lakewood Community Services, distributes meals to needy members of the town of Lakewood and its neighboring communities.

Published by:
    ComteQ Publishing
    A division of ComteQ Communications, LLC
    101 N. Washington Ave. • Suite 2B
    Margate, New Jersey 08402
    609-487-9000 • Fax 609-487-9099
    Email: publisher@ComteQpublishing.com
    Website: www.ComteQpublishing.com

ISBN 978-1-935232-22-3
Library of Congress Control Number: 2010929515

Cover design by Rob Huberman
Book design by Jackie Caplan & Rob Huberman

Printed in the United States of America
10 9 8 7 6 5 4 3 2 1

Written in loving memory of:

My mother, Ruth Peck Botein
*She is clothed with strength and splendor;
She looks to the future cheerfully.
Her mouth is full of wisdom,
Her tongue with kindly teaching.*
Proverbs 31:25-26

My father, Herman William Botein,
who taught me compassion and the joy of laughter.

My grandmother, "Bubbie" Sarah Leonson Botein
A very wise woman who loved a good story.

Dedicated to:
My husband, Allan Furrevig,
*who stands quietly in the background in good times,
but is always there in the front line cheering me on
when things seem to be falling apart.*

Acknowledgements

In loving gratitude to the members of the Orthodox community of Lakewood, NJ for opening their hearts and homes to me during my journey through their world.

I am particularly indebted to the following for their unconditional support and patience as I navigated unfamiliar roads, turning strangers into friends:

My mentor, colleague, and cherished friend, Dr. William Stefan Lavundi, who never fails to energize and inspire me with his insights and humor. His wisdom, strength and spirituality has guided me far beyond the parameters of this project.

Rabbi Baruch B. Yoffe, for his graciousness and good humor in reviewing the manuscript, and sharing his amazing knowledge and love of Lakewood's Jewish history. I am indeed blessed for having met him.

Reisa Sweet, who believed in and encouraged this project from the start. Without her friendship, selfless kindness, and willingness to travel with me on this journey, the idea would not have become a reality.

Heartfelt appreciation to the following for their unconditional support of, valuable time on and interest spent in, this project: Rabbi Aaron Kotler, Rabbi Pesach Levovitz, William Goldstein, Lynne Teitelbaum Bennardo, Ben Heinemann, and Pearl Herzog.

And to my treasured students:

As is said in the *Talmud*: *Much have I learned from my teachers; even more from my friends; but most of all from my students.*

Table of Contents

AUTHOR'S PREFACE...11

INTRODUCTION..13

CHAPTER ONE
    People of the Covenant: Texts and Contexts...23

CHAPTER TWO
    All in the Family: Faces of Judaism 35

CHAPTER THREE
    The New Ezekiel: 350 Years of American Jewry....................................45

CHAPTER FOUR
    Exit 91 S on the Garden State Parkway: Welcome to Lakewood, N.J....52

CHAPTER FIVE
    Beth Medrash Govoha and the *Frum* Community, or,
    What's with the Black Hats? 63

CHAPTER SIX
    A Crown of Prayers 75

CHAPTER SEVEN
    Living Torah: Acts of Kindness, Compassion, and Charity...................81

CHAPTER EIGHT
    The Classroom and Beyond: An Integrated Formula for
    Ethical Living 90

CHAPTER NINE
    Dating and Marriage, or, A Bird May Love a Fish, but
    Where Would They Live? 98

CHAPTER TEN
    To Everything There is a Season: Orthodox Life Cycles 105

CHAPTER ELEVEN
    Orthodox Judaism and the Belief in Afterlife 112

CHAPTER TWELVE
    Orthodox Women and the Mitzvot of *Shabbat*, Challah, and
    Spiritual Immersion 120

CHAPTER THIRTEEN
    Orthodox Women and the Dichotomy of Equality and Place 127

CHAPTER FOURTEEN
    The Orthodox Year in Celebration 135

CHAPTER FIFTEEN
    Yom HaShoah: Remembering the Unforgettable 153

CHAPTER SIXTEEN
    Chaim's Story: A Survivor Speaks 160

CHAPTER SEVENTEEN
    Living with Diversity: Lakewood's Ethnic and Racial Mosaic 169

CHAPTER EIGHTEEN
    And Speaking of Melting Pots, or, Eat Something Mamala 177

AFTERWORD 184

CHAI TIMES TWO PLUS FIVE
    A Teaching Guide for Tolerance and Understanding............................186

A BISSELL GLOSSARY 191

SOURCES CONSULTED AND RECOMMENDED READINGS 195

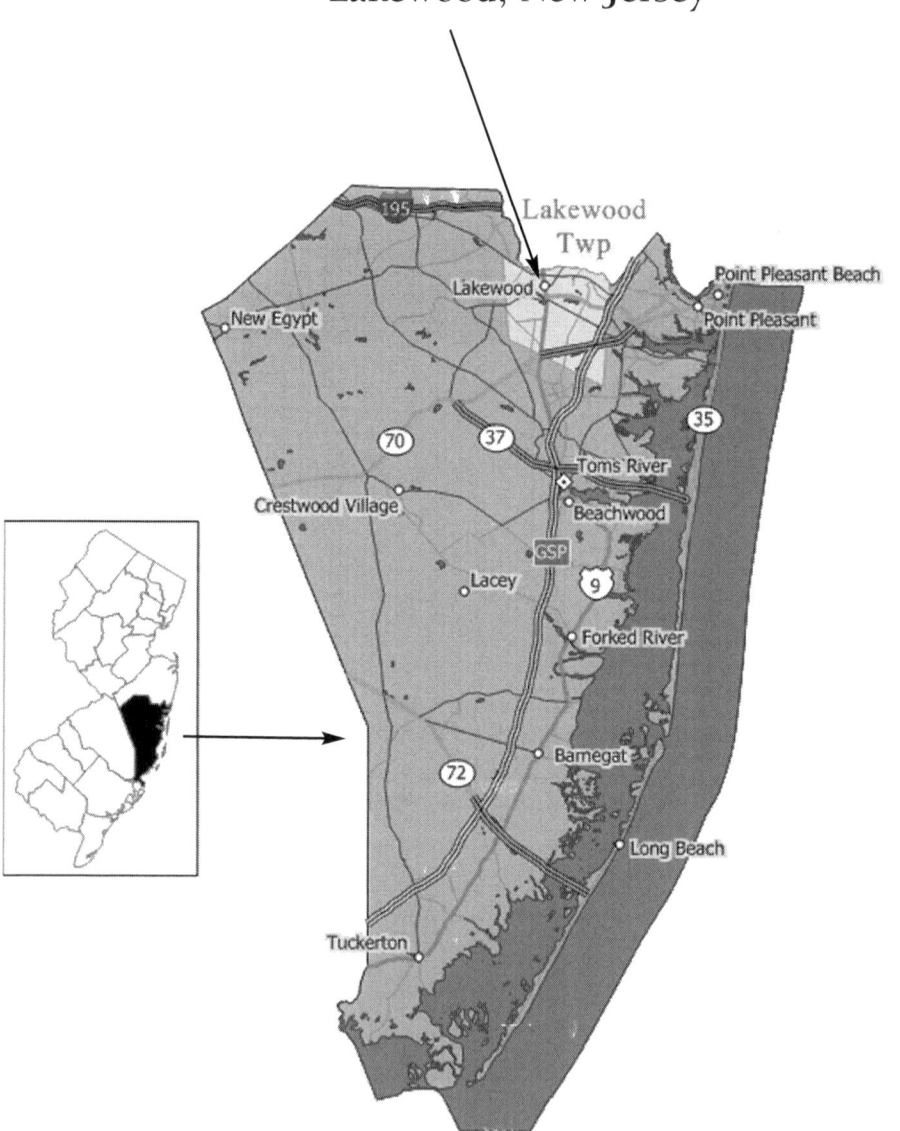

Author's Preface

When leaving sunny Lakewood,
I need no picture art to mind me of her beauties
They're folded in my heart
Her loveliness hath made me whole—
her peace hath filled my very soul.

From an advertisement brochure for the Laurel-in-the-Pines Hotel, c. 1900

A mere ten miles from coastal beaches of the Jersey Shore, and surrounded by lakes, rivers, over one million acres of pristine aromatic pinelands and 1200 acres of parks, Lakewood New Jersey is conveniently situated midway between New York City and Philadelphia. From its rural beginnings of small hamlets, dense pine forests and winding Indian trails, the periods that make up Lakewood's 200 plus year history are, at first blush, seemingly disparate and fragmented.

In the early 19th century, because of its proximity to waterways and its soil discovered to be rich in ironstone, Lakewood's earliest recorded settlements were built around lumber mills and bog iron and blast iron furnace businesses. The late 19th century through the early 20th century marked Lakewood's extraordinary "Golden Era," over four glorious decades that put the once sleepy mill town on the map as a posh winter resort with over 120 magnificent hotels and legendary entertainers catering to the rich and famous. Wealthy businessmen, statesmen, presidents, and literati including Rudyard Kipling and Mark Twain resided or vacationed in this idyllic winter paradise replete with tea parties, dances, sleigh rides, and ice skating on Lake Carasaljo. There were grand mansions belonging to prominent families such as the Rockefellers and Goulds. Architecturally stunning hotels hosted guests including the Astors, Arbuckles, and Vanderbilts.

But Lakewood did not only attract the affluent. Because of its warm climate and balsamic air, Lakewood was touted as the ideal health resort and sanitarium for those suffering from respiratory diseases. Concurrently, in the early 20th century, Lakewood, along with other rural towns in South Jersey, became known as The Egg Basket of America, attracting an influx of East European farmers who would eventually build self sustaining communities.

Embedded within, but analogous to, this larger historical framework is the chronicle of the Jews who settled in Lakewood from the late 19th through the mid twentieth centuries looking to build a new life where they could raise a family and practice their beliefs and customs, free from discrimination and persecution: Farmers fleeing pogroms in the Pale of Settlement; immigrant peddlers, craftsmen, and merchants anxious to provide services to the wealthy clientele of this tony resort town; Jews escaping the rise of Nazism before WW II and later, those who survived the Holocaust; scholars and families looking to join the growing Yeshivish community.

Lakewood: A jig saw puzzle with at once separate and interlocking pieces. When we place the pieces together, we gain an impressionist painting of how the each unique piece contributed to, and the processes that produced, Lakewood in the 21st century: Home to a world renowned yeshiva and the largest enclave (second only, perhaps, to Israel) of Orthodox Jews living an Old World, Torah- true lifestyle in a multi ethnic community and modern world. This book will, among other things, examine the phenomena of how these outwardly disconnected factors intertwine and have fostered the flowering of the Orthodox community in what has been referred to as "The Second Holiest City after Jerusalem." What becomes transparent in this analysis is the ease with which Lakewood, through all of its metamorphoses, seamlessly adapts to change and embraces its ever shifting landscape while maintaining a distinctive character and uniqueness. Much, one might observe, like the Jewish people themselves.

INTRODUCTION

And so the Torah tells us: "You shall not oppress the stranger; you know the heart of the stranger, for you were strangers in the land of Egypt."
Ex. 23:9

Many years ago, when a young student in my English Literature class noticed the small gold Star of David around my neck, he innocently remarked, "Wow, Dr. B., you don't look Jewish." His skewed perception of what all Jews look like was most likely formulated by his exposure to a handful of students at Ocean County College in Toms River from the nearby Lakewood Orthodox community who are easily distinguishable by their dress and appearance.

I could not have set up a more perfect segue into a piece of fiction we would be reading the following week: Eli the Fanatic, the wonderful short story by Philip Roth. Set in the fictional New York suburb of Woodenton in 1948, the tale focuses on the nouveau riche Jewish residents who moved there to escape and forget the old-world Jewishness of the inner city. Their peaceful existence and self-denial is shattered when a small contingent of religious Jews, led by a Rabbi in Hasidic dress, arrive with plans to open a yeshiva for children orphaned by the Holocaust. The new neighbors are not at all welcomed by their intolerant fellow Jews, who ironically consider themselves so liberal and inclusive, all the while looking for every legal loophole to keep the Orthodox out of their pristine world.

One of the villagers expresses his nightmare scenario: "It's going to be a hundred little kids with little *yarmulkes* chanting their Hebrew lessons on Coach House Road." Another wonders whether "the next thing they'll be after [is] our daughters."

To keep the Yeshiva out, they hire one of their neighbors, an attorney named Eli Peck, to "deal" with the intruders by invoking zoning ordinances to block the yeshiva. Peck, a modern Jew, is basically a good and sensitive man who has compassion for Rabbi Tzuref and for the children. But he also has feelings for his community. He has assimilated with his Protestant neighbors and just wishes that the Jewish man in the old black suit would do the same. He is trapped between two conflicting cultures. He confronts the Yeshiva rabbi with "conditions" for peaceful co-existence, one of which is that Yeshiva personnel be attired in more "Americanized and modern" clothing when they are out in public.

To this end he offers the "Greenie," who regularly walks through the main town to shop for the Yeshiva, a gift of his own business suit to replace the Orthodox garb that offends the good folks of Woodenton. Ultimately, Eli is transformed. He comes to respect the Hasids' religious way of life, even wearing their distinctive dress which the greenie had given to Eli as a reciprocal gift.

What Eli is ostensibly asking Leo Tzuref and his group to do is to conform to the customs of the community so as not to offend the other members: Shave his beard, cover up his tattooed concentration camp numbers, hide his *tsitsit*, and trade in his old black coat for a Brooks Brothers suit. Is this, I wonder, any different than the notion that had the Jews in Hitler's Germany been less conspicuous, perhaps the persecution and massacre may not have occurred? In Woodenton, the Gentiles have required that the Jews conform to traditional American practices in order to live peacefully, and the assimilated Jews, in turn, are requiring the yeshiva members to conform to standards of modern society, to "fit in," in order to peacefully co-exist in the mainstream Jewish community.

The story concludes with Eli's simultaneous spiritual rebirth and nervous breakdown in the hospital where his first son is being born. The hospital attendants humor Eli long enough to sedate him which "calmed his soul but did not touch it down where the blackness had reached." Torn apart by two cultures and by his own inner conflict of personal identity, Eli comes to realize the moral and spiritual hypocrisy and vacuous nature of his bigoted neighbors. In his epiphany, he also comes to respect and embrace the Hasidic way of life.

At the time in which Roth's story is set, and after one third of their people had perished in Eastern Europe, American Jews were acculturating into a Gentile world that included, for many, repressing and forgetting the Old World that they or their parents had striven to leave behind. Eli even tells Tzuref that it would have been better in pre-war Europe "for Jews and Gentiles to live beside each other in amity." If Woodenton's vision of sanity and what is normal translates to compromise and alienation from the spiritual and cultural past, then I would conclude that Eli is a fanatic and insane, and that he will never be "normal" again. Perhaps bigotry is ultimately just a short step away from madness.

Today, some sixty years after the publication of *Eli the Fanatic*, discrimination and non-acceptance of the Orthodox Jews by Jews and non-Jews alike are alive and well, still predicated on otherness and difference. When I mentioned to an acquaintance, Bekkah, that I was writing a book about Lakewood's Orthodox community, her shocked reaction was "What? G-d, Ali, you're not even Orthodox! Do you really think that they will even talk with you? They don't look at Jews like us as even being Jews."

"We're all Jews; we just practice our faith in different ways," I replied, somewhat miffed, and said a silent prayer that Bekkah had miraculously refrained from making some convoluted connection between my book proposal and my conservative ideologies. An otherwise informed and bright woman, Bekkah prides herself on her progressive and inclusive politics. She is active in community civic and religious organizations that seek to promote tolerance and understanding. Her mother was a Holocaust survivor. She fights for human rights and dignity around the globe, but yet there is an overt intolerance and disdain towards her own people, a people whose very history is forged in exile and powerlessness.

Indeed, to many outsiders, the Orthodox world is shrouded in mystery and myth. Though many non-Orthodox Jews view that world as idyllic, others deride the *frum* or *haredi* (both conversational terms for strictly observant Jews) as unhealthy, dirty, fanatical, dishonest, old-fashioned, and egregiously unfair to women. They also erroneously categorize all Orthodox Jews as Hasidic.

Admittedly, I suffered some initial angst, even reservations at times, about trespassing into the insulated world that is a mere fifteen minute drive from my home. How would I, born and raised in a family that straddled somewhere between Reform and Conservative Judaism and now married to a non-Jew, articulate to the Orthodox community why I had such passion about this project, and felt *bashert* – destined – to write their stories?

My purpose was and is heartfelt and twofold. It is my hope that learning about the strangers next door will lead to examining and demystifying stereotypes of Orthodox Jews in Lakewood and beyond, and to embracing compassion, tolerating difference, and fostering an appreciation of, and sensitivity to, "other." Certainly, history teaches us about the climate that fueled the genocide, ethnic violence, and abuses of human rights in pre-WWII Europe.

Today, the perpetuation of negative stereotypes and myths about Orthodox Jews has resulted in bigotry and hate, locally as well as globally. New Jersey is second only to California in bias crimes, with Ocean and Monmouth Counties weighing in highest on the state's list. The disturbing incidents in Lakewood alone, albeit isolated, are a matter of grave concern to residents and law enforcement agents. Perhaps, in some way, this book will replace irrational bias and hatred with the Jewish concept of *kavod ha-briyos* – respect for all beings.

This book was generated, too, by my intellectual curiosity and interest in Orthodox Judaism which could not be satisfied by my education or social milieu. Orthodoxy and the Lakewood community, neither of which I grew up in, is uniquely connected to my familial history, my sense of Jewish values and cultural pride, and what Shalom Aleichem's Tevye calls "tradition." I grew up in Far Rockaway, New York, a seaside community bordering Queens and Nassau County, nestled quietly between Jamaica Bay and the Atlantic Ocean. In the fifties and sixties, Far Rockaway was heavily populated by first and second generation Eastern European Jews, mostly reform and conservative, although there was an Orthodox enclave on Reeds Lane in its easternmost part. My parents were first generation Americans of Ashkenazi ancestry. My maternal grandmother, Nana Rose, an exquisite hazel-eyed Austrian widowed when my mother was 17, dutifully sent her three sons and daughter to Hebrew schools in Lawrence and Woodmere, two of the "Five Towns" on Long Island. Her inclination for practicing Judaism at home was limited to dietary laws and observing major holidays.

My paternal grandparents, on the other hand, were more embedded in religion. My *bubbie* (grandmother) was born in a small Russian shtetl, the child and grandchild of rebbes; my French-Russian *zeide* (grandfather) was the son of a Cantor who was part Sephardic. Both were brought up in traditional Orthodoxy and later inculcated in their children an appreciation of, and sense of responsibility for, perpetuating their rich cultural inheritance. Telling stories was one means of educating the children and grandchildren about familial and Jewish history. Of all the stories I heard as a second generation American, the ones I hold most dear and never tired of hearing again and again, were those told by Bubbie Sarah. Most likely romanticized and sacrizied, they told of the Old World shtetl, the trip across the ocean to the "Golden Land," and life on the crowded tenement streets of New York City's downtown ghetto.

Sarah Leonson and Herman Botein each came to America at the turn of the twentieth century, settling, along with other immigrants fleeing the pogroms and poverty of Eastern Europe, on New York's Lower East Side, a colorful subculture of peddlers, intellectuals, radicals, poets, and laborers. My grandmother was approximately fourteen years old. At seventeen, when asked out on a date by an "older and sophisticated gentleman" of 28 who had come to America from France, she pleaded with her mother for permission: "But mama, he's a doctor!" They married shortly thereafter and had two children.

In 1907, while my grandmother was pregnant with my father, her husband died, leaving her with a family to raise on her own. When my father was old enough to be left alone with his older brother and sister, Bubbie worked at the Henry Street Settlement, founded in 1893 by German immigrant Lillian Wald. Sickened by conditions in tenements and a local orphanage, Wald devoted her life to being a nurse, child advocate, and settlement house leader. The Henry Street Settlement provided much needed social and health services to children, families, and the poor on the Lower East Side. Wald also established camp, playground, and cultural programs for children and mobilized the first visiting nurse service.

In 1914, inspired by Wald's work and her own struggles as a young widow, Bubbie joined LC York Agency of Metropolitan Life Insurance Company, becoming part of a growing force of agents offering much needed life insurance to American workers. She eventually bypassed her male co-workers, working her way up to District Sales Manager. Not exactly what her Orthodox father and grandfather would have approved of, but then again, this was America, and she had three children to think of. An article in her company newsletter would later attribute her success to "having started from scratch...having a definite plan of action, and... her resourcefulness. Her work is so earnest and her success is contagious." Yes, quite a talker, my bubbie. She would target potential clients, fathers and husbands, and ask them, "So do you want to leave *your* family like I was left, with three children and no means of support?"

Bubbie was the family legend, a character. Mementos and photos of her later life adventures travelling the globe adorned her small Upper West Side apartment. There was Bubbie, attired in a tailored beige business suit and tan safari pith helmet complete with lace veil, sitting atop a camel in Egypt which she visited en route to Israel. There was Bubbie, five foot two, leaning on a shovel alongside a dozen or so tall suntanned *Kibbutzniks*. That was about the time Israel received its statehood, shortly before I was born, and she would constantly remind my parents that her only granddaughter's given name was 'not Jewish enough.'

"Like Alice in Wonderland?" she queried my parents. And so she opted, to the annoyance of my mother, to call me by my given Hebrew name, Aliya, which means "ascend." Today that word is applied to both the honor of being called up to the Torah, and going to live in Israel. Bubbie instilled in her children cultural pride and the importance of education and old fashioned hard work "so you should make something of yourself and be a *mensch*."

Her eldest son and quintessential *mensch,* my Uncle Bernie, epitomized her ethic. He was seven when his father died. Beginning with a paper route when he was ten, he worked his way through Morris High School, City College, and Brooklyn Law School. He spent years as a lawyer, Assistant District Attorney, a trial judge, was appointed to the New York State Supreme Court by Governor Lehman, and eventually became Chief Justice of the Appellate Division. As the years lined his face and turned his hair white, he truly was the "picture of a judge." He always said that he did not consider himself a "bleeding heart liberal," but he had an amazing capacity for what he called "disciplined indignation."

Frustrated by the dichotomy between the theory of the law being equal for rich and poor, strong and weak, and the reality of the administration and application of justice, he once said that the main difference between Divine justice and the human variety is that in the generality of cases, "G-d knows the truth, the whole truth, and nothing but the truth." He fought against political corruption and briefly considered his party's nomination for New York State Governor. He found time to author many benchmark judicial articles and several books including *Trial Judge, The Slum and Crime,* and a novel, *The Prosecutor.* When he died, he left not only a legacy of major court reform, but a legacy to his children, niece, nephews, and grandchildren founded on personal and social responsibility, making a difference, and never forgetting your roots.

It was through Bubbie's storytelling, holiday dinners, and reading that I learned about my roots. Sitting at our gray marbled Formica kitchen table after school, I was entranced by miraculous tales of biblical heroes. At more formal Seder and *Shabbat* dinners usually held at my Aunt Ethel and Uncle Sam's large Manhattan apartment overlooking Central Park, I would attentively listen to stories about the calamities and history of the Jews from their exodus from Egypt to their arrival in the land of Canaan. The Bible was a seemingly endless treasure of narratives and parables that taught us how to live our lives with kindness and compassion.

The word "holocaust" was not a part of the lexicon of my youth spent in the idyllic fifteen hundred apartment complex, Wavecrest Gardens, which looked south to the Ocean. I had seen some of my friends' grandparents and a local family physician with numbers tattooed on their arms, only to be told that it happened "a long time ago." In junior high school, we read *The Diary of Anne Frank*, focusing on it more as a coming of age story and the conflicts between young Anne, her mother, and her sister Margot. We knew that Anne died in a "concentration camp," but never could we have imagined the brutality and horrors of those death camps.

There was no Holocaust education curriculum then and, in retrospect, the history books in high school gleaned over a dictator named Hitler, with little mention of his systematic murder of six million Jews. It was not until I was out of college that I first read Elie Wiesel's powerful trilogy, *Night, Dawn,* and *Gates of the Forest*. Those works about human suffering, the importance of bearing witness, and communal and personal responsibility profoundly impacted me. I began to read more and more books about Jewish history and culture, as well as the fiction and poetry that came out of the ashes of the Holocaust.

Reading about Jewish history and, in particular, about the Holocaust, compels us to confront truths about human nature and evil. And about intolerance, indifference to human suffering, abuse of power, government propaganda and legalized racism. These stories are vastly different from those endearing ones I was so engaged with when I was young. These stories tell of the sickening human capacity for evil: Roundups, deportations, mass killings, and the unspeakable horrors of the concentration camps —all tragic lessons in individual and global culpability, and moral responsibility. But stories, like that of Chaim Melcer in Chapter Fifteen, can inspire us: Stories of the indestructibility of the human spirit; stories of the countless non-Jews who risked their own lives to rescue and hide their Jewish neighbors, and stories of the irrepressible dignity of a people.

Six years ago and long after my experience with *Eli the Fanatic*, I proposed that a Jewish and Holocaust literature course take its rightful place alongside our other ethnic literature classes. Today, as Ocean County's Jewish population, and interest in that population, continues to grow, Ocean County College has become a forerunner among two year colleges, offering popular classes in Jewish and Holocaust Literature, The History of Jewish Culture, and Modern Hebrew. My goal for the literature course back then was to tell the story of the Jewish people through their own words, in both fiction and non-fiction. The relation of history to literature is often described as a mirror of its soul, reflecting its strivings and desires, its failures and achievements. History without literature seems, to me, to be a dry chronicle of the life of a people. It is the stories and the literature which supply the glow of emotion, the warmth of passion, and intelligent meaning. Of course, this can be said of the literature of any historical people, but so much more to that of the Jews who despite having a nation of their own, had a distinct national character.

The stories that have been handed down to us, and the stories we tell show how the Jews have confronted repression, upheaval, dispersion, and identity, how the Jews have embraced modernity and absorbed foreign influences across the globe without losing who they are. The protean ability of the Jewish people to adapt to wildly different contexts has growing relevance to all of us as we enter an era of globalization and increasingly porous borders. Their stories offer us simple insights into social ethics and personal morality which transcend any one religion or any one people, professing tenets such as living a just and moral life, the uniqueness of human life, the meaning of good will and benevolence.

There is a precept that runs through the very fiber of Jewish life; the concept of *tikkun olam*, which originated in the early Rabbinic period. It is referred to in the *Mishna* in the phrase *mip'nei tikkun ha-lam*, meaning "for the sake of *tikkun* of the world." The term is used in the longer expression *l'takken olam b'malkhut*

Sh-ddai, translated as "to perfect the world under G-d's sovereignty." It is recited in the *Aleinu* prayer where we ask that G-d rectify the world, where we praise G-d for allowing the Jewish people to serve Him, and express the hope that the whole world will one day recognize G-d and abandon idolatry.

The term *tikkun olam*, Orthodox Jews believe, has been hijacked by modern assimilated Jews who speak of it as a biblical commandment and misuse it to justify a wide range of liberal activities advancing social justice, protecting the rights of other minority groups, and fixing the world at large.

It is certainly the Jewish ideal that each person, in partnership with G-d, is accountable for doing his or her part to make the world a better place. To my mind, that is the essence and tradition of Judaism and of humanism, and what must guide each of us in our personal, professional, and religious lives. G-d is not just an idea. He is a moral code. Religion is not merely a faith. It is a prescription for proper human behavior. *Tikkun olam* has to do with transforming ourselves, which ideally leads to transforming the world. And I can think of no better way to achieve a better world than by starting with ourselves; learning about the strangers next door and listening closely to the stories they tell. The Torah tells us: *You shall not oppress the stranger; you know the heart of the stranger, for you were strangers in the land of Egypt.* (Ex. 23:9).

This book is a combination of scholarship and commentary, as well as informal conversations, formal interviews, and guided survey questions with varied members of the Lakewood community. When requested, names* have been changed to respect privacy. It is my hope whether you are a Jew, Christian, or Muslim, that this book will lead to familiarity and tolerance through a more nuanced understanding of, and sensitivity to, our neighbors. That it will foster awareness and respect, and accommodate belief systems and ideologies in contradiction to your own. And that you will, indeed, see the heart of the stranger.

Author's Note: Upon request, and for reasons of privacy, some of the names mentioned in this book have been limited to the first name or have been completely changed, and which is noted by an asterisk (*).

Chapter One

The People of the Covenant: Texts and Contexts

Even after one has achieved the spirituality of an angel, one must still abide by the commandments like a simple Jew.
The Baal Shem Tov

Who are the Jews and what exactly constitutes Jewishness? Is it a cultural, national, ethnic, or religious affiliation, or a hybrid of one or more of those distinctions? The word "Jew" is derived from the Hebrew word *Yehudi*, which means someone from the land of Judea, the tribe of Judah. In contemporary times, the term has come to include anyone who is a part of the Children of Israel; that is to say, the descendents of Abraham, Isaac, and Jacob. Anyone, it is agreed, born to a Jewish mother, or who has converted to Judaism is a full-fledged member of the Jewish people. Some ask the question, "If a Jew doesn't believe in G-d or the Bible, eats pork, and does not observe Sabbath, is he or she still a Jew? The answer is "Of course." Those who observe and those who are non-observant of Torah laws may all consider themselves Jewish.

Dating back almost 4000 years, Judaism is one of the oldest religions, and the foundation of other Abrahamic religions including Christianity and Islam. Given their turbulent history of isolation, persecution and expulsion, beginning with their bondage in Egypt through the destruction of the First Temple by the Babylonians in 586 BCE, and the Second Temple by the Romans in 70 CE, how Jews have managed to survive and maintain their Jewishness is an enigma. Even in ancient times, Jews practiced customs that set them apart such as their belief in one G-d, keeping specific dietary laws, and not intermarrying with other groups. These differences caused suspicion and resentment among their non-Jewish neighbors.

The rise of Christianity, and the Jews' refusal to accept Jesus, who was born and raised a Jew, and to accept him as the messiah led to new conflicts, as many Christians placed blame for Christ's crucifixion on the Jewish people and subjected the Jews to widespread restrictive anti-Jewish laws that affected their social, economic, and political lives. Sadly, it was not until 1965 that this misconception about the Jewish responsibility for Jesus' crucifixion was reversed in Pope Paul VI's *Nostra Aetate* which rejects the false belief that Jews are to be held responsible for the death of Jesus: "…what happened in His passion cannot be charged against all the Jews, without distinction, then alive, nor against the Jews of today…."

It also affirms that the Covenant made by G-d with the Jewish people has never been broken and that the ongoing vitality of the Jewish religion is part of G-d's plan: "The Jews should not be presented as repudiated or cursed by G-d, as if such views followed from the Holy Scriptures…." It rejects prejudice, hatred, oppression, and persecution of Jews: "The church rejects every persecution against any person… and decries hatreds, persecutions, and manifestations of anti-Semitism directed against Jews at any time and by anyone…" (Hoffman and Sievers 236).

During the Middle Ages, Jews in Eastern and Western Europe lived a separate life from the non-Jewish population. They built tightly knit and religiously based communities, developing deep roots in the lands in which they lived. Despite times of relative peace and co-existence with their Christian and Moslem neighbors, the Crusades in the eleventh century led to widespread massacres and forced conversions of the Jews. In the following centuries, Jews became scapegoats responsible for whatever ailed society (real or imagined), were required to wear distinctive clothing, were excluded from guilds, had their properties confiscated, and were victims of expulsions. It was during this period, and because only Jews could become money lenders, that the anti-Jewish stereotype of the greedy Jew was born. During the fifteenth century in Spain and Portugal, despite the threat of imprisonments and torture, there were many Jews who refused to convert, vehemently holding on to their faith and ancestral heritage.

Anti-Semitism continued through the Reformation when Jews refused to convert – this time to Protestantism. Martin Luther issued proclamations that synagogues and books be burned and Jewish property be destroyed. It was not long after that that Jews would again be expelled from the land. It was during this time that Jews moved to lands that were by and large Catholic, and where they were segregated in gated districts called ghettos.

With the European Enlightenment during the eighteenth century, ghettos in Western Europe were eliminated and Jews finally began to finally enjoy equal rights; many even assimilated into the prevailing culture. Unfortunately yet predictably, this emancipation did not have a long shelf life as social and economic upheavals combined with a surge of nationalistic movements led to intolerance of differences within communities. And that did not bode well for Jews regardless of how much they had acculturated. That assimilation was not a panacea for anti-Semitic scapegoating was evidenced by several incidents. First, there was the very public media coverage of the so called Dreyfus Affair which ushered in a new century of virulent anti-Semitism. In France in 1894, a Jewish army officer named Alfred Dreyfus was falsely accused of espionage and not acquitted for two decades. Second, the political, social, and economic infrastructure in Czarist Russia stimulated anti-Jewish propaganda and pogroms.

Finally, there was the growing belief supported by "scientific" studies that Jews and other minorities were somehow genetically and physically inferior in terms of character and behaviors. These "theories" were exacerbated and further fueled by the publication of a fraudulent document in Russia, *Protocols of the Elders of Zion* which suggested that Jews were plotting world domination; a belief, it is safe to say, that is alive and well in the 21st century. It was during the period between 1880 and 1920 that over two million Jews from Eastern Europe fled the pogroms and shtetls for a better life in the Golden Land of America, the new Ezekiel, where they would have religious freedom and economic opportunity.

In the second decade of the twentieth century, Anti-Semitic sentiments resurged in Germany. It was within the context of their defeat in WWI coupled with unbridled inflation, high unemployment, fear and insecurity that gave rise to contempt for the Jews and for the rise to power of the Nazi Party and Adolph Hitler. Hitler immediately imposed anti-Semitic policies and used racial propaganda to justify the supremacy of the Aryan race and the "Final Solution" to the Jewish question. Heinrich Heine had prophesized "Where they have burned books, they will end in burned human beings." And indeed The Holocaust – the systematic genocide of six million Jews – began with acts of violence and book burning. It continued with

Kristallnacht, The Night of Broken Glass, on November 9, 1938, a government sponsored pogrom during which the Nazis shattered the windows of more than one thousand synagogues, desecrating Torah scrolls and burning prayer books. They destroyed hospitals, cemeteries, businesses, and homes. Ninety one Jews were murdered and 30,000 were arrested and sent to concentration camps. *Kristallnacht* marked a turning point in Hitler's campaign against the Jews, marking the beginning of the horror of World War II when men, women, and children would be deported in cattle cars to concentration and death camps where they would die in either gas chambers or from starvation, beatings, and inhumane conditions.

Prior to 1933, Jews had lived in Europe for over 2000 years. Before the Nazis came to power, there were approximately eleven million Jews in Europe. By 1945, six million were dead, one and a half million of whom were children. Today it is estimated that there are almost thirteen million Jews worldwide with roughly five million living in the U.S. and another five million in Israel. Though Jews are for the most part a unified group, there are different denominations or branches with varying, sometimes conflicting, understandings of what principles a Jew should embrace, how one should live as a Jew, and the degree to which a Jew adheres to the teachings of Torah.

But all Jews, despite their affiliation and levels of commitment, accept some fundamental religious tenets, the most important being the belief in a single, omniscient, and omnipotent G-d. According to all Jewish thought, G-d established the universe and established a covenant with the Jewish people, revealing his laws and commandments to them through Moses. What inextricably binds Jews? What has given the Jewish people their resilience, power of survival, and ability to adapt to radically new conditions without losing their identity? The answer to those questions is the two sacred texts of Judaism: The Hebrew Bible and the Talmud. The Hebrew Bible is also called Written Law or Written Torah since it is believed that these are the words of G-d as given to Moses (and written down) at Mt. Sinai. The Talmud is referred to Oral Law or Oral Torah because it includes the commentaries, expositions, and rabbinic explanations of points that were passed down orally from generation to generation beginning with Moses.

The word Torah can be confusing to non-Jews and even non-Orthodox Jews. There are actually two meanings. It is used as the inclusive term for the entire corpus of Jewish law and learning – both Written Law and Oral

Law, as well as all the commentaries produced during the subsequent centuries to the present day. Torah also refers to the first five books of the Bible called The Laws of Moses, or Pentateuch, or *Humash*. As will be further elaborated on in the following section, *Humash* begins with Creation and ends with the death of Moses as the Israelites are poised to cross the Jordon River into the Promised Land.

The Hebrew Bible

The Torah or Hebrew Bible is also called *Tanakh*, the Hebrew acronym for its three sections: The Laws of Moses, Prophets, and Writings. As mentioned earlier, the Laws of Moses (or Torah or *Humash*) consists of Genesis, Exodus, Leviticus, Numbers, and Deuteronomy. It starts with the creation of the world and the history of the patriarchs beginning with Abraham. It continues through the giving of Torah at Sinai until Moses' death before the Children of Israel enter the land of Canaan. Orthodox Jews believe that the words of *Humash* are the words of G-d as revealed to Moses on Mount Sinai 3000 years ago, a sacred anthology of 613 commandments which all Jews accept as the primary text of Judaism, and the prescription for proper human behavior and modes of religious, social, and ethical conduct.

According to Jewish tradition, in 1250 BCE, after escaping Egyptian bondage, Moses and his people, the children of Israel, wandered through the desert, finally camping at the base of Mount Sinai. As related in the Book of Exodus, G-d instructs Moses: *Come up to me on the mountain and I will give thee tablets of stone, and the law and the commandments which I have written that thou may teach them.* And then, *amidst thunder and lightning, a quaking mountain is engulfed by fire and clouds of smoke,* followed by the shrill and familiar sound of the *shofar* (ram's horn), G-d appears atop Mt. Sinai and reveals the Ten Commandments directly inscribed by Him on two stone tablets. He also gives Moses oral instructions on how to interpret the commandments which covered everything from dietary laws, prayer, marriage, and family purity to criminal laws and holiday observance. At the time, it was forbidden to record the oral words of G-d and, so as the Israelites traveled for 39 years through the desert to the land of Canaan, Moses teaches his people G-d's detailed explanations of Torah, His binding words to the Jewish people. He also writes thirteen scrolls, one for each of the twelve tribes of Israel and one that is placed in the Ark of the Covenant as a symbol of G-d's presence. When Moses and his people reach the Promised Land, Moses names Joshua as his successor to preserve the oral instructions for how to lead a just and righteous life.

The Torah is read in the synagogue from parchment scrolls which are always treated with reverence from the time it is written to its use in synagogue services. The scrolls have always been written by hand by a skilled scribe, or *sofer*. A *sofer* must be a religious Jew learned in the laws of Torah, *tefillin* (leather boxes worn by men which contain a piece of parchment with a Torah verse), and *mezuzot* (plural for *mezuzah*, a decorative case or tube containing a piece of parchment with a Torah verse and which is attached to a door frame. The parchment upon which the scroll is written also has to come from a kosher animal. When the scroll is completed, it is checked several times before it is rolled onto handles and can be used in a prayer service. When the person from the synagogue reads from the Torah, he points to the words with a *yad*, or hand pointer, so that the scroll is not damaged.

The second section of the Hebrew Bible is Prophets, or *Nevi'im*, a two part record of the lives and times of the Prophets and their various prophesies. The Early Prophets include Joshua, Judges, and Samuel and traces the history of Israel from the conquering of Canaan and the period of the Judges through the establishment of the rule of the kings in the time of Saul and David. The Book of Kings is about the two Jewish kingdoms of Judah and Israel until Jerusalem's downfall in 586 BCE. The Latter Prophets are a collection of stories from the end of the Kingdoms of Judah and Israel until the early Second Temple period, the eighth to fifth centuries BCE.

The third section of the Hebrew Bible is Writings, or *Ketuvin*. This literature includes religious poetry (Psalms and Lamentations), love poetry (Song of Songs), wisdom literature (Proverbs, Book of Job, and Ecclesiastes) and finally, the historical books (Ruth, Chronicles, Esther, Ezra, Nehemiah, and Daniel).

The Talmud

The second sacred text of Judaism is The Talmud. For seven centuries, the Oral Laws given to Moses on Mount Sinai were transmitted orally down through the generations. When it became clear that the Oral Torah was in danger of being lost and forgotten because of historical factors such as the destruction of the Second Temple and that the Jewish people did not have a homeland, the sages decided to lift the ban forbidding the Oral Torah to be written down. That monumental task was undertaken by the Rabbinical scholar, Judah ha-Nasi, who in 200 C.E. organized the scattered material into six tractates, or laws, dealing with holidays and agriculture. The *Mishna*, as that collection of Jewish laws is called, supplied judges and teachers of religion with a guide to Jewish law; today, *Mishna* remains as Judah ha-Nasi and his fellow scholars arranged it.

Jewish scholars continued to add material until the late fifteenth century. Despite their profound teachings, the Oral Laws were recorded in a rather cryptic fashion and were difficult to decipher; they lacked not only punctuation and vowels, but they also did not provide specific instructions and illustrations as to how to follow those 613 commandments. Jewish law, called *Halakhah* and literally translated as "the path one walks," was intended to be flexible so that its tenets could be debated among scholars to prevent it from becoming obsolete or irrelevant. Often times, the meaning of the words required further explanation by a rabbinical scholar. For example, In Exodus, it says that "For six days, works shall be done, and on the seventh day, it is the Holy Sabbath." So what exactly is work? Opening up your emails? Moving the couch? How about a rabbi doing his job of giving sermons on the Sabbath?

Around 400 CE, the rabbis would engage in informal discourse about passages in the *Mishna*. Those discussions became the *Gemara*, which together with *Mishna*, make up The Talmud. One of the most renowned Biblical and Talmudic scholars was Rabbi Solomon Isaac. Commonly known as Rashi, he was born in Troyes France in 1040, but later moved to Worms, Germany. Rashi is particularly remembered for his phrase by phrase explication of Oral law. Rashi had three daughters, all learned in their own right and well versed in Talmud; it is believed that they contributed to his vast compendium of work. They also experienced the spiritual satisfaction of observing some of the rituals usually performed by men, and this was permitted by their father, as long as the relevant blessing was not recited. A blessing suitable for women was later composed by Rashi's grandson, Rabbeinu Tam, one of a number of distinguished scholars descended from him.

Handwritten copies of the Talmud began to appear in the sixth century CE. Type had yet to be invented and the 2.5 million words of the Talmud had to be copied, letter by letter, into a perfect text by scribes who were both artists and scholars. The first printed Talmud published in Spain in 1508 CE was the model that set up the standard for how the pages of the Talmud look today. Today, a printed copy of the Talmud contains a passage of the *Mishna* followed by *Gemara*, long and often disorganized debates and deliberations on the implications and conclusions derived from *Mishna*. On the top, bottom, and sides of each page are many commentaries written by later sages. It is indeed, as someone described Talmud, "a conversation between generations."

Here is a brief example of a Rashi commentary; the selection is from Exodus 21:

You shall not wrong a stranger or oppress him, for you were strangers in the land of Egypt.

This is Rashi's commentary:

"You shall not wrong" means 'do not vex him with words' (referring to the fact that he is a stranger); contrarier in Old French. "Nor oppress him" – by robbing him of money. "For you were strangers" – if you vex him he can also vex you by saying "You also descend from strangers." Do not reproach your fellow man with a fault which is also yours. Wherever "stranger" occurs in scripture it signifies a person who was not born in that land (where he is living) but has come from another country to sojourn there. (JPS Torah Commentary)

For Orthodox Jews, the *mitzvah* (commandment) regarding the study of the Torah and Talmud involves much more than learning ancient Jewish history and following prescriptive beliefs. Through historical narratives, commentaries, and parables, The Torah and Talmud provide a moral blueprint for how to live a good life; not only are there laws governing an individual's relationship with G-d, but there are also laws about how to treat other people. Several fundamental values addressed in the Torah are the sanctity of life, justice and equality, kindness and generosity, the value of education, and social responsibility.

One of the most famous aphorisms of the great Babylonian scholar, Hillel (30BCE-10CE) is his response to a pagan who said he would become a Jew if he could be taught the Torah while standing on one foot. Hillel's famous reply was "What is hateful to you, do not unto your neighbor: this is the entire Torah. All the rest is commentary –go and study it."

The greatest factor that contributes to the longevity of the Torah is the effort of the great Jewish intellectuals to prevent it from becoming obsolete. In a perpetual search for new meaning, the Torah –every sentence, every word, every letter – was constantly analyzed and probed. Was there a hidden meaning in the text? The result was that the Torah became a "Living Torah" as it's often been called.

Serving G-d and being His instrument on earth are what defines the Orthodox life, and the values observant Jews embrace are as relevant today as they were in biblical times. Who, after all, can dispute the wisdom and relevance of these ageless Talmudic aphorisms?

> On Kindness:
> *Deeds of kindness are equal to all the commandments.*
>
> On the Essence of Religion:
> *The Torah begins and ends with acts of kindness.*
>
> On Charity:
> *Giving tzedakah is greater than all the sacrifices in the world.*
>
> On Hospitality:
> *Let the doors of your home be wide open, and may the needy be often in your home.*
>
> On Charity with Kindness:
> *Whoever gives a coin to the needy is blessed with 6 blessings; but one who comforts the needy with kindness is blessed with 12 blessings.*
>
> On Finding a Good Heart:
> *What is the right path that one should cling to? A good heart for heaven, and a good heart for humans.*
>
> On Jewish Values:
> *The Jewish people are recognized by three qualities: they are compassionate, they are modest, and they perform acts of loving kindness.*
>
> On Kindness to Animals:
> *One must not put food in one's mouth until the animals have been fed.*
>
> On Moderation:
> *Always let your left hand push away, and your right hand pull toward you.*
>
> On Enemies:
> *Who is the greatest of all heroes? One who turns an enemy into a friend.*
>
> On Personal Growth:
> *Improve yourself, and only afterwards try to improve others.*

On the Danger of Projection:
A fault that is in you, be careful not to ascribe to another.

On Private Morality:
Whatever behavior the sages forbade because of "appearance sake," is also forbidden in complete privacy.

On Personal Values:
Your own conduct will command respect for you.

Living in the Now:
Worry yourself and not about tomorrow lest there be no tomorrow. And it turns out that you are worried about a world that is not yours.

On Work:
Greater is one who enjoys physical labor, than one who is pious and idle.

On Marriage:
To acquire land make haste. To pick a mate, deliberate slowly.

On Influence of Family:
Whatever youth say in the marketplace comes from the home.

On Love:
All love that is dependent on a motive, when the motive is gone, the love is gone. Love that is not dependent on a motive will endure forever.

On Our Children:
The world exists only because of the breath of young students at school.

On Greed:
When you grasp too much you lose it all. When you grasp a small portion, you win it all.

The Talmud is not the only work generated during this period. A genre of literature known as *midrash*, meaning to seek or find, were parables or commentaries on specific Biblical passages. *Midrashim* fills in the gaps by giving the reader or listener a sense of the motivations and personalities of biblical characters as well as a moral lesson to be gleaned. There is a *midrash*, for example, about how Abram discovered monotheism and rejected his father's idolatry. He smashes all of his father's idols except the big one and blames the whole mess on the big one in order to prove to his father that the idols really did not have any power. Within *Midrash* are those stories having to do with *Halakhah* or legal rulings and *Aggadah,* other topics such as ethics, medical counsel, and the immortality of the soul.

When asked what force has preserved the courage and vitality of the Jews amidst continual persecution, any Orthodox Jew, any observant Jew for that matter, will answer that it was loyalty to Torah. Maimonides, or Rabbi Moses ben Maimon, also known as Rambam (1135-1204), lived all his life in Islamic society – Spain, Morocco, and Egypt. He was not only one of the most preeminent Torah scholars; he was also a physician and philosopher. Among his writings and commentaries on *Mishnah*, is what he refers to as the *Shloshah-Asar Ikkarim,* the Thirteen Articles of Faith, compiled from Judaism's 613 commandments found in the Torah:

> Belief in the existence of the Creator, be He Blessed, who is perfect in every manner of existence and is the Primary Cause of all that exists.
>
> The belief in G-d's absolute and unparalleled unity.
>
> The belief in G-d's noncorporeality, nor that He will be affected by any physical occurrences, such as movement, or rest, or dwelling.
>
> The belief in G-d's eternity.
>
> The imperative to worship Him exclusively and no foreign false gods.
>
> The belief that G-d communicates with man through prophecy.
>
> The belief that the prophecy of Moses our teacher has priority.
>
> The belief in the divine origin of the Torah.
>
> The belief in the immutability of the Torah.
>
> The belief in divine omniscience and providence.
>
> The belief in divine reward and retribution.
>
> The belief in the arrival of the Messiah and the messianic era.
>
> The belief in the resurrection of the dead.

The Torah (and, by extension, Talmud) is the key to Jewish survival, the most important work of Jewish civilization, with the expression "The Sea of Talmud" aptly describing the vast conversation between different sages that began some 1500 years ago.

Maimonides offers this nautical analogy:

> *We should lay hold of the cord of the law and not loosen our hand from it for we who are living in captivity are like one who is drowning. We*

are almost totally immersed…The seas of captivity surround us and we are submerged in their depths…the waters overwhelm us but the cord of the ordinances of G-d and His law is suspended from the heavens to earth and he who lays hold of it has hope, for in the laying hold of this cord, the heart is strengthened, and is relieved from the fear of sinking into the pit. And he who loosens his hand from the cord has no union with G-d and G-d allows the abundant waters to prevail over him so none is saved from toils of captivity except by occupying himself with Torah, by obeying the precepts, cleaving to it and meditating on it continually. (Heschel)

Chapter Two

All in the Family: Faces of Judaism

The gravest sin for a Jew is to forget—or not to know— what he represents.

Abraham Joshua Heschel

Jews are a people of diverse customs and beliefs, a people not of one land, one time or place, or one language. Across the globe, across centuries, connected by one religion, they are indeed the poster children for diversity and the multicultural paradigm.

Prior to the eighteenth century, and except for regional differences resulting from the dispersal of Jews that existed between the Ashkenazi (Eastern European) and Sephardic (Spanish and Portuguese) Jews, there were historically no different strains of Judaism. What is now referred to as "Orthodox" was, in fact, classical rabbinic Judaism that had evolved over 2000 years of exile and diaspora. Contemporary Jewish religious life is largely defined by the denominational beliefs and practices of the three major religious groupings – Orthodox, Conservative, and Reform – and, to a far lesser extent, by the modern Reconstruction Movement. These movements themselves are not monolithic; each is characterized by a substantial variety of intra-denominational differences in doctrine and practice. What they stand for and how they differ from one another – and from other groupings within their own denomination – is determined primarily by their position on the nature of divine revelation, religious authority, and attitudes to the contemporary situation. These positions determine their relationships to one another and to the outside world.

Orthodox Judaism

The beliefs and customs of what is to referred to as Orthodox Judaism have been observed since the time of Moses. The term applies to those Jews who stress the importance of the preservation of old Jewish traditions and strict observance as dictated in the sacred texts of Judaism, and who view themselves as the true heirs to normative Judaism. At the center of Orthodox Jewish teaching is the conviction that G-d revealed the entire Torah to Moses at Sinai, and that the Torah is unchanging. Although various Orthodox groups articulate the manner of revelation differently – some maintaining that the contents were dictated verbally to Moses, and others maintaining that the method of inspiration cannot be comprehended or articulated within the context of normal human experience – all are united in the conviction that what is recorded in the Torah is of exclusively Divine origin. In the Orthodox view, G-d revealed not only the written Torah, but also the oral interpretation of its contents. The former is incomprehensible without the latter. As the Divine logos, all knowledge and truth is imminent in the Written Torah. Orthodox Jews are committed to keeping the tradition of Judaism as practiced during the 2000 years of Exile. Their central belief is that because the Torah, including Written Law and the Talmud, was given to Moses directly by G-d on Mount Sinai, that those laws are Divine and binding, representing the will of G-d, and can never be altered.

Hasidic Judaism

Hasidic Judaism began as a revivalist movement started in Eastern Europe at the time of the Enlightenment by the charismatic teacher and healer Israel ben Eliezer (1700-1760), also known as Besht, or the Baal Shem Tov, which means Master of the Good Name. The Besht believed that there was no place free of G-d's presence. Directed to both the poor oppressed Jews and the elite Jews of eighteenth century Europe, The Besht demanded that even the simplest Jew achieve *devekut* – uninterrupted communion with G-d. To achieve this communion, he placed joyous prayer, singing, dancing, storytelling, and the sanctification of daily life, on the same level as Talmudic scholarship, thus leading European Jewry away from Rabbi centered Judaism and toward mysticism. At the heart of Hasidic life practice was a rebbe or *tzadik*, which is Hebrew for "righteous man." The *tzadik* became the means by which the uneducated masses could lead more Jewish lives and who helped his followers attain a closer relationship with

G-d. The *tzadik* would pray on behalf of his followers and advise them on all matters. Each spiritual leader had his own court or dynasty that was carried on by sons or close family members. After the Besht's death, his cause was carried on by his followers including Dov Ber, the *Maggid of Meseritch,* who also gathered many disciples who would eventually become revered Hasidic masters in their own right throughout Poland, Russia, and Lithuania. By the beginning of the nineteenth century, over half of the Jewish population in Eastern Europe embraced the Hasidic movement.

Where there is a movement, so goes a counter movement. There were those, called *Mitnagdim,* led by Rabbi Elijah, the Gaon of Vilna in the late eighteenth century, who believed that the traditional way of life was unchangeable. They vehemently opposed Hasidism, arguing that not only was it not scholarly, but that its very core – the belief in miracle workers, and that G-d permeates all physical objects in nature – was heretical. Despite this vocal opposition, Hasidic Judaism flourished. As a social movement, Hasidism sparked a radical reorganization of the Jewish community into a series of collectives centered around charismatic spiritual leaders and, over time, broke up into different groups headed by the different *tzadikim.*

Hasidism has become synonymous with the practice of Kabbalah, meaning, among other things, "tradition" or "that which is received" and which, in our time, has sadly become a farce, a trendy and dangerous fad associated with red string and the superstition and spiritual journeys of celebrities, rather than genuine spiritual elevation. Kabbalah dates back to the Biblical period when Moses received the secret coded meanings from G-d on the summit of Mount Sinai some 3,000 years ago. Passed down orally through generations, it emerged in a body of European medieval Jewish literature, specifically Moses de Leon's text, *The Zohar* (translated as "Spiritual Shining"), which defines Kabbalah as an alternative theological and mystical view of the world based on hidden meanings in Torah.

For the sake of brevity and admittedly a gross simplification of an ancient complex and esoteric tradition, Kabbalah can be explained in terms of ten creative forces called the *sefirot* which are the ten attributes by which G-d created the universe. Mastery of the *sefirot* is a life task and a way to harness Divine energy, achieve profound truths, and connect with G-d. It is believed that one must be at least forty years of age to even begin that daunting task. True Kabbalah, today, is studied as it was ages ago, by select Hasidic and *Yeshivish* scholars as an integral part of a deeply rooted religious practice.

Hasidic Judaism eventually found its way to Western Europe, and then to America in the mass wave of emigration during the early 1900s. In the 1940s, Hasidic survivors of the Nazi Holocaust arrived in America with a dream significantly different from the many Jews who preceded and followed them. Rather than wanting to assimilate into and achieve material success in the New World, they merely wanted to restore their communities from the Old World. New Orthodox Jewish centers were established in the United States, Europe, and Israel and the traditions of the Hasidim and the *Mitnagdim* were revived, continuing to develop along the old lines. Throughout the world today, Hasidism remains a vital movement. The various sects are still organized around a spiritual leader or *rebbe*, viewed as more enlightened than the other Jews, and consulted by his followers about all major life choices and decisions. The *rebbe* rules the court and the soul. There is also a chief rabbi in the community, a scholar educated in Talmudic law and ordained as a rabbi. He is primarily responsible for addressing the congregation, officiating at legal ceremonies, and is considered the expert on ritual law.

There are approximately 25-30 various courts or dynasties, each named after the place of its founding leader: Lubavitch, Satmar, and Bobov are the largest. Other sects include Belzer, Breslov, and Ger. Despite their overlapping affinities, there nonetheless still exist factions and contentions that began in the shtetls of Eastern Europe. In Europe the various Hasidic courts were buffered by geography, but this is not the case in America where Brooklyn, NY became the Orthodox heartland with three separate enclaves, each with its own network of congregations, social service institutions, and yeshivas.

One of the most influential Hasidic courts, Satmar, was founded by Romanian born Rabbi Joel Teitelbaum. Considered the most fundamentalist sect of Hasidism, Satmar takes its name from the town of Satu Mare, Romania. The core phenomena of the Satmar is their deep concern that any change from tradition would be dangerous to the continuity of the sect, and any change in the status and position of women would be the most perilous. Whereas the Lubavitch look to spreading *Yiddishkeit* by interacting with and educating secular Jews, the Satmar sect looks to the past and maintains a distance between believers and non-believers. While they recognize the land of Israel as sacred, Satmar Hasidim do not recognize the validity of Israel as a Jewish state, believing that it is not through secular leaders, but through the coming of the *Mashiach*, or Messiah, that Jews will ultimately be led back to their homeland. When its founder died in 1979, his nephew, Rabbi Moses Teitlebaum, became the spiritual leader and Grand Rebbe. Born in Sighet, Teitelbaum escaped Nazi persecution, and came to the United States in 1946. Despite concern in the sixties that the community would not survive because of an unstable economic structure, today Satmar has over 120,000 followers worldwide, one of the largest congregations being in Brooklyn's Williamsburg and Boro Park sections, as well as in Monsey and Kiryas Joel in New York.

Nearby Boro Park in Brooklyn is home to, among others, Bobov, Belz, Ger, Satmar, and Skver, as well as a minority of non-Hasidic Jews, often referred to as *Litvish* or *Yeshivish*. The Bobov dynasty of Hasidic Judaism is named after the shtetl of Bobvo in Western Galicia. The first Grand Bobover Rebbe was Rabbi Chaim Halberstam (1797-1876), followed by Rabbi Shlomo Halberstam (1847-1905), Rabbi Ben Zion Halberstam (1874-1941), Rabbi Shlomo Halberstam (1907-2000), and Rabbi Naftali Halberstam (1931-2005). Rabbi Ben Zion Aryeh Leibish Halberstam (1955-) serves as the current leader of the Bobov sect. There are currently an estimated 50,000 Bobover Hasidim living in Borough Park, but there are also Bobover communities in Montreal, Toronto, Miami, London, Antwerp, and a number of cities in Israel.

The Bobover sect is known for its music; in the early 1960's, Velvel Pasternak's Chassidic Chorale released the two volume album *Songs of the Bobover Chasidim*, a wonderful collection of *niggunim*, or tunes without words. Another Bobover tradition is the Purim*shpiel*, an elaborate play which originated in pre-war tradition of Eastern European communities and which was a precursor to Yiddish theatre in America. The Bobovers were the first sect to resume the traditional Purim*shpiel* which incorporates slapstick, satire, and homily and is regularly staged at The Bobover Beis Midrash in Borough Park.

A short subway ride away from Boro Park and Williamsburg is Crown Heights, which houses the renowned World Lubavitch Center at 770 Eastern Parkway. The Hasidic Lubavitcher movement is known as *Chabad*, an acronym for the Hebrew words for wisdom, understanding, and knowledge. Today the terms "Chabad" and "Lubavitch" mean the same. The

Lubavitcher philosophy which has existed for over 200 years, was founded by Shneur Zalman of Ladi (1745-1813) based on the teachings of Dov Baer, the Maggid of Meshirech, and then passed down through his dynasty which would later settle in Lubavitch, Russia.

In the 1940s, the sixth Lubavitcher Rebbe, Joseph Isaac Schneerson arrived in America and made Crown Heights the center of Lubavitch Hasidism, which prompted an influx of thousands of Russian Hasidic refugees to that Brooklyn neighborhood. By the time of his passing in 1950, he had laid the infrastructure and foundation for the global renaissance of Jewry. His successor, Rebbe Menachem M. Schneerson (1902-1994) or "the Rebbe" as he is still reverently referred to, became seventh in the dynastic lineage, and turned Lubavitch into a worldwide outreach program. Renowned as a brilliant scholar and prophetic visionary, The Rebbe was a leader who led by example and recognized the wealth of potential in each individual.

For Chabad, thinking about G-d comes before true religious emotion – if one reverses the process, this distorts the worship. Chabad believes that deep in the recesses of the individual Jew is an authentic Divine spark and when a person succeeds in completely bypassing his ego, that Divine spark is awakened. Chabad's emphasis is on outreach education, on making non-observant or non-affiliated Jews more observant and more aware of their Jewish heritage. To this end, the Chabad organization sends out emissaries, or *shlichim*, young Orthodox families, into communities around the world to teach its religious philosophy about the importance and unique mission of each individual. Today, Chabad has cable and satellite broadcasts, Chabad House centers in colleges and universities, as well as Chabad centers in hundreds of communities in over fifty countries.

Ironically, the Russian word Lubavitch, which refers to the town in White Russia, also translates into "city of brotherly love" which conveys the essence of responsibility and love engendered by the Chabad philosophy toward each and every Jew. To date, there remains infighting among the Lubavitch about the true heir to Schneerson's dynasty. Though a spiritual and vibrant sect with a special connection to tradition and Jewish solidarity, there are many traditional Orthodox who view the Lubavitch and their outreach programs as too adaptable and overly involved in the non-Orthodox world.

Beyond dress (discussed in Chapter Five) and ideological differences on family traditions and customs, Zionism, and outreach, all Hasidim share a common fervent dedication to transplanting their European ways and maintaining a distinct separateness from secular American life.

Modern Orthodoxy

Modern Orthodoxy came about as the American Jewish immigrants assimilated into other communities and embraced American social values and cultural institutions including public schools and universities. Though Modern Orthodox Jews have a broad respect for historic traditions, practices, and worship, they accommodate Jewish traditions and laws to living in the modern world. They believe that religious behavior can evolve from generation to generation. Unlike their traditional Orthodox separatist brethren who see the outside western world as threatening, the Modern Orthodox strive to be somewhat more acculturated; choosing, for the most part, to live among diverse cultures and world views.

Reform Judaism

During the eighteenth century, an intellectual, social, philosophical and political movement began in Europe and eventually spread throughout the world. This secular movement, called The Enlightenment, promoted scientific thinking, free thought, and the questioning of religious dogmas. As Jews became emancipated and assimilated into European society, many felt that values of the European Enlightenment would enhance Jewry by encouraging integration with the outside world. The *Haskalah* movement, or Jewish Enlightenment, was a spiritual and literary movement founded by Moses Mendelsohn, an Orthodox Jew who believed that secular studies, in addition to Judaism and Jewish history, should be a part of the education of a Jewish child; that the study of Hebrew should be promoted, and Yiddish, the vernacular language of exile, abandoned. Mendelsohn strongly felt that in order to survive and maintain relevance, the Jewish religion needed to adapt to the modern world, and that the Jews should have their own nation, a movement which would later lead to the modern Zionist movement.

The impact of the European Enlightenment on the secular lives of Jews led to the development of Reform Judaism which was concerned with breaching ghetto walls and harmonizing Jewish tradition with modern life and culture, of bringing it into closer harmony with European standards of decorum. As these "reformers" immigrated to the United States in the mid 19th century, they brought this liberal approach to Judaism which would become the wave of the future. It was first introduced in the United States by one of the most active German reformers, Rabbi Isaac Mayer Wise. Though they embrace the written and oral Torah and *Halakhah*, and accept that the Torah was divinely inspired, Reform Jews believe that it was authored by human hands in the language of its time, and revised over time. Their main principles include the belief in G-d as defined in the *Shema*, the central prayer of Jewish liturgy which declares one's faith in G-d: *Here O Israel, Adonai is our G-d, Adonai is one*. They maintain that the values and ethics of the Torah should be revered and retained, but that each Jew should follow and adapt practices which will foster and enhance his or her life and relationship to G-d.

Because, among other reasons, their children had assimilated, the movement introduced changes to worship including shorter services, more prayers in English than in Hebrew, and the use of musical instruments during *Shabbat*. Reform synagogues have mixed gender seating as opposed to the Orthodox services where there are separate sections for women. The Reform movement ordained the first woman rabbi in 1972. The movement's school is Hebrew Union College and its official rabbinical body is the Central Conference of American Rabbis. Congregations generally belong to the Union of Reform Judaism and are committed to supporting the state of Israel and Jews around the world.

Conservative Judaism

Though they admired the intentions of the reformers, many European Jews were dissatisfied with the Reform approach to reconciling tradition and change and sought a less extreme "middle-ground" break from Orthodoxy. The Conservative movement was born in Germany in the mid-nineteenth century, when the head of the Jewish Theological Seminary, Zacharius Frankel, realized that he could neither embrace old school traditional Orthodoxy or modern day Reform Judaism. He wanted to maintain and preserve traditions central to Judaism and also relate traditional texts to modernity.

The major force behind the rise of this movement in America was Rabbi Solomon Schechter, an English scholar, who emigrated to the United States in 1902. An observant Jew and traditionalist, Schechter headed the Jewish Theological Seminary in New York City which eventually became an international center of Jewish learning and Conservative thought. The Conservative movement is characterized by a commitment to traditional

Jewish laws, including observance of *Shabbat,* or Sabbath. It teaches that Jewish Law is not static and has historically developed in response to changing conditions, but it vehemently opposes extreme alterations or "reforms" to traditional observances. It accepts secular scholarship on sacred texts and allows certain modifications of Jewish law to accommodate the demands of modern life. It holds that the Torah is a Divine and normative document, but rejects strict Orthodox interpretations of the oral law or *Halakhah.*

Many Conservative Jews do not ascribe to the Torah being dictated to Moses by G-d, believing that it was written by prophets inspired by G-d. The main tenets of Conservative belief are that Judaism is a mix of religion and nationhood, that Jewish law is flexible enough to meet the needs of modern people when interpreted by rabbinic authorities, and that there is room within Jewish law for change and for differing opinions. In Conservative services, the liturgy is conducted in Hebrew, but the native language of the congregants is also used. Men and women sit together. Today, Conservative Judaism, organized under the aegis of the United Synagogue of Conservative Judaism, is centered in the United States, but it is also represented in Canada, South America, Europe, and Israel.

The Reconstructionist Movement

The Reconstruction Movement is the youngest and smallest denomination which was founded by Rabbi Mordechai Kaplan in 1935. Their services are similar to the Conservative ones with added creative readings. Reconstructionists are committed to protecting tradition, but "reconstructing" it to contemporary meaning. They emphasize individual responsibility over commandments, and they believe that the Torah was not revealed by G-d at Mount Sinai, but rather, it and other sacred texts, are the creation of the Jewish people over time.

One concern that repeatedly emerged from members of the Lakewood community is the growing schism between the denominations of Judaism. Moishe Gelb*, a 52-year-old grandfather who owns a furniture business in Philadelphia, expresses the prevalent belief that there is a "definite lack of unity and respect between the various sects. Yes, we may observe differently, but we are all Jews." David, his new son-in-law, nodded: "Exactly. The Torah says that all Jews are responsible for all other Jews, and so whether we affiliate ourselves either with the Reform, Conservative, or Orthodox sect, we should never forget that we are all an essential component of the worldwide community of Judaism, of K'lal Yisroel."

Over one hundred years ago, Bezalel Goldstein spoke to The Hebrew Free Loan of Lakewood, N.J. Goldstein, who, as discussed in Chapter Four, played a pivotal role in sustaining *Yiddishkeit* in Lakewood, addressed this same issue, asking that his audience focus on what unites us all:

> *We are living in a time when religious beliefs, religious institutions, are not powerful enough to unite all people because of the free thinkers among us. Nationalism…has not yet inspired the Jewish people sufficiently to cause a united Jewry. On one question, however, we can claim to be united. On one occasion we all assemble and find our hearts throbbing with the same beat. That one question, that one occasion is the consideration of charity of mercy, and the common welfare. In these things we all unite…It matters not on what account one is charitable…Maimonides , in discussing this matter, concludes that the highest commendable cause of charity is a good heart.*
>
> (qtd. in Maurice Levine's Diary)

In a broader sense, the binding force uniting all Jews together is their commitment to the Covenant of the Torah, the foundation and backbone of their religion. Although diversely interpreted, it makes them one people and brings them together as a community of learners and worshippers.

Chapter Three

The New Ezekiel: 350 Years of American Jewry

Yea, Prophesy, the Lord hath said. Again
Say to the wind, Come forth and breathe afresh,
Even that they may live upon these slain,
And bone to bone shall leap, and flesh to flesh.
The Spirit is not dead, proclaim the word,
Where lay dead bones, a host of armed men stand!
I open your graves, my people, saith the Lord,
And I shall place you living in your land.

From The New Ezekiel by Emma Lazarus (1849-1887)

When we read American history textbooks, often times there is not much mention of the Jews. Most might judge from this that the Jewish people have had little to do with the history of the United States, or that the Jews were newcomers who arrived after others had founded the nation and made it great. But this is far from the truth. Jews have been here from the beginning and have been an important part of the American story. 2004 marked the 350th year of Judaism in the United States; over that period, American Jews have made an indelible mark on the American landscape in the areas of pop culture, film, the arts, music, finance, military, science, business, medicine, and academia. American Jews helped to defend and build America in peace and war, from colonial times to the present. Whether descending from Spain and Portugal, or emerging out of the leisure classes of Germany, or the impoverished villages of Poland and Russia, they brought to America the dreams and energies that helped define this nation's character and contributed to its strength.

Historically, the story of American Judaism begins in 1492 with Christopher Columbus' first voyage. The American born poetess and Jewess of colonial Sephardic and Ashkenazi stock, Emma Lazarus, is most known for her sonnet, *The New Colossus,* the poem etched on the Statue of Liberty welcoming the hordes of immigrants arriving at Ellis Island. In another poem, *1492,* Lazarus refers to that year as "two faced," meaning one of exile when Jews were driven from Spain, and one of welcoming, when Columbus discovered America. Columbus' voyage was actually financed by the Marrano Jews of Spain, and at least five members of Columbus' crew, including the ship's physician, were Jewish. It is believed that it was one of these Jewish crewmen who first set foot in North America.

The first major wave of Jewish immigration to America occurred between 1654 and 1830. In 1654, 23 refugees – men, women, and children – from Brazil, which Portugal had just reclaimed from the Dutch, arrived on the shores of New Amsterdam, later to be renamed New York. Descendents of the Marrano Jews who had been forced to convert to Catholicism during the Spanish Inquisition, many came burdened with family and with painful memories. They had witnessed persecution, forced conversions, deaths, and eventually expulsions and scattering of families over separate continents. These Sephardic Jews were seeking a haven where there was religious, political, and social freedom and equality, and where they could express their Jewishness without fear of hostility and ill treatment. But New Amsterdam, they came to learn, was not exactly the utopia they had envisioned. Here, they were still treated as separate citizens, not allowed to serve in the military, hold official posts, practice their religion in public gatherings, or build synagogues.

Even though New Amsterdam was a Dutch possession, Governor Peter Stuyvesant did not exactly put out the welcome mat for the new arrivals. Writes Arthur Hertzberg in *The Jews in America:* "Two weeks after they landed, Stuyvesant heard the complaint from local merchants and from the Church that the Jews who had arrived would be likely to remain" (21). Stuyvesant decided to chase them out. Employing the usual formulas of religious invective, he called the Jews "repugnant...deceitful...enemies...blasphemers of Christ..." and recommended that his directors "...require them in a friendly way to depart" (24). Stuyvesant claimed that the Jews would be a financial burden to the community and conveyed these sentiments in a letter to Amsterdam.

While he waited for a reply, Jews sent their own communiqué across the ocean, addressing their desires to the Jews of Amsterdam who enjoyed a relatively high level of religious tolerance. They begged their brethren in Old Amsterdam to intercede on their behalf with the Dutch West India Company which was heavily dependent upon Jewish investments. The Amsterdam Jews concurred and sent a petition to the directors of the company pointing out the loyalty of the Jews to the Netherlands, and that their trade connections would be helpful. The Company concurred and sent a letter to Stuyvesant giving the Jews the right to live as equals with the other colonists and to establish the first Jewish community in the New World. In 1730, the first synagogue was built in Lower Manhattan. With its red brick façade and Romanesque arches, the Romanian American congregation, then referred to as The Cantor's Congregation with a choir that once included Red Buttons and Eddie Cantor, is today one of the last remnants of religious and cultural life in the late nineteenth century.

By 1776, there were an estimated 2,000 Jews living in America. Not only did many Jewish men fight on the side of freedom, but some, like Haym Solomon, provided significant financing for the patriots. In the now famous letter he sent when the first Sephardic synagogue opened in Newport, Rhode Island in 1790, President George Washington acknowledged the major contributions of the *"Children of the stock of Abraham who dwell in the land"* and that they *"continue to merit and enjoy the goodwill of the other inhabitants...while everyone shall sit safely under his own vine and fig tree and there shall none to make him afraid."* (Chametsky et al 8)

The interesting reference to the vine and fig tree was a phrase used by the Prophet Michah, prophesying the Messianiac utopia. Not a surprising allusion since the Old Testament had an enormous impact on the pilgrims and on the founding fathers of the new nation. Numerous examples can be found which clearly illustrate to what a significant extent the political struggles of the colonies were identified with the ancient Hebrews. The first design for the official seal of the United States recommended by Benjamin Franklin, John Adams and Thomas Jefferson in 1776 depicts the Jews crossing the Red Sea. The motto around the seal reads: *Resistance to Tyrants is Obedience to G-d.* The inscription on the Liberty Bell at Independence Hall in Philadelphia is a direct quote from Leviticus (25:10): *Proclaim liberty throughout the land unto all the inhabitants thereof.* In his February 16, 1809 letter to F.A. Van Der Kemp, John Adams emphatically states:

> *I will insist that the Hebrews have done more to civilize men than any other nation. If I were an atheist and believed in blind eternal fate, I*

should still believe that fate had ordained the Jews to be the most essential instrument for civilizing the nations. If I were an atheist and another sect...I should still believe that chance had ordered the Jews to preserve and propagate for all mankind the doctrine of a supreme, intelligent, wise almighty sovereign of the universe, which I believe to be the great essential principle of all morality, and consequently of all civilization... They are the most glorious nation that ever inhabited this earth. The Romans and their Empire were but a bauble in comparison to the Jews. They have given religion to three quarters of the globe and have influenced the affairs of mankind more, and more happily than any other nation, ancient or modern.

(Letters of John and Abigail Adams, Shuffelton, ed.)

By 1789, Jewish immigrants in America had established small communities in the Eastern seaport cities of New York, Boston, Philadelphia, Charleston, and Newport. By 1820, the Jews were accorded full citizenship with the right to hold public office and to vote. The few Ashkenazi Jews who came to America during the eighteenth century had, by and large, adapted the customs of the Sephardim.

The first of the 250,000 Jews who came to America between 1820 and 1880, were mostly from those countries that had been incorporated into a unified Germany, or from the urban elite of Austria, Hungary, Bohemia, and Moravia who were strongly influenced by German culture. Beginning in the 1840s, there was a trickling exodus to America by Lithuanian, Galician, and Russian Jews. Unlike the wealthier and more educated Ashkenazim and Sephardim who preceded them in the eighteenth century, these German Jews, many widows and orphans, came from Europe; most with little capital, some middle class, and all steeped in German culture which enabled them to adapt to American standards of behavior. They had not undergone the Inquisition and expulsion, but they suffered persecution.

The initial group came to what one rabbi called "The American Jerusalem" for economic reasons because of the scarcity of land, rural poverty, and government restrictions in Germany on marriage, domicile, and employment. In the early part of that century, America was experiencing a period of rapid geographic expansion, and the German Jews became an integral part of the developing Midwest. Many of these new arrivals had been peddlers, shopkeepers, and artisans who had been exposed to the *Haskalah,* or Jewish Enlightenment. They held traditional beliefs, for the most part, but they were willing to disregard the rabbinic leaders back home who viewed American life as a radically different culture that would require Jews to assimilate and lose their Jewish identity.

All of these new immigrants had journeyed to the New World seeking civil rights and economic opportunity but, as their Old World *rebbes* feared, they were indeed ill equipped to integrate into the existing forms of Jewish worship, which were mostly in Reform synagogues with English speaking rabbis. As a result, they innovatively pioneered their own form of religious life, creating the Conservative movement which was designed to retain some of the elements of tradition while embracing more modern ideas.

Unlike the earlier immigrants, they did not embrace Zionism since they wanted to be integrated into the American mainstream. Some chose professions in law and medicine, taking advantage of quality education programs in public universities. Others became entrepreneurs or pioneers in the burgeoning American entertainment industry. Still others remained mired in poverty, eventually making their way into the middle class. During the Civil War, and rarely mentioned in history textbooks, thousands of Jews volunteered to fight and many died on both sides of the conflict. There were nine Jewish generals in the North and several in the South. Jewish soldiers fought not only for the cause, but for equal rights for themselves.

> *The religious freedom for which we have fought for 3000 years is ours at last. But there are two sides to freedom – freedom to observe, freedom to neglect. In the ghetto, it easier to observe; in the larger world, it is easier to neglect.* (qtd. in Weissman- Joselit 85)

These perceptive words spoken by Reform Rabbi Maurice Harris in 1893 acutely prophesized the dichotomy of the mixed blessings of freedom for new American Jews. Worried about Jewish survival, Harris's observations have echoed and rung true across decades and centuries.

The years between 1881 and 1914 are historically known as the Great Tide of Immigration, a mass influx of 2.3 million Jews from Russia and Poland. Unlike their predecessors who came to America for economic opportunity, these Jews were fleeing bloody pogroms in their shtetls and were more "ethnic," conspicuous, and resistant to change. In the Old Country, they were forced to live in the confined and strictly regulated area called the Pale of Settlement where, beginning in 1871, anti-Jewish sentiments led to violence and pogroms. Local mobs attacked, raped, and pillaged Jews and their property and conditions quickly deteriorated from economic and political repression to starvation and death. As word of the plight of Russian Jews reached across the ocean, mass anti-Russian rallies in the United States decried the barbaric and brutal actions in the Pale of Settlement, and impoverished refugees seeking safer haven packed up their family and belongings, bid farewell to neighbors, and began their long journey to America.

The increase in arrivals to the East Coast; in particular, downtown New York, prompted the establishment of immigrant assistant organizations such as United Hebrew Charities of New York. The Lower East Side, with its tenements, poverty, pushcarts, and sweatshops, became a melting pot of Yiddish speaking refugees who transplanted the culture of Eastern Europe to America soil. Yiddish theatre and the newspaper, *The Forward*, nurtured memories of the *Yiddishkeit* culture left behind. But whereas in the shtetls of Eastern Europe, the highest praise was accorded to small *heder* yeshiva education and Torah scholars, here in what author Anzia Yezierska rhapsodized as "the golden land of flowing opportunities," immigrant parents who lived intensely Jewish lives knew that formal secular education was the only means through which their children could realize a better life. Enrolling in New York City's public schools and colleges, these first generation Americans did not necessarily give up their essential "Jewishness," but they did cast aside their parents' Old World traditions and language in order to adapt their Jewish lives and assimilate into mainstream America. By 1924, the total Jewish population in America had skyrocketed to 4.2 million, a significant amount of whom rose to become successful bankers, theologians, writers, composers, journalists, financiers, businessmen, merchants, and scholars.

The Holocaust in Europe opened a new dark chapter in the story of Jewish immigration to America, when visas became an issue of life and death. Most of the countries able to provide protection to immigrants from Nazi persecution, including the United States, ignored the petitions of Jewish refugees and stood silent while millions perished. One of the stories that epitomizes the tragedy of such apathy is the 1939 voyage of the St. Louis, a German transatlantic liner. There were 936 passengers aboard that fateful voyage, all but six of them Jews, attempting to escape persecution and murder at the hands of the Nazi regime. The passengers possessed valid visas to Cuba, but in an eleventh hour turnaround, the Cuban government refused to honor these visas.

Lottie Freund, a former student in my Jewish and Holocaust Literature class, was a young child aboard that ship with her family. She recalls that "we could actually see the lights of Miami as we cruised by the Florida shores while appeals were made to the Roosevelt administration to allow the ship to dock." The appeals, as history proves, were fruitless, and the St. Louis was forced to return to Europe. Except for some 288 passengers, among them Lottie and her family, who found refuge in Great Britain, nearly all of the original refugees would be killed in the Nazi death camps and gas chambers. The Roosevelt administration continued its restrictive immigration policies with respect to European refugees until 1944, when the War Refugee Board was established. But by then, roughly 5 million Jews had been massacred in Europe.

The post World War II era saw another wave of immigrants, this time mostly Holocaust survivors, many of whom lost entire families during the Nazi regime. While some Jews who had immigrated to America abandoned or refigured their religious practices to better assimilate into the New World, most of the Jews, primarily those who came to America right after the War, struggled, despite staggering socio-economic challenges, to keep their traditions alive; indeed, these Jews chose to replicate and sustain their Eastern European roots and Torah true religion and lifestyles in communal enclaves in American Eastern cities such as Brooklyn's Boro Park and Crown Heights, and in the seemingly unlikely shore town of Lakewood, New Jersey.

Chapter Four

Exit 91S on the Garden State Parkway: Welcome to Lakewood, N.J.

Back again to Lakewood fair
Where fly my troubles and despair.
Back to scenes of joys that bear
With them of health, a goodly share.
Here weird and wasting worry pales
'Fore nature's beautied fields and dales.
Here care's sharp stinging blade sure fails
To pierce the happy hopes I hail.
Oh Lakewood, bountifully blessed
With natures' beauties, nature's best,
Continue thus to manifest
Thy benefits to me, thy guest.

February 7, 1907 entry in the unpublished diary of Maurice Levine
(1884-1912)

Driving through Lakewood today, it is difficult to imagine that over a century ago, the city was home to lavish hotels and the spectacular mansions of John D. Rockefeller, Jasper and Rachel Lynch, Charles Lathrop Pack, and George and Edith Gould. Sadly, most of the hotels have since been demolished or destroyed by fire. The Strand Theatre on Clifton Avenue remains probably one of the last vestiges of a grand bygone era. In the early 1900s, architect Thomas Lamb was commissioned to design a theater in Lakewood for vaudeville acts and previewing Broadway shows. Among the then unknown performers who graced its stage were Ray Bolger, Milton Berle, Ruby Keeler, and George Burns and Gracie Allen. When talkies hit the theatre, the live acts were replaced by movies. When the theatre began to face extinction, a coalition of individuals and government officials were able to preserve the building as an architectural treasure and, in 1981, The Strand gained its rightful place in the National Register of Historical Places. The magnificent theatre on Clifton Avenue has since been splendidly restored with superior acoustics and unobstructed stage views. In 1984 Pearl Bailey opened the first show in what was now was called Ocean County Center for the Arts, and which has since become a popular and successful venue for musical and comedy shows, plays, dinner theatre, and showcasing local talent.

But in the glory days of Lakewood, there were over 120 hotels with prestigious guest lists including Oliver Wendell Holmes, Andrew Carnegie, Woodrow Wilson, Ulysses S. Grant, and Mark Twain. Vacationers enjoyed dance and tea parties, hunting, polo, ice skating, boating and sleigh rides along the lake. The four story Laurel House on Main Street was host to, among other socialites and millionaires, the Vanderbilts, Arbuckles, and Houghton and Miflin families of publishing fame. The 700 guest capacity Lakewood Hotel was famous for its curative water and electric baths modeled after the famous Charcoat Institutions at Paris. With entertainers such as comedian Henny Youngman, The Laurel-in-the-Pines hotel on Lake Drive was recognizable by the spectacular copper rotunda over its entrance. The famous Lilyan Lodge was located on Forest Avenue and Fifth Street. Madison Avenue was peppered with hotels: the Ritter Hotel on Sixth Street, The Hotel Grossman on Eighth Street, and the Irvington Hotel on Ninth Street. Jerry Lewis played to crowds at the Hotel Belmont on Forest Avenue and Sixth Street. The Plaza Hotel on Seventh Street and Clifton Avenue was where the New York Giants stayed during their training at the baseball diamond on John D. Rockefeller's estate on Ocean Avenue which is now the site of Ocean County Park. The majestic Jay Gould estate with its European fountains and sunken gardens is now the campus of Georgian Court University, a Roman Catholic College.

In the late nineteenth and early twentieth centuries, a good percentage of hotels and boarding houses were owned and operated by non Jews. There were, of course, exceptions such as Charles Hecht who ran the Manhattan Hotel in 1895 and Nathan Jacobs who owned the only kosher hotel in Lakewood, The Lilyan Lodge. But over time, more Jews would build hotels and rooming houses. Predictably, however, the guest registry at some of the non-Jewish owned establishments was clearly restricted, eerily foreshadowed by a sign 60 year resident Rabbi Pesach Levovitz remembers on County Line Road announcing "No Jews or Dogs." In 1907, vacationer Maurice Levine from Liberty, New York, reflected on why the Jews were hated, writing that "...it is because [others] look upon us and judge us from the exterior, refusing to see what is in us." Then there is the oft told story about President Woodrow Wilson bringing his White House team on retreat to The Laurel House around 1911. Among Wilson's distinguished entourage was Nathan Strauss, a diplomat and a Jew who was, no surprise, turned away from lodging at the hotel. Several years later, a syndicate headed by Strauss would build the fifteen acre seventeen story Lakewood Hotel, which in later years was converted into a hospital for WWI veterans.

Because of its warm climate, porous soil, ocean breezes, and aromatic pine trees that absorbed the humidity thereby creating dry conditions, Dr. Paul Kimball, the house physician for the Laurel House and for whom Kimball Hospital would be named, promoted Lakewood as an ideal rest resort and health haven for those with malaria, typhoid fever, tuberculosis, and other lung diseases. This is corroborated by Maurice Levine, who regularly spent summers in the mountains, and October to May in boarding houses and sanatoriums in Lakewood. Suffering from advancing tuberculosis that would claim his life at age 28, the young Levine enjoyed the benefits of the balmy balsamic air as he judiciously recorded his keen observations of people he met, and of life and impending death. He voraciously read Emerson and Longfellow, taught himself Hebrew, and penned poetry and articles for local papers. "City life has destroyed my health," Levine writes in 1906, "and I must stay in the country...this refuge, close to nature."

It would hardly seem that this turn of the century, primarily WASP paradise and meeting place for the elite would be, beginning in the last decade of the nineteenth century, a magnet for immigrant Jews. It was, however, precisely the hotel business, along with the simultaneously growing chicken farming industry, the early formation of religious and educational institutions (which would culminate in the establishment of the famed Beth Medrash Govoha), and, ironically, the Great Depression that are the intertwining roots of Lakewood's rich Jewish life and history and, which is, as Rabbi Levovitz puts it, "a reflection of the history of Jews and Judaism in the United States." By first isolating, as best one can, each of these key trends, one can appreciate the intersecting and symbiotic relationship responsible for the unique history of Judaism in Lakewood from the mid-nineteenth century through what the township is today.

Since the mid to late nineteenth century, even before Lakewood was the playground of American aristocrats, Jews were instrumental in building up the chicken and egg (whichever one came first) farming business; not only in Lakewood and its surrounding areas, but throughout Southern New Jersey. The history of farming in Southern and Central New Jersey is a complex story and this is not intended as an all inclusive scholarly absolute, but rather as a general and contextual overview. As early as 1855, there were efforts to transplant immigrant Jews who had been farmers in the Old Country from overpopulated cities to more healthy rural areas. Between the 1870s and 1890s, with assistance from The Jewish Agricultural Society and Hebrew Emigration Society, Eastern European Jews seeking to flee the pogroms in the Pale of Settlement, were urged to come to the United States to work the land. Baron Maurice de Hirsch, one of the wealthiest Jews of his time, founded the Jewish Colonization Association in England which encouraged young Jews to join agricultural colonies in rural cities such as Woodbine and Alliance in Salem Counties where the new farmers were able to purchase land and buy homes. These thriving small farming and merchant communities such as Woodbine became self-sustaining with their own public schools and cultural programs. Woodbine was actually the first Jewish borough incorporated in the United States, and The Brotherhood Synagogue, built in 1896, still stands there today.

In the 1890s, the first Jewish families arrived in Lakewood, settling in the section called "Sugar Hill" on John Street and Fulton Avenue. The new arrivals included Louis Mayers, Abram Byer, Moses Silverman, and David Sall. Most of them earned livings as peddlers. One of these immigrants was Lithuanian born Charles Goldstein, known as Bezalel, who would later own the Goldstein Carlton Hotel in Lakewood and Belmar, and become legendary for upholding *yiddishkeit* in Lakewood. As noted by his grandson, William Goldstein, Bezalel had a threefold vision for Lakewood: To help establish a *Torah Talmud*, a Hebrew Day School, and a Yeshiva. He was, as we shall see, successful on all accounts.

A peddler who arrived in Lakewood in 1893, Goldstein rented a room in a boarding house and would travel twenty miles each week by horse and buggy, trudging over cobblestone roads to Asbury Park to purchase kosher meat, chickens, rye bread, and other supplies for the then small Jewish community. Out of the 600 or so families residing in Lakewood at this time, about twenty five were Jewish. The men worked painstakingly hard during the week, peddling their goods and services by foot, horse drawn buggy, or bicycle, but remaining true to having a *minyan* (required quota of ten men for community prayer) on the Sabbath which was held without a *Sefer Torah,* a Torah Scroll, at the Jones Street home of Moses Silverman. Upon learning that a *Sefer Torah* could be borrowed from Joseph Cohen of Point Pleasant, who later moved to Lakewood and opened a Jewish boarding house, Bezalel travelled by horse and buggy to pick it up. He returned to the small congregation gathered at Mrs. Charmes' large house on Meadow Avenue, where one of her guests was a rabbi who officiated at that service. When subsequent religious services resumed at the residence of Moses Silverman, he served as reader and cantor.

To comfortably accommodate more worshippers, Louis Mayers offered the apartment over his dry goods store. As the Jewish community grew, attracting congregants from other parts of Ocean County, Bezalel called a meeting to discuss establishing a more permanent structure with their own *Sefer Torah*. In attendance were Louis Mayers, Abram Byer, Moses Silverman, Benjamin Leet, David Sall, Zussman Rabinowitz, Max Friedman, Samuel Effros, and Rev. Abraham Tarshish. A charter was drawn up and members contributed one hundred dollars to rent space over a Chinese laundry in the Cooper Building. A *Talmud Torah* was established with classes taught by Rev. Isaac Zinkin, who also served as the reader and cantor at holiday and Sabbath services.

As Lakewood's general population markedly grew, so did the number of Jewish families drawn to that community, confident they could lead a Jewish life and earn livings by providing much needed stores and services to the town's wealthy clientele. Henry Kantor, Abram Alpert, Jacob and Sam Newman, Jacob Brown, Louis Traub, Barney Shapiro, Sam Cohen, and Abraham Jaffe were just some of the new arrivals. Some were tailors; some worked as carpenters, painters, and butchers. Some opened small grocery and furniture stores. Some continued to be peddlers. When the rental hall could no longer accommodate the growing congregation, a campaign began to establish a permanent house of worship.

Captain Bradshaw, a local realtor and Civil War veteran, was able to obtain a lot from the Bricksburg Land and Development Company at the intersection of East Fourth and Park Avenue and the railroad tracks. As Rabbi

Levovitz tells it, even though Bradshaw was instrumental in getting the property for the Jewish community, he was also determined to keep the Jews away from the hotel districts and, literally, "on the other side of the tracks."

To build a *shul* (synagogue) on that property, the group enlisted help from those who patronized the kosher hotels. In 1907, Mrs. Bertha Frank, a wealthy woman from Baltimore and the wife of Dr. Raymond Frank, who spent winter months in Lakewood gave the Jewish community of Lakewood $5,000 to engage an architect. In his diary, Maurice Levine compares Mrs. Frank, who sent the young man and other lung disease sufferers to the mountains in the summer months, to *"one of Abraham's best and noblest daughters...and who like Queen Esther and Deborah, is imbued with that same spirit of justice, righteousness, friendship, and bountiful charity."* Mrs. Frank also elicited donations from the Strauss family which was followed by generous contributions from John D. Rockefeller, George Gould, and State Senator William Harrison.

In 1907, the cornerstone for Congregation Sons of Israel, built at a total cost of $9,500, was dedicated, with Bezalel Goldstein as its president, Rev Isaac Zinkin as its cantor, ritual slaughterer, and teacher, and Joseph Kaplan as sexton. In 1912, land on East Seventh Street was purchased for a Jewish burial ground which would be named Mount Sinai Cemetery. In 1917, through the efforts of Simon Jacobsen, Morris Levin, Jacob Jacobson, among others, a *Talmud Torah* named The Lakewood Hebrew Institute, was constructed on Fourth Street and Monmouth Avenue to provide after school religious education for Jewish children. The first Rabbi of Sons of Israel was Rabbi Judah Damasek in 1919, followed by Rabbi Joseph Levine in 1921, and Rabbi Mordechai Reisman in 1925.

As word of the Jewish resort of Lakewood spread, it attracted affluent clientele from the Northeast. More kosher hotels opened and more small businesses emerged to accommodate the Jewish guests and the growing Jewish resident population. The membership of Congregation Sons of Israel continued to expand and, in 1920, an addition was built. In 1924, The Ladies Benevolent Society donated a grand chandelier which still hangs in what is now referred to as the "Old Shul of Park Avenue." During those early years, the *shul* served not only the small Jewish community, but prominent Jewish guests staying at nearby hotels who made generous contributions to The Congregation Sons of Israel which had begun with barely a *minyan* in Moses Silverman's home.

In 1932, Rabbi Nisan Waxman became the *shul's* spiritual leader, followed by Rabbi Pesach Levovitz who officiated from 1943 through 1993. He was succeeded by Rabbi Baruch B. Yoffe, who still remains the rabbi of that original *shul*. In 1963, because of changing demographics and the need to accommodate the population shift to the western section of Lakewood, a new Congregation Sons of Israel was built on the corner of Madison Avenue and Sixth Street. Rabbi Shmuel Tendler currently officiates at this modern structure which houses a sanctuary, daily chapel, youth lounge, library, kitchen and auditorium. An impressive monument memorializing the six million Jews who perished in the Holocaust stands at the front entrance on Madison Avenue welcoming congregants, many of whom are survivors and descendents of those murdered at the hands of the Nazis.

Rabbi Baruch Yoffe probably knows more about Lakewood's Jewish past and present than anyone; it is hard to believe that this spry, fast-talking man, and admitted history buff, recently celebrated his seventieth birthday. As he effortlessly provides a meticulous historical[1] monologue, he periodically and nonchalantly produces documents from his pockets and desk drawer to authenticate his facts.

Rabbi Yoffe guided me on a tour of his *shul*, which still stands alongside the old railroad tracks on the triangular intersection of Fourth Street and Park and Ridge Avenues. The neighborhood has deteriorated considerably over the decades, and there are pieces of fencing, tree branches, and debris littering the yard. As he bends down to remove a street sign which has fallen onto the property, he points to the original entrance and the Ten Commandment tablets carved over the wooden doors. He shows me where the addition from 1920 begins, the carved Star of David, and the small plaque at the building's foundation paying tribute to the generosity of Dr. and Mrs. Frank. I see the steep narrow stairs that lead down to what was the community's first *mikvah*, or ritual bath. If one closes his eyes, he can imagine that bygone glory era and the congregants, both working class residents and well dressed men and women staying in local hotels, walking up the steps of this white stone structure to pray.

The walls inside the synagogue are covered with brass plaques; I struggle with the Hebrew, but see that many are engraved with names I have encountered in my research. On the *bimah* (the platform) and to the right of the Torah scrolls, is a chair reserved in that place of honor for a distinguished congregant. The plaque on it reads "Bezalel Goldstein." The chandelier donated by the Ladies Benevolent Society hangs majestically in the center of the room.

There is something "other worldly," I think, about older houses of worship; a history, of course, but specifically in this *shul* a reminder of life with horse drawn carriages; a time without endless strip malls, soccer fields, and modern cookie cutter houses. The Old Shul today boasts a loyal congregation of 150 which surprises even the rabbi: "Had you asked me how many members we had twenty years ago or what our future was," he says while carefully locking up the building, "I'd have told you we would probably be closing these doors." This one-hundred-year-old iconic building serves as a reminder of how it all began; how the dream of 25 immigrant Jews came to be realized, and how one structure that started with dollar donations, symbolically and historically forever transformed the fabric of the surrounding neighborhood.

To be sure, during those formative years of Congregation Sons of Israel, chicken farming remained a major industry, earning Southern and Central Jersey, through to the fifties, the reputation as "The Egg Basket of America." It certainly continued to be a significant factor in the history and development of Lakewood's Jewish population and of its *shul*. Among the immigrants who were here before and shortly after the erection of Congregation Sons of Israel, a substantial amount were farmers. In the late twenties through the early forties, more Jews, many German immigrants, flocked, no pun intended, to South Jersey from the steaming sweatshops and crowded tenements of the Lower East Side, to be trained for farming and other trades.

One impetus for the revitalized egg farming business was The Great Depression. The ten year economic crisis that devastated the United States beginning in 1929 resulted in unprecedented unemployment, homelessness, and people not being able to afford adequate food, clothing, shelter, and medical care. President Roosevelt implemented, among other recovery plans, legislation for food subsidies; for basic staples of milk, eggs, and poultry. This required farms and people to farm the land, and was a needed means to bring Eastern European Jews who were farmers or businessmen in the Old Country as well as immigrants already living in the Northeast to rural cities such as Lakewood where many built bigger and more technologically advanced farms.

Ironically, the Depression's effect on the hotel industry in Lakewood was a marked shift in ownership from the WASP elite to the Jews. In 1929, when the stock market crashed, owners of the lavish estates were anxious to sell their properties at economically driven deflated prices. Word of the available estates and mansions travelled to Jewish chambermaids and cooks in the Catskills, who bought them and converted the thirty to forty room mansions into kosher hotels and apartment houses, among them The Stanley and The Irvington. The new owners brought with them their Catskill clientele seeking a vacation spot during the winter months.

Throughout the thirties and forties, many renowned *Roshei Yeshiva*, heads of yeshivas, from the United States and Europe would visit Lakewood to raise funds for Talmudic study from the wealthy visitors to the shore. They would speak at Sons of Israel and stay at one of the myriad of local kosher hotels that graced the town. At this time, there were some 120 hotels in Lakewood; one of the hotels that housed these distinguished scholars was Goldstein's Carlton. William Goldstein has fond memories of his grandfather:

In the winter, I remember being in his vast semi circular library on Shabbos afternoons when my grandmother served tea and cakes and my grandfather hosted the weekly shiur and halakhic discussion. He was respected and revered, and was friends with Rav Moshe Feinstein who married my parents, and with Rabbis Twersky, Silver, and Teitz. He died when I was ten years old, but I can still hear the sound of his voice. He comforted me when I was upset. He taught me how to play chess when I was seven. His beautiful ivory chess set sits in my studio and keeps me company every day inspiring my own creative spirit.

Writing in his journal in 1908, Maurice Levine remorsefully lamented about the future of Judaism: "My heart breaks as I witness the encroaching assimilation [of the Jews]. The inevitable result will be that generation after generation will continue to weaken in Judaism and [the race] will be extinguished. What is the remedy? What is the preventative?" Levine, decidedly ahead of his time, believed that Zionism was one answer. But Levine's anxiety over the impending end of a race and culture would be echoed by many over the succeeding decades, and answered with one solution some thirty years later: The formation of traditional Jewish education. "When you defend land," the venerable Rav Kotler once remarked, "you need armies. When you need to defend a faith and Jewish continuity, you need schools."

Indeed, the influx of Eastern European immigrant Jews to America in the post WWI period raised tremendous concern among Jewish leaders as to the future of childrens' religious education. These Jews, the least acclimatized of the various waves of immigrants over the decades who had reconstituted itself in America, had given up some of its Old World attachments, not as much for assimilatory reasons, as for economic realities: providing for family and ensuring their children a good education that would improve their lives. When Rav Aharon Kotler arrived in America from Lithuania, where there had been a solid foundation for Torah learning, here he found that "the spirit of pragmatism, goal, and career reigned supreme" (qtd. in Bunim). His concerns were twofold: Who would ensure the perpetuation of *Yiddishkeit* and who would teach Torah to future generations?

At that time, boys and girls in public schools would participate in after school Jewish education programs, such as those offered in Lakewood's *Talmud Torah*. Now, in the wake of the decimation of Eastern European Jewry and Jewish culture, and coupled with the assimilation of Jews into American life, the call went out trumpeting the need for Jewish Day Schools that would ensure that Jewish parents would have a means whereby their children connect with the language and core of Judaism in a full day dual curriculum of religious and secular education in one building, under the shared supervision of an ordained rabbi and an "English principal."

Discussing this with Rabbi Levovitz in his modest home on Sixth Street, the rabbi confirmed that "Yes, sixty years ago, the projection for Jewish life and culture was lower than Obama's poll numbers. It was literally near the level of extinction." But that would change with the establishment of *Torah Umesorah*, the National Association for Hebrew Day Schools. This network of Jewish Day Schools was co-founded by Rabbi Shraga Feivel Mendelowitz, the head of Brooklyn's Yeshiva Torah Vodaas, and Rav Aharon Kotler, with the encouragement of their Eastern European-educated colleagues.

In 1947 and with the help of Rabbi Pesach Levovitz, Bezalel Goldstein who was one of the early founders of Congregation Sons of Israel and The Talmud Torah, was able to fulfill his second mission: Establishing the first all day Hebrew School in Lakewood, dedicated as The Bezalel Hebrew Day School, and which still stands in the same location today. Rabbi Levovitz admits that at first it was difficult to attract students because free public schools were attractive to the new immigrants, and because of the stigma of separation from the mainstream population. "But," he tells me, "the miracle of the Almighty changed minds over the course of the year and there was an awakening of the Jewish soul." That, and as we shall see, the tireless efforts of Rav Kotler, created a *Yeshivish* community to uphold and sanctify Torah learning.

William Goldstein remembers when his legendary grandfather was stricken with a fatal heart attack following a trip to New England to raise funds for the Day School: "On his deathbed, he turned to his children and whispered, '*Mein arbeit fa the Day School is fartik: yetz meg ich gain*' – "my work for the Day School is finished; now I'm ready to die." But before his death, Bezalel would also be one of the driving forces in helping to establish a European model Orthodox Yeshiva in Lakewood, laying the groundwork for a cultural resurgence of traditionalist or "black hat" Orthodoxy in America.

Upon his death in 1952 and, according to his wishes, Bezalel Goldstein's vast library was donated to Beth Medrash Govoha and in April of 2010, I was honored to be invited by the Goldsteins to the dedication of the Bezalel Library plaque in one of The Yeshiva's original buildings. The ceremony was attended by Bezalel's grandchildren, great-grandchildren, and a handful of close friends. It was a bright and crisp Sunday afternoon. Rabbi Kotler spoke of the loving friendship between the two families down through the generations as he gave us a personal tour of the expansive and growing campus. A few students were reading in the large study halls; others were strolling on the grounds. We visited the newly dedicated Kleinman Campus which can serve 1,000 students, and walked gingerly through ongoing construction sites. One of the buildings under renovation was the old Irvington Hotel that had its heyday during the time Bezalel lived in Lakewood, a time when the possibility of one day having a preeminent Talmudic institute and thriving culture of *Yiddishkeit* in this then sleepy town was but a dream. Today, Bezalel would be proud.

Chapter Five

Beth Medrash Govoha and the *Frum* Community, or, What's with the Black Hats?

The words of Torah are like golden verses; the more you scour and rub them, the more they glisten and brighten and reflect the face of him who looks at them. So it is with the words of Torah; whenever you repeat them over and over, they glisten and enlighten/reflect the face of the one (who studies them).
Midrash Nate

The Nazi regime sought to murder all the Jews in Europe – 50 to 70 percent of whom were Orthodox – and tragically succeeded to the extent of six million. So too did they aim to destroy a whole culture, or way of life. That culture was embodied in, and perpetuated by, a broad spectrum of communal organizations, congregations, and educational institutions that transmitted the culture the Nazis were intent on destroying. In pre-war Europe, there were approximately 800 yeshivas for boys and young men at the elementary, secondary, and post secondary levels serving students in excess of 200,000. Girls' schools encompassed 250 institutions with a student population in the neighborhood of 40,000. Despite the devastating destruction, there were a determined number of survivors who managed to rebuild many of the yeshivas and *kehillas* (Jewish communities revolving around a synagogue and its schools) that existed in Europe.

Certainly, the most legendary figure who set the standard for traditional yeshiva study in the United States was Rav Aharon Kotler who, out of the burning ashes of Eastern Europe, brought the light and perspective of Torah to Orthodox Jews in America. Rav Kotler was considered by the sages of his time, including Chofetz Chaim and Rabbi Chaim Ozer Grodzienski, one of the *gadol ha-dor*, Torah giants, of his generation. According to William Heinrich in his book *The World of the Yeshiva*, Rav Kotler was a dominant Torah personality who "embodied the yeshiva in all its aspects: He had dramatic presence, was brilliant, selfless, and incredibly hard-working. Uncompromising in his principles, he won people over to his cause by the sincerity and force of his convictions" (42). Among his other contributions to Orthodox Jewry, Rav Kotler was the founder and *Rosh Yeshiva* of Beth Medrash Govoha in Lakewood, today the most prestigious institute in the world for rabbinical study based on the European tradition of yeshiva learning and having a satellite network of *kollelim* (institutes for advanced Talmudic study) all over the globe.

Rav Kotler was born in Sislovitz, White Russia (present day Belorussia) in 1890 into a distinguished rabbinical family. A brilliant student at the renowned yeshiva in Slabodka, Rav Kotler "exhibited a rare combination of intellect and charisma." (Bunim). After finishing his studies and marrying Chana Pearl Meltzer, he worked as an assistant to his father-in-law, Rabbi Isser Zalman Meltzer at a yeshiva in Slutsk, which he headed for twenty years. In 1936, Rav Kotler came to America to meet with prominent leaders of the Orthodox community and raise funds for educational institutions in Europe. They discussed, along with the future of Talmudic scholarship, how to build and finance a Torah sanctuary in the United States. Rav Kotler and several American Orthodox students returned to Europe. When, on the precipice of the outbreak of WWII, the American government announced that they could not take responsibility for any American citizens living in Europe, students returned home, and scholars from yeshivas throughout Eastern Europe sought refuge either in safer cities throughout Europe, or in the United States or Palestine. Kotler and his yeshiva relocated to Vilna. Through the efforts of a rescue committee, *Vaad Hhatzalah*, Rav Kotler and his wife were among those who, in 1941, were able to secure passage to America via Siberia.

Lakewood's Rabbi Yoffe relates the story about Rav Kotler who, on the eve of *Pesach* (Passover), stepped off the boat in San Francisco where he announced to his welcoming party: "I'm going to organize traditional Torah learning in the United States." Rav Kotler's deep concerns about the future of traditional Torah study following the destruction of Torah centers throughout Europe was shared amidst World Jewry who saw the lofty task of rebuilding the ruins falling upon the Jews of America and Israel. Rabbi Yoffe considers Rav Kotler, "[who was] known as *Rosh of Etz Chaim Yeshiva*, the greatest Jew who ever lived in America, and the one who had the most profound influence on the American Orthodox landscape."

Without question, Rav Kotler was a visionary whose dedication to the continuity of Jewish tradition and *Halakha* (law) and to the rigorous growth of Torah scholarship, reshaped American Orthodoxy. Amos Bunim, in his eloquent biographical tribute to his father, Irving Bunim (1901-1989), who worked closely with Rav Kotler in his rescue work, maintains that Rav Kotler, along with Rabbi Silver, President of Agudah Harabonin, brought a spiritual revolution and the enlightenment of Torah to Lakewood, which, in turn, charted a different course for Orthodox Jewry throughout America. Rav Kotler, Bunim asserts, knew a great deal about American Jewish history when he arrived in 1941. He was painfully aware that the early Sephardic and German communities saw their children assimilate, and that at the turn of the century, Eastern European immigrants, even more religiously inclined but who had experienced poverty in the Old Country, also became engulfed in assimilation; with little political and economic clout, they hoped for inclusion with Reform and Conservative Jews. Their lives, says Bunim, "stressed the supremacy of overall social good and charitable work, rather than living life with a Torah perspective in all actions [and Kotler warned that] Jewry stands or falls in direct proportion to the measure of its devotion to Torah study."

Meanwhile, Lakewood was experiencing a growing Jewish community of mainly Russian, German, and Polish immigrants. Rabbi Hillel Bishco, founder of a small White Plains, NY yeshiva *kollel*, was invited to Lakewood to speak to the well -to -do winter vacationers to raise funds for yeshiva education. Rabbi Pesach Levovitz, one of the attendees, recalls that Bishco, after alluding to the Nazi annihilation of European Yeshivas, startled the audience: "Dear friends, I am here to invite you to the funeral and burial of Torah." Indeed, in the United States, there were then but two schools of advanced Torah study, one in Brooklyn and one in Manhattan. The guests asked Rabbi Bishco what could be done to reverse the projection about the end of Orthodoxy, to which he replied: "The promise of the Almighty was that Torah was eternal." He suggested that they begin the process in Lakewood by establishing a yeshiva which would follow the classic approach to Torah study. An ad was placed in the papers for anyone interested in traditional yeshiva learning but, because there was no scholar affiliated with the planned yeshiva, no one responded.

The wealthy Jews who had put up the initial financial backing started to question their investment decision, but soon word spread that there was a need for a Torah scholar in New Jersey. Rabbi Gordon, the original President of the White Plains kollel had emigrated to Israel. Rabbi Mordechai Yoffe was instrumental in persuading Rav Kotler, who was in the United States at that time, to run the kollel. After considering several possible new locations for the kollel, Rabbi Yoffe then worked with Rav Kotler, Bezalel Goldstein, and Rabbi Waxman to establish it in Lakewood. Rav Kotler's conditions were that he would stay in the shore town Thursday evening through Monday morning, and then return to his apartment on New York's Upper West Side, where he could continue carrying on the work of *Vaad Hatzalah* which, through the war, had kept many refugees in Europe, Russia, and Shanghai alive.

When the Holocaust began, the American State Department hindered efforts to rescue Jews and, as David Wyman points out, most of the leaders of American Jewry failed to protest against the abandonment of the Jews by the "democratic" nations. One of the critics of this passive attitude was Rav Kotler who issued a fierce call for all Jews to take immediate action: "We must not abandon hope or remain silent," he warned, "…[and] it is our sacred duty to go to Washington…." (Bunim).

And so in 1943, several hundred rabbis from the *Vaad Hatzalah* and other activist groups, many wearing long black coats and black hats, marched from Washington, DC's Union Station to the nation's Capital to pressure politicians and government officials to admit more refugees and to take other forms of action to help the Jews of Europe. The rabbis met with members of Congress to read the group's petition to the President. Worried about his upcoming reelection campaign because most Americans were opposed to letting in more refugees, President Roosevelt wanted to avoid the rabbis, and was curiously unavailable that day. But his political calculation backfired since the next day's headlines read: *Rabbis Report "Cold" Welcome at the White House.*" The impact of the negative publicity about the march resulted in the creation of a Federal government agency to rescue people from the Holocaust, The War Refugee Board, which was instrumental in saving the lives of tens of thousands of Jews (Wyman).

At the same time Rav Kotler was busy in New York City, Bezalel Goldstein and Rabbi Waxman were convincing David Shapiro, a guest at the Carlton Hotel, to purchase the first building for a yeshiva. They then approached Lakewood businessmen to commit to financial support for the yeshiva. Beth Medrash Govoha (BMG), opened its doors the day after Purim in 1943 on the first floor of a large home in Lakewood. Some of the first students were from Rav Kotler's yeshiva in White Plains and other American students. Shortly thereafter, students from the White Plains yeshiva, also named Beth Medrash Govoha, relocated to Lakewood. It was not easy to sustain religious education at any level, and during its formative years, BMG sometimes lacked sufficient money to pay basic bills. The Sons of Israel community, the Lakewood Branch of the National Council of Jewish Women, and B'nai Brith, helped to cover the Yeshiva's immediate financial needs.

Rav Kotler also was instrumental in establishing *kollels*. A *kollel*, generally defined as a community of learners, is an institution where veteran and married yeshiva students receive a stipend in order to continue to devote themselves to full time Talmudic studies after their marriage, in a program that requires rigorous ten hour a day programs. While individual enrichment through advanced study remains a central focus of *kollel*, there also is the community *kollel* which has been transformed into an informal educational institution geared toward addressing the intellectual and spiritual interests of local Jewish populations throughout the United States and Canada. Some of these community *kollels* focus on Jewish education of children and adults who are already active members of their communities; others are more "outreach" directed, seeking out individuals who have more limited connections to Jewish life, offering them a variety of Jewish learning experiences.

Explaining how Rav Kotler succeeded in establishing *kollels*, an area in which others had fail, Rabbi Eliezer Goldstein, director of BMG's Division of New Kollelim, attributes Rav Kotler's success to "one of the unsung heroes of Torah growth"—Lakewood's Rabbi Nosson Wachtfogel –who worked under the guidance of Rav Aharon Kotler and who would travel to each community, convincing its Jewish leadership of the benefits of hosting a *kollel* and recommending married scholars from Lakewood who would be successful in each city (Feitman).

Rav Kotler was also one of the rabbinical leaders of Agudath Israel. This organization, founded in Poland in 1912, promoted the ideals of Orthodox

Jewry and was the political arm of Eastern European Ashkenazi Torah Judaism. A confederacy of Orthodox Jewish communities throughout the world, its core mission is the protection of human rights such as freedom of religion, and the preservation of the Jewish cultural heritage. Rav Kotler and other members of the Sages of Agudath Israel in Israel, founded *Chinuch Atzmai*, an alternate school system for Orthodox children in Israel which emphasizes Jewish studies and which include *Bais Yaakov* schools for girls, *Talmud Torah, Cheder* (or *Heder*) and *Yeshiva Ketana* for boys. The school was only partially supported by the State and Rav Kotler was extremely influential in fundraising efforts. Today, *Chinuch Atzmai* which has an enrollment of 80,000 students, is dependent upon donations from outside Israel, particularly the United States.

Rav Aharon Kotler died in 1963. "Torah," he once stated, "is the lifeblood of the Jewish people, the goal of Jewish existence… [and]…the perpetuation of our people depends on the development and growth of authentic Torah scholars." (qtd. in Dershkowitz). Rav Kotler believed that Torah should be studied because it was G-d's revealed truth; his dream for *Torah lishmo*, study for its own sake, rather than because it provided the possibility of employment, was carried on by his son, Reb Shneur Kotler until his untimely death in 1982. Today Rav Kotler's eldest grandson, Rabbi Aryeh Malkiel Kotler is the spiritual leader of BMG and his youngest son, Rabbi Aaron Kotler, serves as its CEO.

I had the pleasure of sitting with Rabbi Aaron Kotler in the study of his Lakewood home. An eloquent and humble man with sparkling china blue eyes, Kotler attested to the fact that the examination and admissions process for acceptance into BMG, which is fully accredited and licensed, is grueling and competitive. Though it has an operating budget of twenty million dollars, the school is completely funded by charities, individuals, and scholarship endowments. Tuition for a full time undergraduate is approximately $13,000 per year, but when a student marries, he does not pay tuition, and is granted a stipend for his studies. Graduate tuition for a full time student is approximately $5,000 per academic year.

Though called a yeshiva, BMG is a college which is fully accredited and offers undergraduate and post graduate degrees on a fifteen acre campus consisting of dormitories, residence halls, study halls, classrooms, libraries, dining rooms, and visitor facilities. The 5000 plus student body represents the United States as well as 22 other countries. BMG has branches in major communities in the US, Canada, and Israel. The average age of a BMG student is 23. Many of those who come to BMG have already had one to two years of college, some abroad. There are over 230 study programs at BMG as compared to other yeshivas which offer two to eight. Some of the students are in a joint program with Farleigh Dickenson's CPA program. The academic year, based on the Hebrew calendar, is divided into three semesters or terms. The academic week is Sunday through mid-day Friday and is rigorous. Most students' days begin at dawn and are 12-14 hours long, with breaks only for breakfast, lunch, and dinner. BMG's study halls are large and there are benches or tables for books, chairs for seating, and lecterns, or *bimahs*, for the lecturer. Students learn through lecture, or *shiur,* and also by working with a study partner, a *chavrusa;* together, they read and analyze the nuances of Talmud and rabbinical commentaries and engage in scholarly debates about ethical and legal issues.

According to Rabbi Moshe Chaim Lussatto, an eighteenth century Italian scholar and teacher, virtually every Talmudic discussion between study partners is built from seven principle elements of reasoning, almost hairsplitting logic:

Statement: Speaker states a fact

Question: Sage asks for information from speaker

Answer: Speaker responds to question directly, or

Contradiction: Speaker disproves a statement and contradicts or refutes it

Proof: Original speaker presents evidence from which truth of a statement is made obvious

Difficulty: Sage points out something untrue in a statement or idea

Resolution: Original speaker or some other sage reconciles the difficulty raised against statement or idea and everyone goes home happy

Study partners, a distinct feature of yeshiva life, are not chosen lightly. *Chavrusa Tumult* is an annual event at BMG when thousands of students gather in hallways and in the parking lot in search of the perfect *chavrusa*. Common to large yeshivas such as Mir in Israel, *Tumult* is an intense and competitive day when, in addition to considering their educational goals, students must choose a partner with whom they feel they can have a successful personal and academic relationship. Students also must arrange to join a particular study group, called a *chabura*.

Like the majority of the student body at BMG, Yussie* does not mind BMG's demanding schedule. "However small my existence is," he says, "I am serving *Hashem* by studying Torah. Torah is considered the light because it brings light and enlightenment to one who studies and interprets it." Yussie's study partner, Mordechai*, agrees: "It's a *mitzvah* to observe the commandments and struggle for righteousness in the world. To study Torah is a distinction rather than a burden."

But when young men feel that they are not growing in their study of Torah, they will seek other avenues of maintenance and support. David Berg*, a young Hasidic student currently enrolled in Ocean County College's Liberal Arts program, with a concentration in Psychology, often stops by my office to visit. David studied at BMG for a few years and says that the most remarkable aspect of his experience was the nurturing environment for, and student dedication to, learning for learning's sake. "A few of my friends," relates David, "will become Torah scholars and others will use the argumentative and critical thinking skills they developed at BMG through Talmudic discourse to pursue a career in law," but David's goal is to ultimately work in the area of forensic psychology. "But," he assures me, "I will continue to lead a Torah true life."

Rabbi Kotler is justifiably proud of the fact that his school's learning focused programs allow motivated students to grow intellectually and in life, with the freedom to develop how to think. Some go on to be successful in business, the rabbinate, academia, medicine, finance, law, or technology; most do not become rabbis, but all are there for the sheer love of learning. BMG has a successful job placement service for their graduates, many of whom are awarded posts in *kollels* around the country.

"Look, I'm third generation and have the huge benefit of having the groundwork," Rabbi Kotler tells me modestly, "The model is done and I just tinker with it." Over the period in which BMG has existed," he continues, "two percent of Jewish history has taken place. Jews are an integral part of civilization; human history would be unrecognizable without the Jewish people."

Today, the total population of Ocean County surpasses 450,000 and, according to the Ocean County Jewish Federation's statistics, fifty thousand are Jewish. Forty thousand of that figure are Orthodox who reside in

Lakewood, making that city home to one of the largest clusters of Orthodox Jews in the United States. One of the many misconceptions about Lakewood's Jewish population is that they all fall under the banner of "black hat Hasidim" or "black hats." "Black hats," for starters, refers to the yeshivish. The term Hasidic, in itself, presents somewhat of a conundrum. On one hand, it comes from the Yiddish word for "pious or pious one" and therein lies the problem. One might argue that technically, the entire community by definition is pious, but the label Hasidic, correctly used, describes a follower of Hasidism.

Simply put, there are three groups of Torah observant Jews in Lakewood: Those affiliated with the Yeshiva (called *Yeshivish*), those not affiliated with the Yeshiva, and the Modern Orthodox. The first two categories include Hasidim who represent about 20 percent of the Lakewood Orthodox population. While all groups are considered Orthodox, living according to Torah commandments, there are subtle nuances in customs and appearances dictated by family customs.

The Orthodox, individually and as a group, are often referred to as *Frum or Haredi*. The word *frum* comes from the Yiddish word for "religious." *Haredi* (pl. *Haredim*) is a term meaning "devout." For purposes of clarity, I refer to the collective Lakewood religious community, including Hasidic, as Orthodox, *haredim*, or *frum*. Only when necessary do I make specific references to yeshivish or Hasidic.

There are some outside the Orthodox enclave who mistakenly refer to Lakewood's *haredim* as "Ultra-Orthodox," a seemingly redundant term. To my mind, "ultra" is a judgmental term negatively suggesting fanaticism or extremism. Orthodox, by its very essence, implies the highest adherence to a belief. It does not get any higher. Are there Ultra Reform Jews? Ultra Protestants? Ultra Buddhists?

Manner of dress is a means to ensure Jewish identity, tradition, and distinctiveness. Certainly, clothing is but the outer garment, not an indication of what is within the soul of the person, but a simple understated mode of dress is viewed as conducive to inner reflection and spiritual growth. It is difficult to broad brush a picture of what a "typical" Hasid or yeshivish Jew looks like. Often times, Hasidic men will follow the specific dress style of their sect which may include a long coat, called a frock coat, or a full length suit jacket called a *rekel*. This mode of attire was common to Hasidic and non Hasidic Jews in pre-World War II Europe, though many

Hasidim, especially those who have businesses, opt to wear a black business suit with a conservative light colored shirt and tie.

Payos, or side curls, and beards are worn by most Hasidim and the vast majority of Yeshivish. Both Hasidim and *Yeshivot* men wear a *kippah*, or *yarmulke*, to cover their heads. The *kippah* is made out of black material or black velvet. Very few members of both groups do not wear hats over their *yarmulkes*. Yeshivish men will wear a fedora or trilby style hat made out of felt. The Hasidic men wear hats that, depending on dynasty affiliation, range from fedoras (often with the brim turned down) to bowler hats made out of felt or beaver. The formal *shtreimel*, a wide and flat fur hat is reserved for the holidays, Sabbath, and special occasions. Some sects of Hasidim may wear a *spodek*, which is a higher and narrower fur hat. Whatever the style, the hat is worn out of respect for G-d by showing that there is a higher power.

Modesty in dress and behavior, one of the most fundamental of Jewish values, is viewed by some outsiders as provincial, prudish, and chauvinistic when, in fact, it nurtures individuality and relationships based on wisdom and good deeds which are, one might say, the garments of the soul. Both Hasidic and *Yeshivish* women's modest attire is limited to conservative dark colors and skirts that at least cover the knees, blouses with high necks, and sleeves which cover at least the elbows. There are some Hasidic women who wear ankle length skirts, and some yeshivish women who do as well. You will find teenage Bayis Ya'akov girls garbed in long denim skirts and hoodie sweatshirts or conservative sweaters congregating in places such as Jerusalem Pizza or Taste Buds on Route 9, or Barnes and Noble on the Howell border. Once married, both yeshivish and Hasidic women are required to wear a *sheitel*, or wig, and some may wear a hat or head scarf as well. The fitting rooms in clothing stores for women in Lakewood, as well as in Boro Park and Williamsburg, post charts with appropriate rules of attire.

It is certainly not unusual for Hasidim and yeshivish to pray together in a common *shul*, or synagogue. Some Hasidim do, however, have their own *shtiebel*, a smaller and less formal *shul* in the basement of a house, where there is more exuberance with singing and dancing. Many yeshivish opt to *daven*, or pray, in a *shtiebel*. While it is possible to find a Hasidic young man or woman in a yeshivish school, the majority prefer to attend schools more in keeping with family traditions. Hasidic and yeshivish men study side by side at Beth Medrash Govoha where such distinctions disappear with attention to advanced Torah study.

Today, Lakewood's Orthodox abide by secular civil law, but they also have their own governing body called the *Vaad*, a tradition that comes from Poland and other countries where it played a major role in giving East European Jews as sense of community and people-hood. The Council of the Four Lands (*Vaad Arba Aratzot*) consisted of lay leaders and rabbis whose major function was to defend Jewish interests and to interpret, modify, and adapt the legal code of Polish Jewry which required a great deal of rabbinic expertise in Talmudic law and commentaries. Lakewood's *Vaad* is composed of Rabbis and leaders of the Orthodox community, and one of their functions is to ensure that any planned secular legislation is not harmful to the entire Lakewood Jewish community. Since the Torah discourages going through the secular court system, the The *Vaad* has a tribunal or rabbinical panel, called *Batei Din*, located on Forest Avenue, which oversees a myriad of Orthodox legal and civil disputes.

Though Lakewood appears, to the outsider, to be a cloistered community with regard to its internal experience *vis-a-vis* Jewish life and Torah study, the Orthodox community's deep roots branch out to the needs of fellow Jews throughout the world. For over six decades, they have been able to create and sustain a Torah-true lifestyle and ensure Jewish continuity through education and preservation of family tradition. Far from the restrictions of the Old World shtetls, they can maintain the traditional practices of their Eastern European ancestors with the conveniences of modernity.

Asked about the different strains of Orthodox Judaism in Lakewood, Rabbi Aaron Kotler explains that yeshivish and Hasidim live and pray side by side: "The basic difference is that Hasids are centered on dynasty *rebbes*, many of whom studied at BMG. Yeshivish Orthodox are affiliated with synagogue rabbis. All go to *shuls*. There are subtle differences in customs, but it is important to recognize that we share more similarities than differences. Ultimately, all of us are bound by Torah, Jewish history, language, and by following the 613 commandments."

As to the future of American Orthodoxy, the young CEO of BMG believes that "Orthodox Jews are the keepers of ancient tradition [and that the] Orthodox experience in the United States is very successful, more so than the European model insofar as the latter had little diversity and was monolithic. Jews were the perpetual minority where American culture is more hospitable to diversity." And when it comes to fostering diversity, as will be discussed in Chapter 16, Rabbi Kotler has had enormous success. He is committed to improving relations and building bridges with the other ethnic groups that reside in Lakewood, and for fulfilling the core values of BMG for excellence in Torah education and service to community.

Over the six and a half decades since Bezalel Goldstein and Rabbi Waxman welcomed their beloved colleague, the venerable Rav Kotler as *Rosh Yeshiva,* Beth Medrash Govoha has been the centerpiece, the heartbeat, of Lakewood's religious and social life. From its inception with under fifteen students, the now sprawling BMG campus in central Lakewood with a student body of six thousand – and still growing – stands as a tribute to, and reflection of, Rav Kotler's dream for future generations of Orthodox Jews to study and live Torah, and to become immersed in intellectual activity for a higher spiritual purpose.

Chapter Six

A Crown of Prayers

Teach me my G-d, a blessing, a prayer
On the mystery of a withered leaf
On ripened fruit so fair
On the freedom to see, to sense
To breathe, to know, to hope, to despair.
Teach my lips a blessing, a hymn of praise
As each morning and night
You renew Your days
Lest my days be as the one before
Lest routine set my ways.

Leah Goldberg, tr. Pnina Peli

Beth Medrash Govoha is not only a world renowned institute of Talmudic learning and studying; it also serves as the largest *shul*, or house of worship, in Lakewood where Orthodox Jews from the entire community can come together for prayer services. Reform Jews use the word "temple" for a house of worship because they consider every one of their meeting places to be equivalent to, or a replacement for, The Temple. The use of the word "temple" to describe modern houses of prayer offends most Orthodox Jews because it trivializes the importance of The Temple. Conservative Jews will usually refer to a "synagogue," which is a Greek translation of *beit k'nesset* and means "place of assembly" (it's related to the word "synod"). The Orthodox use the Yiddish word *shul*, derived from a German word meaning "school," and which emphasizes the shul's role as a place of study. They will also use the term *beit midrash* meaning "house of study" or *beit tefilah*, a house of prayer; again, a constant reminder of the close relationship between prayer and Torah study. Devorah was sitting alongside of me during a recent *Shabbat* dinner. The discussion turned to study and prayer: "The difference between prayer and Torah study," she maintained, "is that when you pray you speak with G-d; when you study Torah, G-d speaks to you."

The *shul* is the place where Orthodox Jews satisfy the obligations of daily prayer. Though they can pray alone, there are certain prayers that can only be said in the presence of a *minyan,* a quorum of ten adult men. Too, tradition teaches that there is more merit to praying with a group than there is in praying alone. The sanctity of the synagogue for this purpose is second only to The Temple. In fact, in rabbinical literature, the synagogue is sometimes referred to as the "little Temple." Lakewood has over one hundred *shuls*, the majority of which are *yeshivish*, but some of which are strictly Hasidic. In *shul*, men and women are segregated, separated by a wall or curtain, called a *mechitzah*. One reason is that it helps ensure the main focus is on the prayers without any distractions, not only from the opposite sex, but also from any beautiful inanimate object such as a painting. Referring to Talmud, the distinguished scholar, physician, and philosopher Rambam cites: *One must disengage himself from this world and free his mind of any thought which will distract his attention from prayer.* Too, as discussed in Chapter Twelve, men and women are very different human beings; not only physically, but in our thought processes, emotional states, and psychology. Why? Because our souls are different – they come from complementary, but opposite sources. The prayer experience is meant to be an opportunity to be with your true self, to communicate with your soul; men and women need space from each other to help them connect to their higher selves. Distractions also include inanimate objects such as pictures which might distract congregants from prayer.

Probably the most important feature of the *shul's* sanctuary is the Ark, a cabinet or recession in the wall that holds the Torah scrolls. The Ark is generally placed in the front of the room; that is, on the side facing towards Jerusalem. The Ark has doors as well as an outer curtain called a *parokhet,* and which is a replica of the curtain in the Sanctuary in The Temple. During certain prayers, the doors and/or curtain of the Ark may be opened or closed. Opening or closing the doors or curtain is performed by a member of the congregation, and is considered a great honor. All congregants stand when the Ark is open. In front of and slightly above the Ark, you will find the *ner tamid*, the Eternal Lamp, which symbolizes the commandment in

Exodus to keep a light burning in the Tabernacle outside of the curtain surrounding the Ark of the Covenant.

In the front of the synagogue is the *bimah*, or raised platform, from which the Torah is read. The portion of the synagogue where prayer services are performed is commonly called the sanctuary and is designed so that the front of the sanctuary is on the side towards Jerusalem, which is the direction that one is supposed to face when reciting certain prayers. In addition to the eternal light, many Orthodox *shuls* have a menorah, symbolizing the menorah in The Temple. The menorah in the synagogue will generally have six or eight branches instead of The Temple menorah's seven, because exact duplication of the Temple's ritual items is considered improper. Because the study of sacred texts is a life-long task, Orthodox *shuls* normally contain a well-stocked library for members of the community to study.

Recitation of prayers is the central characteristic of Jewish worship. In *A Letter for the Ages*, an ethical letter Ramban wrote to his son, the philosopher and scholar comments that

> *Prayer is the pathway to G-d... Prayer is a moment of transformation. Before he speaks to G-d, man is alone and frightened, weak and torn by worries which threaten to overwhelm him. When the moment of prayer arrives, man understands that he has a sympathetic and caring ear to talk to...One should seriously take to heart that he stands before his Maker, and should carefully choose both the words and the themes he intends to contemplate...The words of prayer ...are merely the shell. The heart's meditation upon these words is the inner kernel. Words are like the body of prayer, while meditation is the soul... [Prayer] is nothing less than the passionate yearning of the soul for G-d, and its utter surrender before him.*

There are three types of prayers; those from the Bible, mainly the Book of Psalms; those composed by the rabbis of the Talmud, and liturgical poetry for the holidays. While all branches of Judaism use the same set of prayers and texts, the frequency of prayer, the number of prayers recited at various religious events, and whether one prays in a particular liturgical language or the vernacular differs from denomination to denomination. The Orthodox pray solely in Hebrew from the traditional Jewish prayer book called a *siddur*. The word *siddur* means "order" because the blessings and prayers are written in the order in which they are said for the services during the year. It also reflects the fact that G-d created the world in a particular order. Orthodox Jews are obligated to recite three prayers daily and more on the Sabbath and Jewish holidays. They believe that the name of G-d is one that should be reserved for prayers and spoken with reverence. For that reason, in casual conversation, they will use the term *Hashem* (or *Ha-Shem*).

The morning prayers are called *Shacharit* and take anywhere from a half hour to an hour. Many men go to the synagogue at the crack of dawn and then head straight to work or study. There are three morning blessings. *Amidah*, a plea to G-d to fulfill spiritual and physical needs, as well as those of the Land of Israel, consists of 19 blessings and is recited while standing. *Tachanun* is the penitential prayer of repentance. The daily *Shema*, the central prayer of Jewish liturgy, is the basic statement of the Jewish faith: "Hear O Israel, the Lord is our G-d, the Lord is One."

Mincha are the afternoon prayers that contain readings from Psalms, *Amidah*, a shortened version of *Tachanun*, and *Kaddish*, praising G-d and asking for the speedy establishment of G-d's kingdom on earth. *Kaddish* is also said by mourners at the grave of close relatives and during the eleven month period following the death of a parent. These prayers last about fifteen minutes and should be completed before sunset. *Ma'ariv* are the evening prayers conducted after sundown. This service begins with the *Barechu*, the formal public call to prayer, and an expanded series of prayers relating to the *Shema Yisrael*. This is followed by the *Hashkiveinu*: "Lay us down to sleep, Ad-nai, our G-d, in peace, raise us erect, our King, to life, and spread over us the shelter of Your peace." The prayers end with *Kaddish*.

Men's appearance and attire for praying is dictated by commandments in the Torah. In addition to wearing *kippot* (skullcaps) at all times as a symbol of respect and observance, during weekday prayers men wear a large prayer shawl, called a *tallit*, which is made of wool and worn over the shoulders. The *tallit* helps the worshipper create a sense of being enveloped in the Divine. Some men cover the tops of their heads with a large *tallit* to avoid distractions while praying. The white fringes or tassels, called *tsitzis*, are tied to each corner of the shawl (or of any four cornered garment) as a symbol that G-d is everywhere – North, South, East, West, and to fulfill the commandment: *Speak to the children of Israel, and bid them that they may make fringes on the borders of their garments throughout their garments.* (Numbers 15:38). Each tassel has five knots as a reminder of the Five Books of Moses. Young boys receive their first fringed garment at age three, the same day as their first ceremonial haircut.

Orthodox men wear *tefillin,* a pair of small black leather boxes that contain pieces of parchment inscribed with passages from the Torah. The manner in which the *tefillin* are strapped spells out *Sh-ddai,* one of G-d's names. The men wrap the straps of the *tefillin* to their arm and forehead as a symbol of binding their minds and deeds to the devotion of G-d.

The meaning behind *tefillin* comes from the commandment in Deuteronomy 6:5-8:

And you shall love the Lord your G-d with all your heart, with all your soul, and with all your might. Take to heart these instructions. Recite them when you stay at home and when you are away…Bind them as a sign on your hand and let them serve as a frontlet between your eyes.

The Orthodox practice of swaying the body back and forth during prayer is referred to as *shokeling* in Yiddish and is not mandatory; in fact, the Kabbalist Isaac Luria felt that it should not be done. On the other hand, the medieval German authority Maharil, also known as Rabbi Jacob Molin, pointed out a story in the Talmud that the *Mishnaic* sage Rabbi Akiva would sway so forcefully that he ended up at the other side of the room when praying.

Proper concentration, *kavvanah,* is considered essential for prayer, and there are certain prayers that are invalid if recited without the required awareness and intention. Ben Menachem, a student at BMG refers to the Torah instruction about prayer: "To pray loudly is not a necessity of devotion," he quotes, "and when we pray we must direct our hearts towards heaven. Even when the gates of heaven are shut to prayer, they are open to those of tears."

Water is a universal symbol of life and spiritual cleansing. The traditional Orthodox ritual of washing the hands upon awakening and before eating bread involves taking a cup of water in one hand and pouring it over the other hand, then switching hands and repeating the process. This is usually done three times for each hand. Many restaurants in Lakewood and other Orthodox communities have a sink in the front or back of their establishment for washing the hands, prior to saying a blessing before eating.

Through prayer, the Jew expresses devotion, gratitude, praise and contrition. And in the daily *Shema*, the basic message of Judaism is repeated in the words of Deuteronomy, the focal book in the formation of the Hebrew Bible: "Hear O Israel, the Lord our G-d, the Lord is One. And thou shalt love the Lord thy G-d with all thine heart and with all thy soul and with all thy might."

One of the most insightful and beautiful metaphors for prayer is offered by Rabbi Michael Strassfeld:

Standing on an empty beach, we look back across the sand stretching as far as the eye can see. Lost from our sight is not what lies beyond the horizon but rather the millions of grains of sand lying at our feet. All those millions make up this sandy vista, but we only perceive the mass whole. A life of prayer is to make us aware of the millions of moments that make up the sandy beach of our individual lives. (206)

CHAPTER SEVEN

Living Torah: Acts of Kindness, Compassion, and Charity

What does G-d ask of you? To do justice, to love kindness, and to walk humbly before G-d."
Micha (ch. 6:8)

Woe to the person who says 'Peace be upon my soul' and doesn't join the community in its hour of trouble.
Shevet Musar

In all of its many dimensions, Judaism is characterized as a religion of deed, a means by which human beings are capable of understanding and responding to G-d's teaching. The religion of the people of Israel was and is the loving and faithful Covenant devotion to one G-d who revealed Divine Teaching through the matriarchs and patriarchs of the people of Israel, through Moses and the Prophets and Sages whose spirituality is documented in the 24 books of the Hebrew Bible. The goal of this Covenant consciousness in partnership with the Divine is the defining characteristic of any Orthodox community, and is clearly affirmed in *Ethics of Our Ancestors*: "The world rests on three things: Torah study, *avodah* (worship), and *gemilut hasadim* (acts of loving kindness)."

The guiding tenet of Orthodox life is that studying Torah in and of itself is not sufficient; that study must ideally result in living the words of Torah in one's spiritual lives and ethical and everyday behavior by observing the 613 *mitzvot*, or Divine commandments. *Mitzvos* which define the *frum* lifestyle are acts of kindness and good deeds, especially for those less fortunate. This includes *tzedakah*, donating money for charitable purposes, and donating time and effort to help others.

The concept of kindness and community is not a new idea. Over 2000 years ago, Rabbi Hillel issued a warning to the Jewish community of his day: "Do not separate yourself from the community." Each time an individual performs an act of *gemilut hesid*, Hillel taught, he or she strengthens the community and Jewish continuity. Jews lived without a homeland for thousands of years, and they know what it is like to be a stranger in a foreign land.

One of the commandments and virtues of Judaism is to look after the welfare of others, just as G-d had done by visiting Abraham when he was sick. Abraham and his wife Sarah were always hospitable and set the tone for future generations. During the Middle Ages, because individual family homes were very small, many Jewish villages had a guest house where travelling beggars could stay free of charge. Today, Jews can welcome guests in their own homes.

The *mitzvah* of loving your neighbor as yourself is a biblical instruction; because man was created in the image of G-d, individuals must be treated with the utmost respect and honor. Too, Judaism emphasizes the value of human life, that the life of one person is no less important than the life of another. This concern for life extends to animals and one of the oldest laws prohibiting cruelty to animals is found in The Torah.

Tzedakah is seen as the duty of every person to share what G-d has given them. Every week, before the start of *Shabbat*, coins are dropped into a charity box, called a *pushka*, which will be donated to philanthropic and educational institutions, as well as to the poor. According to Maimonides, the best act of *tzedakah* is helping people to help themselves by providing them with employment. Even though the word *tzedakah* is associated with "charity," it also means righteousness. Beyond the basic responsibility of *tzedakah* is *rachamim,* or mercy; caring about others personally and getting involved. That may mean collecting food for the poor and clothes for the homeless, creating religious schools, visiting the sick, caring for the elderly, or standing up for justice. Sometimes it is merely giving an attentive ear or a warm smile.

True to the tenets of their religion, Lakewood's Orthodox have established a host of exceptional volunteer services and organizations for both the Jewish community and the community at large. BMG takes its core mission, not only for education, but for community service, seriously. The

Lakewood Community Services Corporation (LCSC) was founded in 1994 by BMG alumni and is government subsidized. Among its overwhelming number of economic, educational, medical, and communal services offered to all residents of Lakewood, regardless of faith or religious affiliation, is Kosher Meals on Wheels. From Monday to Friday, freshly prepared meals are delivered to needy and homebound residents throughout Lakewood and Toms River by *frum* volunteers who also spend a little time socializing with the clientele. LCSC also provides job placement services, business and career seminars, as well as an English as a Second Language (ESL) program for Hispanic members of the community.

The Chemed Medical Center complex on Madison Avenue was established in 2007, after Rabbis Kotler and Halberstam identified a need for a comprehensive medical facility to serve the entire Lakewood population, particularly those without insurance. After meetings with liaisons for the black, Orthodox, and Hispanic communities, and writing grant proposals, what began as an ambulatory service grew into an unparalleled state-of-the-art integrated model for providing pediatric, internal, general practice, dental and behavioral health services.

All of the doctors are employees of Chemed, which is a federally granted and qualified health center under the auspices of its parent company, LRRC. Chemed accepts patients with insurance and Medicaid and determines fees for non insured patients based on an income based sliding scale computation. Because of its connections to social services organizations, Chemed can assist clients in applying for other programs. Chemed is not an impersonal clinic or walk-in facility, but rather a one stop medical complex which has child friendly décor and pediatric professionals to serve the needs of families with many children. The CEO and one of the founders of Chemed, Dr. Dovid Friedman, disclosed that Chemed has begun plans for an expanded dental program and to add a full service pharmacy and Ob-Gyn center.

Bikur Cholim is an organization founded by the wives of BMG alumni which provides one-on-one assistance to the areas sick and elderly. They implemented an "Adopt a Bubbie" program where volunteers pair up with residents at area nursing homes to engage in conversation and participate in various activities. Over the years, *Bikur Cholim* has expanded substantially. They have on site offices in local hospitals such as Ocean Medical Center in Brick, Community in Toms River, and Kimball in Lakewood to provide patients with books, Kosher food, and other services. They also maintain a residence that accommodates the patients' families and loved ones.

Hatzolah, which, in Hebrew, means to save someone, is a mobile emergency medical service. An independent branch of a worldwide umbrella organization, *Hatzolah* was founded in the late sixties in Williamsburg, Brooklyn, where there was a dire need to improve first responders to medical emergencies, and to address cultural concerns of the religious Yiddish speaking community. *Hatzolah* has expanded to orthodox communities throughout the United States and the world, where they respond to major incidents and crises, medical emergencies, and fires. *Hatzolah's* response is not limited to the Jewish community, but is always there to respond to any major incident including terrorism, providing first aid, medical advice, and treatment to area residents, often stabilizing victims before they are able to reach a hospital. *Hatzolah* volunteers were some of the many heroes who risked their lives to help rescue and treat victims of the September 11, 2001 terrorist attack on the World Trade Center in New York City.

The Lakewood *Hatzolah* team includes trained and licensed paramedics, EMS specialists, and drivers available at no charge to serve its community. A recent partnership with MONOC, Unit 270, pairs hospital personnel with *Hatzolah* volunteers. There have been times when a crisis has occurred on a Friday night. Since the Orthodox are not permitted to work or drive on the Sabbath, most of the time there is a non-Jew who is the designated driver for *Shabbat* and Holy Days. But as dictated by Torah, when it is a life and death situation, one is not only permitted to break with the laws of Torah, but is obligated to place human life over Jewish law.

Since 1987, *Chai Lifeline* has been helping children with lifelong or life-threatening illnesses including cancer and hematological diseases. With the slogan "Fighting Illness with Love," *Chai Lifeline's* core belief is that seriously ill children need and deserve to have as normal and happy a childhood as possible. To that end, the organization's myriad services include helping the families with advocacy and case management, insurance support, and transportation. They also work to integrate, when appropriate, chronically ill children into schools and provide training for educators, clergy, and mental health professionals on how to help the child, family, and community cope with crisis, and handle untimely death. Each summer, *Chai Lifeline* sends 400 children to Camps Simcha and Simcha Special in Glen

Spey, NY, where they enjoy traditional camp activities including concerts, talent shows, and modified sports.

The volunteers in *Mikimei* visit hospitalized children with life threatening illnesses. They cheer them up by providing puppet shows, magic acts, and other entertainment. *Tomchei Shabbas* is an organization that ensures all households have basic food staples to feed their family with dignity by discreetly distributing food packages, especially for *Shabbat* and the holidays, to needy families in Lakewood and the surrounding areas. *Aim Habenim* helps mothers with caring for their newborns. *Chevra Kadisha* provides burial services for families. They arrange for the funerals since, by Jewish law, burial must occur before the next sundown and on Sabbath, after sundown. They will provide low chairs to families sitting *shiva*, when they receive guests at their home. *Chevra Kadisha* also ensures that the bodies are cleaned according to strict *Halakhic* law. *Chaverim* is a sort of Jewish Triple A that provides assistance to whoever's car breaks down on the road.

The term, *Oorah*, generally known as the enthusiastic greeting and spirited cry of the US Marines is also the Hebrew word for "to awaken." As such, it is the name of a Jewish outreach organization founded thirty years ago called *Oorah Kiruv Rechokim*, meaning "to awaken and bring in those who are far;" far, that is, from Orthodox Judaism. *Oorah's* mission is to awaken Jewish children and their families to their heritage. To this end, *Oorah* offers summer camp programs for boys and girls, as well as scholarships for yeshiva education to Jewish children from non-Orthodox homes. To encourage simultaneous Jewish education for parents, *Oorah* sponsors *Torah Mates*, a telephone study partnership that pairs Torah knowledgeable adults with less knowledgeable men and women.

Without marriage, considered the Holiest of *mitzvahs*, there is no perpetuation of the Jewish nation. The Orthodox communities in Lakewood, as well as those in Monsey, Brooklyn, and Cedarhurst, NY, are committed to continuing the tradition of *bayis ne'eman*, or faithful Jewish homes. The cost of a wedding and setting up a new home can be enormous and certainly more than most large families can afford to provide. Donations from members of the Orthodox community and the organization, *Tiferes Devorah L'Kallah*, ensure that financially needy brides begin life in their first home with all the necessities – linens, dishes, cutlery, towels, pots and pans. They are given the opportunity to visit a furniture warehouse and pick out dining room, bedroom, and living room sets.

Hillel's assertion that "All of Israel is responsible for one another" serves as a reminder that for Jews, Jerusalem and all of Israel are considered as one's own community. In 1948 when Israel won its statehood, Abba Eban (1915-2002), the South African born Israeli diplomat who served as Deputy Prime Minister and Foreign Minister, came to Lakewood to speak at the Laurel in the Pines fundraising dinner for Israel where tens of thousands of dollars were raised for the *Haganah*. *Haganah*, meaning defense, was founded in 1920 during the British Mandate for Palestine to protect the Jewish *Yishuv* (settlement) from Arab riots and violence. Their doctrine stressed loyalty, secrecy, and devotion to humanitarian and Jewish values including the sanctity of life. The *Haganah* evolved into an effective military force by 1948 and was able to hold its own against the Arabs of Palestine and the invading armies of Jordan, Lebanon, Syria, Egypt, and Iraq despite inferiority in arms and numbers during the initial fighting. The *Haganah* was merged into the IDF following the foundation of the state of Israel in May of 1948.

Though *Haganah* eventually came to be associated with the Labor Zionist ideology and movement and the *Histadrut* labor union federation, Lakewood's Orthodox community today is overwhelmingly non-Zionist, by the more modern definition of that term. The term "Zion" historically refers to the Land of Zion, *Eretz Yisroel*, or Israel. The first Jewish community of Lakewood (discussed earlier) whose population was more Modern Orthodox, conceptually embraced Zionism in terms of the establishment of a homeland, of Jewish colonies in Israel, founded on socialist principles in a network of agricultural settlements and cooperative communities.

It was Theodor Herzl (1860-1904) who is credited with transforming the Zionist idea into a political movement which achieved, with efforts of Jews worldwide, the realization of the State of Israel. Zionism, today, is a national, secular, and political ideology to help all of Israel, Jews and non-Jews, develop and prosper. Orthodox Jew' overwhelming support of, and enormous financial contributions to, *Eretz Yisroel*, is founded upon history and religion, and geared towards sustaining religious life and education.

Most Lakewood families have relatives in Israel and children studying in Israeli schools and universities. They believe that every Jew has a share in and obligation to the homeland and take seriously their duty to perform individual and communal acts of *gemilut hesed* for Israel.

Throughout the year, women in Orthodox communities volunteer to host parties in their homes to raise money for local charities as well as those in Israel. I was invited to Rachel's home in Lakewood for one of these events. With twenty or so exquisitely wrapped items, and a beautifully decorated table replete with every imaginable homemade pastry and dessert, Rachel, a spirited woman with 8 children, auctioned off each gift and, by the end of the evening, had raised over $1,000 that will go to *Girl's Town Jerusalem*, a girl's orphanage.

A representative from this organization was among the guests that night. Elisheva, an Israeli woman in her late 60's, travels to Orthodox communities throughout the United States to talk about this charity and about the importance of building Jewish homes in Israel. *Bayit Lepletot,* which means a home for refugees, was founded in 1949 to accommodate the stranded, broken, and orphaned children whose parents or entire family were killed in the Holocaust and who were in dire need of a warm and understanding home. Then housed in a small basement apartment, the institution started with seven little refugee girls who were raised, cared for lovingly, cured, married off, and started on their way to raising new families.

Today, there are over six hundred children, many from tragic backgrounds, in three dormitory buildings: *Bayit Lepletot*, in the heart of Jerusalem, a smaller building behind it, and *Girl's Town Jerusalem*. The children there come from over thirty countries all over the world: Iran, Morocco, Yemen, Tunisea, England, Belgium, South Africa, Russia, Ethiopia, as well as local Israeli children. Elishever explains that some of the girls who come to *Girl's Town* understandably arrive with psychological and emotional issues, and some with learning or physical disabilities.

The audience listens silently to their stories: Ronit is a young woman crippled shortly after her bas-mitzvah. Saralech came from what was formerly the USSR with her mother and brother, both of whom totally disowned her when she adopted a lifestyle of Torah. Shani's father died, leaving her mother stripped of emotional strength to take care of her daughter. Chaiky spent most of her early childhood with her mother on the streets collecting charity from passers-by. Elishever tell us that their "home" has grown with the needs of the times and situations. "The refugee children have grown and are today happy mothers and grandmothers."

Today children enter *Girl's Town* from the tender age of 3 and up and stay until they are married and or old enough to go out and start independent lives of their own. An average of 25 to 30 weddings are celebrated annually. The Home's licensed educational program enables the girls to choose from a variety of subjects – both academic and vocational. "When leaving the Home," Elisheva proudly tells us, "the girls are secure in their confidence of being self-supporting." Some of the money raised also goes to families in Israel who otherwise could not afford the costs of a wedding for their daughter.

Brachie grew up in a poorer section of Jerusalem. Her parents had already sent six children to the *chuppah* (wedding canopy). With the assistance of the *Bayis Ne'Eman Hachnasas Kalla Fund*, Brachie had the wedding of her dreams. When the time comes to be married, all of these young women are generously provided with a complete wardrobe, beautiful wedding, and, as Elishever put it, "all the necessities for building a true Jewish home in, and rebuilding the ruins of, *Yerushalyim*."

At another fundraiser, it was Rivka who graciously opened up her home in an upscale section of Lakewood to some 75 or so Orthodox women. The guest speaker that evening was Bambi, a charismatic Israeli woman in her sixties who works with the impoverished population in Israel, "helping them to survive each day." She told the audience that the poverty rate in Israel is "alarming and increasing, and that most of the poor are only able to get by because of the generosity of donors in Israel and the United States orthodox communities." She spoke about individual plights: Shanie, who has MS and six children, and who left her drug addicted husband; Micha, a widow with 8 children; Bluma and her husband, Raffi, have seven children, one of whom is severely learning and emotionally disabled. They lost their home and business in a fire. The fundraiser brought in several thousand dollars for this worthy cause.

Ultimately, all of these programs at home and in Israel, these acts of *gemilut hasadim,* are integral components of *tikkun olam*, a concept that comes from the 16th century Kabbalist, Rabbi Isaac Luria, who saw us living in a shattered world, littered with broken hopes and dreams. They maintained that we all live in exile from ourselves and each other. According to Rabbi Luria, G-d concentrated himself to allow space for the world to be created. In the process, vessels of light shattered and their shards became sparks of light trapped in the material world.

Contemplating the aspects of divinity in the *sefirot* relases these sparks and allows them to reunite with G-d's essence. The global Orthodox community lives by the Torah principle that ignorance and tolerance darken the world, and that understanding and love bring light and help to restore the world. In partnership with G-d, and by *mitzvahs,* acts of *tzedakkah,* and caring concern, they believe that each person can help move the universe a bit closer to G-d's vision of a spiritually perfected world. Living by and not just studying sacred texts *vis-a-vis* active engagement in a life of ethical, social, and moral responsibility, the Orthodox community in Lakewood serves as reminder of the true essence of any faith.

Chapter Eight

The Classroom and Beyond: An Integrated Formula for an Ethical Life

You shall teach them diligently to your children"
The Torah

What the child says outdoors, he has learned indoors.
The Talmud

The Torah stresses the importance of knowledge. Above all and at every level, Lakewood is a learning-oriented community; as such, and like other Orthodox communities, both boys and girls receive a quality religious and secular education. By extended definition, Orthodox education is a holistic endeavor; not only a means of achieving a good quality of life and worthwhile career, but also as a way of inculcating moral and ethical values, encouraging observation of the Torah commandments, and transmitting knowledge of the sacred texts. While disseminating Torah knowledge to children was once the sole domain of parents, it has over the years been handed down to teachers and schools. As far back as the rabbinic period following the destruction of the Temple in 70 CE, there have been houses of Torah study called *beth midrashos* or *yeshivos*.

As discussed in Chapter Four, most non-Orthodox Jewish children in the twentieth century, if they received a Jewish education, did so as I did, in synagogue after-school or Sunday school programs as an extension of secular study in public schools. For the Orthodox, schools are integral to their efforts to protect their children from the perceived evils of secular America and a modern public educational system with teachings that are considered anti-religious, assimilating, and immoral. Jewish day schools are private institutions that provide Jewish children from kindergarten to twelfth grade with rigorous dual curriculums in English and Hebrew, and secular and religious studies. Though the first Talmud Torah and Hebrew day school in Lakewood were co-ed, partially due to financial constraints, observant communities today have separate schools for boys and girls.

Boys' schools are called yeshivas, and girls' schools are called *Bais Yaakov*. The etymology of the word yeshiva is from the Hebrew word for "seat." Jewish tradition lays down that students should sit while learning from a master. Many in Lakewood, when referring to BMG, say *"The Yeshiva."* In its broadest sense, a yeshiva is the generic name for the entire system of schools for boys and men that teach *Mishna* and Talmud to all ages.

There are several institutions within the yeshiva system for boys. *Yeshiva ketana,* or *cheder,* meaning junior yeshiva, refers to institutions for primary school children. The *Yeshiva mesivta* is for high school boys aged thirteen to sixteen. The school day for *ketana* boys begins at 9:00 in the morning and ends at 5:00 p.m. Once a week, the day is extended to 6:00 p.m. for the study of *Tanach* (Hebrew Bible). *Ketanas* have a dual curriculum combining secular studies with religious education.

Once young Orthodox boys begin high school, their day begins at 7:00 a.m. and goes until 10:00 in the evening except, of course, on *Shabbat*. Half of the school day is devoted to moral teachings. Approximately two hours are spent reading Torah and Talmud in ancient, or Biblical Hebrew. Five hours are spent in reading and analyzing Talmudic commentary in concert with a study partner as in the higher yeshivas, and also with the teacher or lecturer. The day is broken up by morning, afternoon, and evening prayers. There are two to three hours dedicated to secular subjects.

Gadola, or higher yeshiva, comes from the word *gadol* meaning "big," and refers to the post high school institution dedicated to the study of Torah, Talmud, and rabbinical literature. Some men take the additional step of joining a *kollel*, an advanced yeshiva often housed in the same facility as the yeshiva and designed for men beginning their married lives immersed in learning. *Kollel* students, choosing not to pursue the formerly *de rigeur*

Jewish professions of medicine, law, business, and education, receive a small stipend for their dedication to Talmudic study.

The nature of girls and womens education in Orthodox Jewish society in America has gone through a tremendous metamorphosis. For Jews, mostly Sephardic, who arrived on the shores of colonial America, there were few Jewish schools; those that did exist were co-ed and short lived. The Orthodox Jews who immigrated to the New World from Eastern Europe in the 1930s would eventually establish, in America, the Old World *Bais Ya'akov* model of girls' education founded in 1917 by Sarah Schenirer in Cracow, Poland.

Schenirer saw the high rate of assimilation amongst these girls as due to the secular influences of the non-Jewish schools they were then attending. She concluded that providing young Jewish women with a thorough, school-based Jewish education was the only way to combat this phenomenon.

She started a school of her own, trained other women to teach, and set up similar schools in other cities throughout Europe. *Bais Ya'akov*, which means House of Jacob, grew rapidly and provided a religiously acceptable alternative to secular schooling where young girls were being educated and assimilated for life in modern, Western-oriented, secular society – believed to be poor preparation for marriage and motherhood in a strictly observant Jewish community.

Today, from Israel to England to Canada to Brooklyn, Monsey, and Lakewood, the term *Bais Ya'akov* is the generic name for elementary and secondary schools for girls from Orthodox families, both *Yeshivish* and Hasidic. Students are required to uphold a dress code or wear uniforms which conform to the rules of modesty. While uniforms differ from school to school, they typically consist of a long pleated skirt, conservative oxford blouse, and either a sweater or sweatshirt. Girls attend elementary school from 9:00 a.m. to 3:30 or 4:00 p.m. Like the yeshivas, the *Bais Ya'akov* school day is divided between secular and religious studies, but the curriculum differs from that of male yeshivas insofar as the core component of study for males is the Talmud.

Girls in *Bais Ya'akov* do not learn law from the text of the Talmud itself, but may study *Aggadah* portions. *Aggadah* refers to the non-legalistic exegetical texts in classical rabbinic literature as recorded in Talmud and *Midrash,* a compendium of rabbinic homilies that incorporates folklore, historical anecdotes, moral exhortations, and practical advice in various spheres from business to medicine.

The secondary level Bais Ya'akov has seven hour days. Half of the day is devoted to *Tanach* which is studied through the lens of commentaries, especially those of Rashi, because Orthodox Judaism teaches that it is not possible to fully comprehend Written Torah without the commentaries. They also study Hebrew, Jewish history, and practical *Halakha*, Jewish law. That girls' education in today's Orthodox communities is of less concern than that of boys is the very antithesis of the spirit of Jewish family life. Admittedly, *Bais Ya'akov* schools' primary purpose is to prepare young women to be good Jews, mothers, teachers, and wives, but Lakewood psychologist Lauren Roth maintains that *Bais Ya'akov* girls are in fact "better educated and more proficient in secular studies than their male counterparts" whose education is more religious-intense.

A significant and ever increasing number of *Bais Ya'akov* graduates are electing to continue their education at colleges, referred to as seminaries, within the *Bais Ya'akov* system. The course program lasts between two and three years and prepares women to teach. Many young women participate in Bachelor's and Master's Degree programs at TTI (Training and Testing International) in Manhattan affiliated with various accredited universities throughout the United States. The *Raizel Rite* Program offers credits for knowledge of Jewish studies based on intensive testing. Both classroom and distance learning courses offer flexible alternatives. The BA program is affiliated with Excelsior College; depending upon the graduate curriculum, TTI works in conjunction with other universities.

Twenty-one-year-old Sheina* is completing her Masters degree in special education through Daemen College in Amhurst, N.Y., and hopes to teach at Lakewood's celebrated SCHI School. SCHI (School for Children with Hidden Intelligence) on Oak Street is a top tier, state approved private school that educates multiple handicapped, learning disabled, and underprivileged Orthodox and non-Orthodox children with special needs, and which encourages independence and academic achievement. One of the most remarkable and innovative aspects of this school, Sheina tells me, is that it mixes mainstream students from other schools into the classes to afford both student populations an opportunity to meet and learn together.

Some women may decide to attend a secular college, such as nearby Georgian Court, Richard Stockton College in Atlantic County, or Ocean

County College in Toms River, for degree programs, or to take core courses that will prepare them to study at TTI, Touro, or other four year universities where they pursue careers in teaching, information technology, speech pathology, physical therapy, law, or medicine – all flexible occupations allowing them to have a rich and spiritual family life while fulfilling the mitzvah of sharing full responsibility with their husbands for religious observance in the home and guiding the academic and religious life of their own children.

As such, and as was the case in Europe, education does not stop at the end of the school day but continues in the home. A non-Orthodox friend of mine recently related a story about a young Orthodox boy from Jackson who was roughed up by some students at a nearby public school. "That happened," Shari explains, "because these kids don't have a rec[reation] center to keep them busy after school lets out." Aside from my indignation that here was yet another convoluted example of excuses and misplaced sympathy for the perpetrator, I marveled at how people have come to believe that the government or others are responsible for keeping our children out of trouble and discouraging juvenile criminal behavior. I could only imagine how an Orthodox mother or father would respond to Shari's declaration.

In the Orthodox world, both parents are obligated to not only care for a child's physical needs; they must provide emotional support, moral guidelines, and educational opportunities to prepare their child to live in the world. Both parents are obligated to teach their children. However, in most homes it is the mother who is the children's first teacher. After all, when the Torah was given at Mount Sinai, it was given to the women first so they would transmit it to their children. As soon as the child can speak, it is the obligation of the father, specifically, and the mother generally, to begin teaching the child Torah. By teaching the child Torah, it will lead him/her to perform *mitzvot*. As soon as the child is old enough, the parents must provide him/her with teachers.

It is said in Torah that *A child owes his life to three; to G-d, to his father, and to his mother.* Children are taught reverence for G-d by the living examples of their parents. Duty to family is stressed in the Orthodox home, especially children's obligations to parents. It is taught that a child must love and honor his parents while they are living and after they pass. Grown children whose parents are aged or needy have responsibility to feed, shelter, clothe, and care for them graciously, and not begrudgingly. They are duty bound to honor and revere their parents after death by reciting *kaddish* for 11 months, keeping *yarzheit,* giving charity in their names, and living a life that reflects credit on those who birthed and raised them so that, as the Torah instructs, "[the parents] live again in his or her good deeds."

Although biblical tales may suggest the lack of brotherly or sisterly love between the likes of Cain and Abel, Jacob and Esau, and Rachel and Leah, Orthodox parents instill in their children a sense of responsibility of each child to his younger siblings. It is not uncommon to see mothers pushing double strollers along Madison Avenue or County Line Road while three of four children follow along. The older girls, some as young as seven, carefully watch and hold the hands of their younger brothers and sisters.

Orthodox women learn their roles early. They are taught that the Jewish woman has a most noble role designated to her, that she is the focal point and essence of her home. The Jewish mother, it is taught, strives to instill in her home a love for Torah and *Yiddishkeit.* Even the mundane and routine take on a new dimension when performed with a higher aim in mind. Young girls are taught to honor their mother and aspire to be like them. Strict regulations regarding modesty and decorum, or *tzniut,* dictate how Orthodox girls and women dress, interact with the opposite sex, and behave in an appropriate manner. Rules of modesty are maintained from a very early age. Orthodox women wear skirts that cover at least the knees, and long sleeved, high necked blouses. There is no commandment for a woman to cut off her hair after marriage, though some women choose to, but because of the laws of modesty and decorum, she is required to wear a *sheitel* (wig). Hair is regarded as a sex symbol which might make her desirable to other men. Hasidic women, in addition to the *sheitel*, also wear a hat, snood, or scarf.

Dietary laws are also learned in the home. Orthodox Jews all over the world follow the same dietary traditions rigidly observed by their parents and grandparents, a tradition that dates back to when Kosher laws (those foods judged fit to eat according to biblical and rabbinic law, as well as the proper supervised slaughtering) were passed down from G-d to Moses to the Israelites. Food is necessary for anyone's survival, but in the Orthodox home, food is symbolic, and a means towards good health, family celebration, and praising G-d. Jewish foods reflect a multitude of savory ethnic influences from as far afield as Spain, Germany, Poland, Russia, and the Middle East. Whether feast or famine, food appears often in stories from the Torah. Abraham and Sarah use food as an expression of hospitality, Joseph reveals himself to his brothers and they break bread together, G-d provides the Israelites leaving Egypt with a mysterious food called *manna*. Orthodox Jews recite prayers (*berakhot*) before eating and drinking to encourage awareness and give thanks for bread, meals, cake, cheese, meat, fruits, vegetables, grapes, and of course, for wine. The *Birkat-ha-mazon*, or Grace after Meals, is recited after meals or after any bread is eaten.

To the outsider, an Orthodox home may be enviable for their large kitchens with two stoves, refrigerators, and sinks. The reason for the separate appliances is not a materialistic one, but one that ensures strict adherence to *kashrut*, or dietary laws. Passed down from mother to daughter, these laws require separate dishes, cooking utensils, ovens, and sinks for dairy and meat products. Foods of dairy (*milchig*) and animal (*fleishig*) origin cannot be combined either in the cooking or the serving of a meal, and dairy foods can be eaten after a meat meal only after several hours have lapsed. Fruits, vegetables, and grains are considered *pareve*, neither milk nor meat, and as such may be eaten or mixed with either meat or dairy.

The term *kosher* is used to describe those foods that are acceptable according to Jewish dietary laws. There are many prohibitions set forth in the laws of *kashrut* in the book of Leviticus in Torah: no shellfish, no pig, no carrion, no birds of prey, nothing that crawls on its belly. Then there are strict categories of food that are permitted: only those fish that have fins and scales; only those animals that chew the cud and have cloven hooves. There are also many cooking and serving instructions. Meat and poultry must be soaked and salted to purge it of blood before it is cooked. Non-Orthodox Jews, on the other hand, even if they maintain a kosher home, may or may not choose to eat anything in a restaurant or at another person's home.

Because they reject and avoid many Western norms, including public secular schooling which they believe to be founded on an anti-religious and materialistic foundation, most Orthodox families do not have televisions in their homes, nor do they attend public movies. Many families do have monitors to allow playing of videos or DVDs of their own choosing. If there is a computer in the home, use of the internet is very carefully monitored because of the uncontrolled and inappropriate material that is accessible or that may appear as pop ups. For this reason, there are several Orthodox websites that are educational and which cover news and stories of interest.

No matter what your belief system, it would be difficult to argue that there are valuable lessons to be learned from Orthodox families about responsible parenting, and that spiritual teachings and character development begin in the home. Today's society, one might reasonably argue, has an absence of moral underpinnings, values, and role models. Too often do we see children being shuttled after the school day and on weekends, to dance lessons, with minimal family time in homes lacking serenity and stability. To be in an Orthodox home where Torah is integrated with life, and children are taught the ethics of individual, family, social, and spiritual responsibility, is to sense an exhilarating aura of joy and peace. These timeless ethics, values, and behaviors have proven relevant across the centuries and remain, today, an essential part of any good life – and of any democracy.

Chapter Nine

Dating and Marriage, or, A Bird May Love a Fish, But Where Would They Live?

To be unmarried is to live without joy, without blessing, without kindness, without religion, and without peace.
The Talmud

G-d did not create woman from man's head, that he should command her; nor from his feet, that she should be his slave; but from his side, that she should be nearest his heart.
Adapted from The Talmud

Perhaps it's because of the memorable character, Yente the Matchmaker in *Fiddler on the Roof,* the musical based on Sholom Aleichem's stories, that many outside Orthodox circles have the notion that marriages are arranged and that young women are forced to marry someone they do not want to, or someone whom they have never met. Nothing could be further from the truth. In speaking to her mother about Yente, Tzeitel complains, "But Mama, the men she finds. The last one was so old and he was bald. He had no hair." To which Golde replies, "A poor girl without a dowry can't be so particular. You want hair, marry a monkey." But even in the musical and film, Tzeitel chooses the poor but earnest Mottel the tailor over Yente's selection of the older and wealthy butcher Lazar Woolf, an act of rebellion signaling the beginning of the collapse of the pillars of Tevye's world.

In the Jewish religion, a woman is never forced to marry someone who is not her choice. As the Bible makes clear in the story of Rebecca's courtship with Isaac, her family says that they must 'ask the maiden' if she wishes to follow Eliezer, the matchmaker, and marry Isaac. Only with her consent can the marriage take place. To the Orthodox, every marriage is Holy and must be based on the exercise of the human free will to choose life partners. What is arranged are meetings between young men and women.

In modern Western culture where men and women interact on a daily basis, young people are able to easily and informally meet at schools, parties, social settings, through family and friends, or on-line. They may date (and have sex) casually, date several partners at once, have a three year engagement, or choose to live together in a committed relationship without the formality of marriage.

By its very nature, the Orthodox lifestyle limits contact between the sexes. The codes of modesty, or *tznius,* which dictate appropriate dress, also govern conduct and relations between men and women to prevent promiscuity. Women do not shake hands with men (or men with women) unless they are married, and in that case, only in a private setting. This is not because women are spiritually unclean, or might be menstruating, as is the common belief, but because they consider the human body sacred and not for anyone else's touch. Men and women do not look directly into the eyes of a person of the opposite sex unless it is his or her own spouse.

To Orthodox Jews, marriage is more than a contractual agreement or social arrangement. It is a *mitzvah* and the very essence of a spiritual bonding. The first step is finding a suitable life partner. As Tevye says to his young daughter, Chava: "As the good book says 'Each shall seek his own kind.' In other words, a bird may love a fish but where would they build a home together?"

Finding one's soul mate is serious business and is done through matchmaking, called a *shidduch*. Though many couples are introduced by a close friend or family member, there are also professional matchmakers or marriage brokers called *shadchanim,* who charge a fee for recommending a match. The matchmaker will make discreet inquiries about the prospective partner such as his or her character, intelligence, educational background, financial status, health, appearance, and religious observance. Once a match has been proposed, the prospective partners meet one or two times to engage in casual conversation to determine if they are intellectually and emotionally compatible. While The Talmud explicitly states that the man and woman must also be physically attracted to each other (which can only be determined by meeting), physical contact, except for certain close relatives, is not permitted between a man and a woman until they are married. If at the first one or two meetings, the couple discovers that they share the common goals and values necessary to a happy life together, they will then discuss more serious issues such as marriage, children, and finances. It is not unusual for the couple to undergo genetic testing to identify whether either one carries a potential life threatening genetic disease that may be passed on to a newborn. At the request of the couple, the *shadchen* may intercede in the first few meetings to resolve any issues that arise. If the match does not work out, the *shadchen* is contacted and tells the other side that the relationship will not be moving forward. If it works out –*mazel tov!*—the couple informs the *shadchen* it was a success.

Many Orthodox are open about negative aspects of the *shidduch,* when it comes to young people with medical, physical, or psychiatric issues, financial or family problems, those from broken homes, and those who have returned to Orthodoxy. Leah is a mother of four daughters and two sons. She is frustrated by her futile efforts to find a match for her eldest daughter, twenty-five-year-old Miriam, because of the family's current shaky financial situation since her accountant husband was laid off from his job. Her brow furrows as she stirs a pot of soup, and rhetorically asks "So how am I to afford three more weddings?"

Interestingly, no one I spoke with sees the *shidduch* process as "unromantic" or too closely related to arranged marriages. Most will proudly point to the very low divorce rate in the community even though it is possible to get a divorce. Knowing Leah and Aaron are happily married, I ask her what marriage means to her. She doesn't even think about her answer. "Marriage? Marriage is Holy. It is about growing together in a loving and caring relationship and having faith in each other and in *Hashem* [G-d]."

Once the couple agrees to marry, it is traditional and expected that the parents of the bride and groom meet, and that the couple asks for their approval and blessings. The families usually announce the engagement at a small reception, known as a *vort,* where friends and family wish the couple *Mazel Tov* (good luck) in their new life together. During the engagement period, some families sign a contract, the *tenaim,* meaning "conditions," that delineates the obligations of each side regarding the wedding and a final date for the wedding. When the *tenaim* is signed, the mothers of the couple break a plate.

According to Jewish law, sex before marriage is forbidden. One week before the wedding, the bride and groom, the *chosson* and *kallah*, stop seeing each other, in order to enhance the joy of their wedding through their imposed separation. During this time, the couple participates in marriage counseling and classes where they are each taught the laws of family purity. Men learn their obligation to honor their wives and to never force them to have sexual relations against their will or if they are not "in the mood." They are instructed in the importance of creating a loving, caring, and comfortable climate for intimacy. Before the wedding, the bride and groom will visit a *mikvah*, which is discussed in the following chapter.

The first thing that is done on the day of the wedding is the completion, signing, and witnessing of the *ketubah*, or marriage contract. Written in Aramaic, and dating back to Biblical times, the *ketubah* details the husband's obligations to his wife: first of which is to honor her. He promises to work to feed, clothe, house, and pleasure her. It also creates a lien on all his property to pay her a sum of money and support should he divorce her, or predecease her. The obligations outlined in the document are explained to the groom and signed by two witnesses. A *ketubah* has the standing of a legally binding agreement, that in many countries is enforceable by secular law. The *ketubah* is often written as an illuminated manuscript, and becomes a work of art in itself, and which many couples will frame and display in their home.

Once the *ketubah* is signed, and before the actual ceremony under the canopy, there are light refreshments and hard liquor for the traditional *L'Chaims*, meaning "To Life," and which is the Jewish salute when drinking and toasting. The groom, together with his father and future father-in-law, accompanied by musicians and male guests, proceed to the room where the bride is receiving her guests for the *bedekin*, or "veiling" of his bride who he has not seen for a week. The bride is seated, like a queen, on a throne-like chair surrounded by her family and friends. The groom covers her face with her veil, a custom that goes back to Biblical times. Rebecca was the first bride in the *Torah Chumush*, and the first one to use a veil. When she first approached her fiancé, Isaac, Abraham's son, she lowered her veil across her face as a sign of modesty. Later on, their son Jacob had his bride switched on him by his father-in-law Laban, who used the thick covering over his daughter's face to replace Rachel with her sister Leah. The custom for the groom to personally veil the bride emerged, in part, to guard against future nuptial surprises.

The canopy under which the couple will be wed, is called a *chuppah*. The *chuppah* is a decorated piece of cloth held aloft as a symbolic home for the new couple. The *chuppah* is placed under the stars, as a sign of the blessing given by G-d to the patriarch Abraham, that his children shall be "as the stars of the heavens." Short of holding the ceremony outdoors, wedding halls have an opening in the ceiling to allow for the sky to be seen. The groom is accompanied to the *chuppah* by his parents, and usually wears a white robe, known as a *kittel*, to indicate the fact that for the bride and groom, life is starting anew with a clean white slate, since they are uniting to become a new entity, without past sins. Before standing together under the *chuppah,* the mood of the day is solemn and serious. The bride and groom fast until they are married, since for them it is like Yom Kippur, the Day of Atonement.

But as the beautiful blushing bride walks to the *chuppah* with her parents, it is a joyous occasion. She is preceded by members of the wedding party carrying candles as a cantor sings a selection from the *Song of Songs*. The bride and groom pray that their unmarried friends find their true partners in life. When the bride arrives at the *chuppah,* she circles the groom seven times with her mother and future mother-in-law, while the groom continues to pray. This symbolizes the idea of the woman being the protective, surrounding light of the household, illuminating it with understanding and love from within and protects it from harm from the outside.

The number seven has several significances. First, it parallels the seven heavens where G-d dwells as well as the seven days of creation. It also symbolizes the fact that the bride and groom are about to create their own "new world" together.

Under the *chuppah,* a Rabbi or honored family member recites a blessing over wine, and a blessing that sanctifies the day, and praises and thanks G-d for giving us laws of morality to preserve the sanctity of family life and of the Jewish people. The bride and groom then drink from the wine. The blessings are recited over wine, since wine is symbolic of life: it begins as grape-juice, goes through fermentation, during which it is sour, but in the end turns into a superior product that brings joy, and has a wonderful taste. The full cup of wine also symbolizes the overflowing of Divine blessing, as in the verse in Psalms, "My cup runneth over."

The ring ceremony is called a *kiddushin*. The groom places a plain gold ring on the bride's finger, and in the presence of two witnesses, recites:

"Behold you are sanctified (betrothed) to me with this ring, according to the Law of Moses and Israel." The *ketuvah* is now read aloud, usually by another honoree, after which it is given to the bride for safekeeping. After the *kiddushin*, comes the recitation of the seven blessings, or the *sheva brachos*, over a full cup of wine. The blessings can be said by the presiding Rabbi, or by people whom the families wish to honor. The blessings begin with praising G-d for His creation in general and creation of the human being and proceed with praise for the creation of the human as a "two part creature," woman and man. The blessings express the hope that the new couple will rejoice together forever as though they are the original couple, Adam and Eve in the Garden of Eden. The blessings also include a prayer that Jerusalem will be fully rebuilt and restored with the Temple in its midst and the Jewish people within her gates.

At this point, the couple again share in drinking the cup of wine, and the groom breaks a glass by stomping on it with his foot. This custom dates back to Talmudic times, and symbolizes the idea of our keeping Jerusalem and Israel in our minds even at times of our joy. Just as the Temple in Jerusalem is destroyed, so we break a utensil to show our identification with the sorrow of Jewish exile. The verse, *If I forget thee O' Jerusalem, let my right hand forget its cunning: If I do not raise thee over my own joy, let my tongue cleave to the roof of my mouth,* is sometimes recited at this point. With the breaking of the glass the band plays, and the guests usually break out into dancing and cries of "*Mazel tov! Mazel tov!*" My father used to say that this defining moment is "the last time the groom gets to put his foot down."

The married couple is accompanied by dancing guests to the *cheder yichud*, "the room of privacy," where their entry into the room must be observed by two witnesses. Usually the groom will present his bride with a gift such as a strand of pearls. While the bride and groom are alone together eating, after having fasted all day, the guests sit down to eat a festive meal. The meal is preceded by ritual washing of the hands, and the blessing over bread. At some point, the band announces the arrival "for the very first time, Mr. and Mrs. _____!!!" and everyone joins in dancing around the bride and groom.

The dancing, in accordance with Jewish law and modesty, requires a separation between men and women; hence, there is a *mechitzah* or partition between the men and women. The main focus of the dancing is to entertain and enhance the joy of the newlyweds. Large circles are formed around the "king and queen," and different guests often perform in front of the seated couple. It is not unusual to see jugglers and acrobats at a wedding. The meal ends with the *Birchas Hamazon*, Grace After Meals, and again the seven blessings are recited over wine, shared afterwards by the bride and groom.

This seems an appropriate time to debunk the myth that Orthodox Jewish lore requires married couples to use a bed sheet with a hole in the center when having sex. This is not only a falsehood, explains psychologist Lauren Roth, "but the very antithesis of all things Orthodox – and Jewish for that matter. Of all the religions, Judaism views lovemaking and sex as something spiritual and to derive pleasure from." Sex between married couples not only may bring forth life, but it binds two people with one flesh and one soul. Nor does Judaism dictate the incompatibility of sexuality and spirituality. Human sexuality is a primary force in the lives of the married couple, the foundation of their own family unit, and integral to the world at large. As long as there would be human beings in the world, G-d assured Abraham, there would always be Jews. Marriage and bringing children into a loving, spiritual, and peaceful home are what will ultimately ensure the continuity and communal nature of the Jewish people.

Chapter Ten

To Everything There is a Season: Orthodox Life Cycles

Youth is a crown of roses, old age is a crown of rosemary.
The Talmud

The birth of a child begins the cycle of life rituals steeped in religion and tradition that continue through *Bar/Bat Mitzvah*, engagement, marriage, death, and mourning. The Orthodox observe these life-cycle events today much as they were followed 4,000 years ago.

Like most key life events in Orthodoxy, the birth of a child is a *simcha*, a joyous event marked with special ceremonies and customs. It is marked by passing on the names of ancestors, though Sephardic Jews name the newborn after someone living. The celebration also provides an opportunity to celebrate and give thanks to G-d. There are differences in celebratory customs for boys and girls. Giving the newborn girl or boy a Hebrew or Yiddish name is considered important and what identifies him or her with the Jewish people. The name of the baby girl is announced at a special baby-naming ceremony at the *shul* on the first Torah reading, or the first *Shabbat* following her birth. Baby boys are named at the *Brit Milah*, or, circumcision ceremony.

The naming ceremony and celebration of the birth of a daughter parallels the *brit* ceremony for Jewish boys, albeit without the circumcision. After the birth of a girl, it is the father's obligation to go to the synagogue as soon after the birth as possible on a day when Torah is read (Monday, Thursday, or *Shabbat*) in order to name his daughter. The father will be honored with an *aliyah* (being called to the *bimah* to read a portion of Torah). After the *Parsha* is read, the *Mi She'Berach* is recited and the daughter is named. After the service, a toast to *l'chayim* (to life) is given. It is customary for the parents to invite family and friends to the synagogue or their home for *Kiddush* on the *Shabbat* directly after their daughter's birth.

There are subsequent rituals reserved for a newborn boy. On the *Shabbat* evening immediately following the son's birth, family and friends gather after the *Shabbat* meal at the new parent's home. This ritual, called *Shalom Zachor*, welcomes and honors the newborn, and expresses gratitude to G-d for his safe birth. The gathering is also to "console" the child." It is believed that while the baby is in the womb, an angel teaches him the entire Torah; therefore, the guests console the newborn who is mourning the Torah he has forgotten. Lentils, beans, or chick peas, foods symbolizing mourning, are customarily served. The guests touch the lips of the baby, signifying that he will relearn Torah. The *Shema* is recited, songs of welcome are sung, and good wishes for the recovery of the mother and well-being of the son are offered. The son will not be named until the *Brit Milah*, the Covenant of Circumcision.

Circumcision is the first commandment given by G-d to Abraham and is central to Judaism. On his eighth day of life, the baby is circumcised as mandated by G-d's covenant with the Jewish people in the story of Abraham in Genesis 17:9-14:

> *This is My covenant that you shall observe between Me and you and your children after you, to circumcise your every male. You shall circumcise the flesh of your foreskin, and it shall become the sign of a covenant between Me and you.*

The circumcision can be performed in a synagogue, but usually takes place in the hospital or at home. The circumcision is viewed as a religious ceremony, rather than just surgery and thus is performed by a *Mohel*, an Orthodox Jew trained in the physical procedures of circumcision and who understands the religious significance of the ritual. If a *Mohel* is not available, then a Jewish physician can perform the circumcision. It is customary to invite a rabbi to conduct the service. The circumcision is performed in the presence of a quorum of ten adult Jewish men. The service begins when the *Mohel* asks that the mother hands the baby over to the *kvatatterin* (godmother) who then brings the baby into the room in which he will be circumcised and hands him to the *kvatter* (godfather). People stand up when the baby enters the room and say "*Baruch HaBa*" (May he who cometh be blessed). The *Mohel* recites a prayer which mentions the covenant with Abraham. The baby is placed in a chair that symbolizes the presence of the prophet Elijah, who emphasized the importance of maintaining G-d's covenant with the Jews. He is then handed to the *Sandak*, who holds the baby on his cushion during the circumcision; this honor often goes to the grandfather. Prayers are recited and, after the circumcision, the father will say the blessing that acknowledges the child's entry into the covenant. A prayer for the well-being of the child and family is recited. The *Mohel* then takes the child and blesses him, and gives him the name chosen by his parents, while putting some wine to the baby's lips. At the end of the ceremony, the baby is passed back to his mother. A family celebration follows that includes a festive meal called the *Seudat Mitzvah* and after the meal, *birkat hamazon* is usually recited with special blessings for the child and his parents.

The term *Pidyon ha' Ben* refers to the ritual of Redemption of the Son and is based on the Jewish concept that first and best things belong to G-d. In Numbers 8:17, G-d declares: *Every firstborn among the Israelites, man as well as beast, is mine.* When the first-born son (of a mother) is thirty-one-days-old he goes through the *Pidyon HaBen* (Redemption of the First-Born Son) which in biblical times was overseen by a *Cohen, or Kohen.* The *Cohen* is any man who is a descendant from the *Cohanim* (priests).

The Jewish people are divided in three groups: Cohen, Levi, and Israel. The group to which the son belongs is transmitted by the father and the knowledge of which group you belong to is transmitted orally in the family. Ever since the incident with the Golden Calf in Exodus 32, the Levites took upon themselves the function of assisting the *Cohanim*, and the first-born son of an Israelite was redeemed for the sum of five silver biblical coins.

Today, during the Ceremony of Redemption, the son is dressed in special clothes. The father presents the child to the *Sandak*, a honored guest, usually the grandfather, who fulfills the duty of the *Cohen* and who presides over the ceremony. The father gives the money to the *Sandak*, who holds five silver coins over the child's head and exchanges the child for the money and blesses the child. The coins can be given back to the father or given to charity depending upon what the *Sandak* decides. The ceremony ends with the *Kiddush* prayer over wine, and a lunch celebration.

At the age of three, a boy gets his first haircut in a ritual called the *upsherin* which, in Yiddish, means "to shear off." The *upsherin* is the third in a series of "cuts" symbolizing a child's movement from babyhood to childhood. First when the umbilical cord is cut after the birth, and then when the foreskin is cut during the *bris*. The custom of *upsherin* is based on biblical verses (Deut.20:19 and Lev. 19:23, 27) that compare man to a tree; just as a tree matures from a tiny seed to fruit-bearing tree, likewise a child grows more knowledgeable and bears fruit via good deeds. Just as the Torah requires newly planted fruit trees be allowed to grow unharvested for three years, a child's hair can be left uncut for three years.

At age three, he begins to learn the *Aleph-Bet*. A tradition at the *upsherin* is for the child to lick honey off of Hebrew alphabet cards and sing the song *Torah Tzivah Lanu Moshe, U'morasha Kehillat Yaakov."* It is also traditional that he receives his first *kippah* and *tzitzit*, which begins the child's formal introduction to Torah education and *mitzvot*. At some *upsherin* ceremonies, each of those attending snip off a lock of hair, at others charity is given equal to the weight of the hair, or for each snip.

Under Jewish law, children under thirteen are not obligated to observe the commandments, though they are encouraged to do as much as possible to learn the obligations they will have as adults. At the age of thirteen (twelve for girls), they become obligated to observe the commandments. In Hebrew, *Bar Mitzvah* literally means "son of the commandment." The word *bar* means son. The late comedian Sam Levenson used to tell the story of the nervous *bar mitzvah* boy standing at the *bimah* who announces, "Today I am a fountain pen." The *bar mitzvah* is really not about presents such as fountain pens, but about taking on the responsibilities of an Orthodox man accountable for his own actions, for fasting on certain holidays, and for being able to participate in a *minyan*. For girls, it means being subject to all laws of Torah as they apply to women. The popular *bar mitzvah* ceremony is not required to confer these rights and obligations, nor does it fulfill any commandment. It is a relatively modern invention, not mentioned in the Talmud.

On the day after his thirteenth birthday, according to the Jewish calendar, the young man attends the *Shacharit* service with his father and formally puts on *tefillin* (boxes containing biblical verses and used for morning prayers), which he has practiced wrapping for several months. On the first Monday, Thursday, or *Shabbat* after his thirteenth birthday, he is called to *aliyah* for the first time. This *aliyah* may include the reading of the *haftarah,* literally meaning "conclusion, and referring to a reading from the Book of Prophets. Following this, the father is called to the *bimah* where he confers responsibility for his son's observance from himself to his son. Depending upon the synagogue's rituals and the *bar mitzvah's* education, the *bar mitzvah* may also chant all or parts of the *Shabbat* service, read the Torah portion, and offer a *d'var Torah*. After the service, the parents host a *Kiddush*, a luncheon celebration with wine (grape juice for the children), cakes, and sandwiches, for the entire congregation. Separate celebrations may also be hosted after *Shabbat*. The most important party, however, is the day of the thirteenth birthday. If a school day, the parents will provide the class with refreshments such as cakes, ice cream, or bagels and lox. Above anything else, this event is more than just one day in the life of a young man or woman—it is a rite of passage and a lifetime commitment.

Judaism encourages us to acknowledge our mortality and embrace the sacredness of life on earth. Jewish law has developed a system of mourning that honors the dead and comforts the bereaved, from a public and dignified eulogy to burial in a plain casket to the week-long ritual of mourning.

Orthodox Judaism decrees that the body must be buried no later than 24 hours after death and also forbids the viewing of the loved one after death. The body of the deceased is carefully prepared for burial by members of *Chevra Kadisha*, a Jewish society made up of Orthodox volunteers in the community. They perform the ritual washing of the body and clothe it in a simple white shroud. Since Jewish tradition holds that all people are equal in death, the deceased is placed in a simple pine coffin. Orthodox Judaism believes that the soul hovers near the body shortly after its separation, and thus the body of the deceased is never left alone without the soul being comforted by the recitation of prayers. The mourners *Kaddish*, the most powerful ritual for mourners is recited for eleven months after the death of a loved one and is a source of blessing to both the mourner as well as to the soul of the deceased. Interestingly, the *Kaddish* makes no mention of death or of the deceased, but serves more as an affirmation of the justice of G-d and the meaningfulness of life. It expresses hope for the redemption and ultimate healing of all those who suffer. The ancient observances of reciting *Kaddish*, lighting a memorial candle which symbolizes the soul, and giving charity on behalf of the deceased are ways of honoring ancestors after death and fulfilling obligations of those who have since passed.

The mourning process has five stages. The first stage, the period of the *onen*, is the period between the death notification and the funeral. The mourners are restricted from certain activities and from performing certain *mitzvot*. The second stage, the period of the *avel*, is the first three days after the funeral. This is an intense period of grief. The third stage is the seven-day (including the period of the *avel*) period of *shivah*. The fourth stage, *shloshim*, occurs during the first thirty days after the funeral. The final stage, *yahrtzeit*, is the observance of the first year anniversary after the death at which time an upright stone, a *matzevah*, must be erected at the gravesite.

One notable feature of the graveside service (although it can take place earlier) is that of *keriah*, the ceremony of tearing one of the outer garments of the direct mourners. The garment is torn on the left side for a parent and on the right side for other relations, because of the presence of the heart on the left. The origin of this idea appears to be biblical. Jacob tore his clothes when he was confronted with the evidence of Joseph's death, (Bereishit 37:34) and David did the same when he heard the news of the death of Saul and Jonathan (II Samuel 1:11). The powerful symbolism and impact of the tear are clear: Something that was whole has been torn apart. This can relate to the dead body that has been torn away from its soul; it could refer to the relationship between the person that died and those that have been left behind; it could also refer to the internal tearing in the heart of the mourners themselves. The Orthodox look upon the modern variation of wearing a ready-made piece of black fabric on a pin as disrespectful, improper, and an example of Western materialism.

When the patriarch Jacob lay on his deathbed, he conveyed to his children gathered around him his deepest principles and wishes. This tradition has been handed down in the manner of writing an "ethical will"— a letter to one's children and descendants expressing one's convictions and the most important actions and beliefs we hope they will carry on. The following is a touching example of an ethical will that was written over 2000 years ago by Judah Ibn Tibbon, and which is emblematic of the Jewish tradition of moral education and of the wisdom of the old being offered to younger generations:

> *My son, when I have left you, devote yourself to the study of Torah and the study of medicine. Chiefly occupy yourself with Torah, for you have a wise and understanding heart and all you need is ambition and application. Let your face shine on people: tend their sick and may your advice cure them. Take money from the rich but treat the poor without*

money. The Lord will repay you. In this way, you will win the respect of people high and low and your good name will go forth far and wide...My son, I command you to honour your wife as much as you can. She is intelligent and modest, a daughter of a distinguished and educated family. To act otherwise is the way of the contemptible...Never refuse to lend books to anyone who has not the means to purchase books for himself, but only act thus to those who can be trusted to return the volumes. Cover the bookcases with rugs of fine quality and preserve them from damp and from mice, for your books are your greatest treasure.

(Qtd. in Abrahams)

Chapter Eleven

Orthodox Judaism and Belief in the Afterlife

There are three sounds which go from one end of the world to the other, yet the creatures therein hear nothing. These are: The day, the rain, and the soul when it departs the body.
    Midrash *(Exodus Rabbah)*

One of the fundamental tenets of Judaism is that life does not begin with birth nor end with death. This belief is articulated in the verse in Ecclesiastes: *And the dust returns to the earth as it was, and the spirit returns to G-d, who gave it.* Several distinct conceptions about the fate of man after death relating to the immortality of the soul, the resurrection of the dead, and the nature of the World to Come after the Messianic redemption exist side by side within the major denominations of Judaism. The philosophies have also varied historically from period to period and though these concepts are interwoven, no generally accepted theological system exists concerning their interrelationship.

Indeed, many non-Orthodox Jews reject some of the doctrines embraced by their Orthodox or more mystically inclined brethren, but what is indisputable is the fact that over the course of millennia, Orthodox Judaism has always affirmed a belief in life after death and that death is not an endpoint of conscious existence but simply a transition to another state of consciousness. Though the physical body ceases to function and exist, and as evidenced by the various prayers said in memory of the dead, the soul that had been contained within that body is liberated; she departs the physical world and lives on.

What is the Soul?

Every person is infused with a Divine soul. The Soul is spiritual and immortal and as the prophet Job calls it, *a part of G-d above*. As such, the soul is considered the part of the human being most like G-d; the seat of the intellect, spirituality, creativity and the Divine spark implanted within. Simply put, the soul is the "self," the identity that inhabits, but yet is distinct from, the physical body. The body is the medium for the soul's improvement and development. Gershon Winkler explains this partnership as one of union and cooperativeness, emphasizing that the role of the body is to facilitate the journey and fulfillment of the soul in this life, and that the role of the soul is to "overcome the glaring distractions of this life so they do not distort its reality and purpose." (Winkler 6)

In Jewish sacred literature, there are many terms for soul and soul qualities such as reasoning, curiosity, innovation, intuition, emotion and awe – all of which become possible once a child has been born. The human soul has five levels or gradations: *Nefesh* is the lowest and physical part of the soul identified with energy and vitality; it is a spark of G-d that man shares with everything from a rock to an animal. *Neshamah* is totally spiritual; the higher soul, the intellect which separates man from other life forms. Literally meaning "breath," it is the part of the soul that G-d blew into the nostrils of Adam so that he became a living being (Gen. 2:7). *Neshama* (feminine noun which is why the soul is referred to as "she") is the immortal part of the soul that survives the death of the body and returns to G-d. *Ru'ach* has been described as the middle transitional soul connecting the former two and allowing the physical and spiritual to coexist in one body. *Ru'ach* contains the moral virtues and the ability to distinguish between good and evil. Above *Neshama* are two levels of soul that are rarely fully internalized by humans: *Chaya and Yechida*. *Chaya* is the life force, that inner breath of G-d. *Yechida* is identified with pure faith and absolute devotion.

Pre-Physical Life of the Soul

An often-cited commentary relates that all the souls that will ever exist were "created during the six days of Creation, and were in the Garden of Eden, and all were present at the giving of the Torah [at Sinai]." (Tanhuma, Pekudei 3) This perspective is reflected in Jeremiah 1:5: *I knew you, before I formed you in the belly, before you left the womb.*

Before a soul descends to this world from "beneath the throne of glory," to animate a human body, it exists in a purely spiritual realm and pre-physical state during which time it is fortified with the Divine wisdom, energy, vision and Torah knowledge to empower it to accomplish its mission in the physical world. It is only in the physical world and in a body that a soul can perform G-dly deeds and connect the Divine with the mundane. While In the spiritual realm, the soul is formed with a distinct identity and purpose to improve herself and to correct and better her surroundings. The soul's lofty role on earth is to work as a messenger of, and in partnership with, G-d to bring His presence into this world through Torah learning and performance of mitzvoth.

Physical Life of the Soul

Most often in Jewish sacred literature, a fetus in the womb is considered a human life "under construction." Though it does not enter the body until birth, the soul is believed to hover over the developing fetus and is often symbolized as a candle or flame burning over the fetus' head. The soul is usually described as arriving when the first breath of life is taken at birth. Ironically, *neshama* also means "to breathe" and indeed, Gen. 1:27 describes the newborn's "breath of life" coming directly from G-d. The primary Jewish imagery for the beginning of universal life also comes from the Biblical passage where breath hovers above the waters of earth before life emerges from that cosmic womb. Then, in Genesis 2:7, after the body of Adam is fashioned from the clay of the earth, G-d is described as breathing life into him. These stories frame the basis for the Jewish view that the fetus gains full human rights and status only once the baby's head has emerged from the birth canal. (Ohalot 7:6)

The soul a baby will receive is traditionally understood to be unique and pre-destined. The combining of the particular soul with the particular body it enters results in a human. There is a *midrash* that explains that the fetus has cognitive ability while in the womb. It goes like this: While the fetus is gestating in its mother's womb, and while the soul hovers over it, an angel is teaching the child the entire Torah. When the child is about to be born, the angel slaps the child just above the lip, causing everything that was learned to be forgotten. [Niddah 30b] Just enough residual memory remains for the human to experience the urge to seek, savor, and believe we can find and connect again to that sweet, deep learning in our lives. It is free will, the human choice, to either pursue that knowledge deeply embedded in our soul or to suppress it.

The word *mitzvah* in Aramaic means "a connection" and thus there are 613 ways for man to act as a Divine spark on earth, to connect his entire being with G-d. Upon achieving this task thorough Torah study and mitzvoth, he creates an abode, a dwelling place, for G-d in this world, hence fulfilling the purpose of creation. As mentioned earlier, each soul is unique and therefore whatever special abilities and talents belong to that individual soul become another tool to fulfill *mitzvoth*, and to repair and perfect the world.

Reward and Punishment in the Afterlife

In the Talmud, the distinction between body and soul is particularly clear in this passage: *When the time arrives for a person to depart from this world, G-d takes His portion back and leaves the portions contributed by the parents.* (T. Niddah 31a) The concept of reward and punishment in the *Olam Ha-Ba,* the afterlife, is extensively discussed in Jewish traditional sources and is one of the "Thirteen Principles" of Judaism enumerated by Maimonides.

The soul is immortal and, thus, the incorporeal soul survives bodily death and is transported to a spiritual realm beyond the dimensions of time and space where, after the final Divine judgment, it enjoys eternal repose. Depending on Torah learning and good deeds done while in a human body, the soul may ascend directly to *Gan Eden,* literally the Garden of Eden, the place of spiritual reward where the soul enjoys the "rays of the Divine Presence."

Descriptions of *Gan Eden* vary. Some sources compare the bliss of the afterlife to the warmth of a sunny day. Others describe it as the place where one finally understands the true nature of G-d. But only the most righteous go to *Gan Eden*. Those less virtuous souls who have sinned descend to a place of punishment known as *Gehinom* to be cleansed for elevation to *Gan Eden.*

In the Talmud, *Gehinom* is pictured as a dark region with fire and sulfurous fumes; other sources describe it as a time when Jews review the actions of their lives and experience remorse for their sins. *Gehinnom* is given much attention in Rabbinical literature and is central to Jewish belief in the afterlife. According to one mystical view, every sin we commit creates an angel of destruction, a demon, and after we die we are punished by the very demons we created. For most souls, punishment is not eternal and they ascend to *Gan Eden* within twelve months; only the most wicked remain. This twelve month limit is repeated in many places in the Talmud and is connected to the Jewish mourning cycles and particularly recitation of *Kaddish* for only eleven months; to do more would suggest that the deceased is one of those who require the longest purification before elevation to *Gan Eden*. Only the utterly wicked do not ascend at the end of this period; their souls are punished for the entire 12 months. Sources differ on what happens at the end of those 12 months: some say that the wicked soul is utterly destroyed and ceases to exist while others say that the soul continues to exist in a state of consciousness of remorse.

Reincarnation of Soul

The term for reincarnation, *gilgul neshamot,* is a belief held by Orthodox Jews for thousands of years. The process, and this is a gross simplification, is based on the following: G-d creates the soul; the soul exists prior to entering the body after conception; the soul, with the help of the body, tries to complete its unique task on earth and repair the world while also experiencing and savoring life; if the soul does not complete its task, it is reincarnated to finish its mission.

The term *gilgul neshamot* literally means "the judgment of the revolutions of the souls." In this view, souls who did not accomplish their mission in one lifetime, or people who had committed extraordinary sins, were given an opportunity to return to life in order to set things right. More particularly, they were reincarnated in circumstances similar to those of their previous incarnation. Thus, Moses and Jethro, for example, were supposed to be the *"gilgulim"* of Cain and Abel. In the Zohar, the authoritative text of Kabbalists, it states the following: *All souls are subject to revolutions. Men do not know the way they have been judged in all time.* That is to say, in their "revolutions," they lose all memory of the actions that led to their being judged. Belief in reincarnation would explain the traditional Jewish belief that every Jewish soul in history was present at Sinai and agreed to the covenant with G-d.

The Jewish understanding of reincarnation and transmigration of the soul is different from Buddhist doctrines. It does not imply pre-determination; rather, it is an opportunity for rectification and soul-perfection, a chance for a soul to achieve a goal not achieved in a previous life and a chance to reward man for fulfilling the desires of his Creator. In the liturgical poem, Keter Malchut, The Crown of Glory," Rabbi Shlomo Ibn Gabirol writes *"If she, the soul, be pure, then she shall obtain favor...but if she has been defiled, then she shall wander for a time in pain and despair...until the days of her purification."* The rabbis explain this verse to mean that the defiled soul wanders down from paradise through many births until the soul regains its purity.

The holy Ari Zal explained it most simply: Every Jew must fulfill all 613 mitzvot, and if he doesn't succeed in one lifetime, he comes back again and again until he finishes. Rabbi Haim Vital, a student of the Ar'I, has compiled a list of those reincarnated in Jewish history. There is a cycle of reincarnations beginning with Dinah and Shechem. Dina, the daughter of Jacob was raped by Shechem. Shechem did not take responsibility for his actions and blamed them on his upbringing and the fact that Dinah was a noble woman. So the roles were reversed when Shechem was reincarnated as Zimri, an Israelite general, and Dina as Cuzbi, a Midianite woman. Zimri was found consorting with Cuzbi and both were killed by the zealot, Pinhas. Thus when Shechem/Zimri was a noble man and of good birth, he could no longer blame outside sources for his own faults and was punished accordingly. The story continues when Pinhas was reincarnated as Rabbi Akiva and Cuzbi, as the wife of the Roman general Turnus Rufus. She converted to Judaism and helped establish the yeshiva of Rabbi Akiva. By promoting Jewish learning in her next life, she atoned for her sins with Zimri.

Resurrection

While reincarnation is associated with the phenomenon of the soul, the concept of resurrection concerns the body. Belief in the physical resurrection of the righteous at some time in the future was considered by the rabbis in the Talmud to be a basic principle of the Jewish faith and was prominently enshrined in the liturgy. While Maimonides included resurrection of the dead as one of his 13 Principles of Faith, he maintained that the righteous who will be resurrected will live a full life and then die a natural death. In his view, the ultimate destiny of the deserving human being is communion with G-d in a spiritual World to Come.

The Orthodox belief in the resurrection of the dead as part of the messianic redemption figures in the liturgy at a number of points, including the morning prayer expressing the believer's trust that G-d will return his soul to his body in time to come.

Orthodox Jews believe that the souls who have achieved their place in the Garden of Eden will stay in their heavenly abode until the time of the Resurrection of the Dead. At that time all souls will descend once again into this world to be enclothed in their resurrected bodies. There are references to resurrection or *techiya* (enlivening) when body and soul are reunited and which will herald the first step in the perfection of the world. The Prophet Isaiah proclaims, *Your dead shall live, dead bodies shall arise, awake, and sing you who dwell in the dust.* And in the Book of Daniel (12:2), it is said, *Many who sleep in the dust shall awake, some to everlasting life, and some to reproach and everlasting abhorrence.*

The Messianic Age and the World to Come

According to Orthodox Judaism, The World to Come is a time when the world will be perfected following the coming of the Messiah. Orthodox Jews may hold the belief that souls are reincarnated through many lifetimes, or that they simply wait until the Messiah comes to initiate the perfect world of peace, when the righteous dead will be brought back to life and given the opportunity to experience the world that their righteousness helped to create. The wicked dead will not be resurrected.

It should be noted that the Jewish idea of redemption differs from the Christian idea of salvation since Jews reject the belief that humans are born condemned (original sin) and require a messianic figure to "save" them. Rabbinic Judaism teaches that every Jew has a share in the World to Come. Many Orthodox Jews also believe in a communal redemption in the Messianic Age, an era of universal peace and justice *when the wolf shall live with the sheep and the leopard lie down with the kid, the calf with the young lion shall grow up together, and a little child shall lead them.* (Isa. 11:6) According to this belief, the Messiah will be a descendent of King David. Under his rule, the city of Jerusalem and the Temple will be rebuilt and all Jews throughout the world will be gathered to the Land of Israel. Yearning for the coming of the Messiah is a core belief in Judaism and plays a major role in Jewish festivals and liturgy. The Sabbath has always been considered a foretaste of the Messianic Age and the World to Come.

Orthodox Judaism teaches that we should work actively to hasten the arrival of the Messiah by doing everything possible to repair and perfect the world rather than simply waiting passively for him to come. Even the advent of the Messiah will not absolve human beings of responsibility for taking care of the world. This is illustrated in Rabbi Yochanan ben Zakkai's statement: "If you are planting a tree and you hear the Messiah has come, finish planting the tree and then greet him."

Orthodox Jews prepare themselves for both the world of reward in Gan Eden and the universal world of the World to Come through Torah study and deeds of loving kindness in this life, the *Olam ha-zeh*. The Rabbis compared *Olah ha-zeh* to an antechamber to the future world where one was urged to "prepare yourself so that you may enter the palace (Avot 4:21). But to deduce from this belief that the Orthodox Jews try to "earn their way" into *Gan Eden* by performing the mitzvot is a gross misinterpretation. It should be remembered that above all, Judaism is focused in the here and now. This life, with all its frustrations and tribulations, is a gift from G-d.

It has been said that the *performance of a mitzvah is a mitzvah*. Maimonides is emphatic that while every *mitzvah* has an overall purpose, there is no rational reason for the specific "how to" details (Guide to the Perplexed 3:26). For the Rambam, the overarching purpose of the *mitzvot* is the perfection of the human soul, and all of the commandments ultimately serve this purpose. Maimonides himself insists that the way to achieve the eternal life of the Coming Age is to observe all the commandments of the Torah out of perfect love and for no ulterior purpose. BMG alumnus, Heschel A., succinctly explains: *"This is not a point system with a check off list. As did our ancestors, we fulfill mitzvot because they are good for us and help us grow in holiness and character. Performance of mitzvot is a privilege and sacred obligation. It is done out of a sense of love and duty, not with the goal of getting something in return. The highest good in Orthodox Judaism is living a moral life. And that is its own reward."*

Chapter Twelve

Orthodox Women and the Mitzvot of *Shabbat* Candle Lighting, Spiritual Immersion, and *Challah*

Forget not the day of the Sabbath
Its mention is like a pleasant offering.
During it the dove found resting place,
And there the weary may relax.

Yehuda ha-Levi

A *mitzvah* (pl. *mitzvot*) literally means a commandment, one of the Torah's Divine 613 religious precepts. It is used also as a word to mean a good deed. "You did a *mitzvah*," someone might tell you after you bring a hot meal to a sick neighbor. Etymologically, the root of *mitzvah* stems from *tzavta*, which translates to "attachment." Thus, a *mitzvah* creates a bond between G-d who commands and man who performs. There are, at minimum, three *mitzvot* required of women in the Jewish tradition: *Nerot* (lighting the *Shabbat* candles); *Challah* (separating a portion of dough before baking the bread); and *niddah* for married women (going to the *mikvah*, or, ritual bath). Though not required, men can bake *challah* and light *Shabbat* candles in the absence of women, and men also go to the *mikvah*.

Should you find yourself in the center of Lakewood on a Friday morning, you will see Orthodox men and women crowding into Gelbsteins Bakery on Clifton Avenue or the Haimeshe Bakery on Second Street to buy *challah* breads and sweets for the *Shabbas* meal. Heading across County Line Road to Route 9, the parking lot at Shop Rite Plaza is filled to capacity. Men and women crowd into The Kosher Experience to select foods for the evening's special dinner. Throngs of Orthodox women laden with shopping bags, children trailing behind, scurry into Judaica Plaza for last minute items. Men emerge from small shops with flowers which will grace the evening's *Shabbat* table. Of all the Jewish festivals, *Shabbat* is probably the most essential to Jewish observance, remaining a constant and compelling aspect of Jewish life. The origin of the Sabbath can be traced back to Genesis, when G-d completed His work and *rested on the seventh day*. The commandment to observe the Sabbath is also a part of the Ten Commandments: *Remember the Sabbath day and keep it Holy*. (Exodus 20:8) Because the Sabbath is a day of rest, relaxation, and reflection, there are voluminous texts on Sabbath laws that prohibit the use of electrical appliances, driving a car, lighting fires or gas stoves. Lights are controlled by time switches.

Many Orthodox people keep food hot by using a *blech*. This is a piece of metal that goes over a burner on the stove. It conducts heat and prevents a pot from coming in direct contact with the heat source, which is prohibited according to strict *Shabbat* observance. The temperature of the *blech* must keep food at a minimum of 180 degrees but must not allow the food to reach the boiling point. A *Shabbat* favorite using a *blech* is *cholent*, a combination of meat, beans, and vegetables that cooks for hours.

The laws and customs that have developed over the centuries to commemorate the Sabbath and pay tribute to G-d's covenant with the Jewish people include special prayers, lighting of the *Shabbat* candles, the blessings over bread and wine, singing, and eating a festive meal prepared earlier in the day. Late Friday afternoon, the table is meticulously prepared for the Sabbath meal by covering it with a beautiful white tablecloth reserved for *Shabbat*. Two braided *challah* loaves protected by a cloth or silk covering, a silver *Kiddush* cup, and *Shabbat* candlesticks (often heirlooms passed down from mother to daughter), symbolizing the welcoming of the royalty of *Shabbat*, are placed on the table. While men are permitted to light candles if they are living alone, or travelling, traditionally it is the women who will light at least two candles and say the blessings. Candles are lit no later than eighteen minutes before sundown and there is a list of candle lighting times provided by the Orthodox Union for all areas of the United States and world.

The significance of two *Shabbat* candles is to honor the dual commandments to remember and keep the Sabbath. While two candles are the minimum, most Orthodox will light a candle for each of the children. After lighting the candles, the woman, wearing a head scarf, encircles her hands around the flames, usually three times. This custom serves to usher in the *Shabbat* bride as the light of *Shabbat* fills the room and surrounds the person; it symbolizes the culmination of the six days of creation with the seventh day of rest and draws the warmth and light inside oneself. She covers her eyes so as not to see the candles before reciting the blessing, and then uncovers her eyes, looks at the candles and prays: "*Baruch atah Adonai, Elohenu melekh ha-olam*" meaning "Blessed are You, our G-d, King of the Universe." Continuing with "who sanctifies us with His commandments and commands us to light the candles of *Shabbat*." It is customary for the mother to say a blessing for their children, and most families light a candle for each child.

For Rachel, a young mother of two, lighting the candles "symbolize bringing light into the world and into my home. It is a time I connect to all of my ancestors and it just gives me a sense of warmth and harmony."

Shabbat services in the *shuls* begin on Friday evening. Among other prayers is the song *Lekha Dodi*. Composed by Solomon ha-Levi Alkabetz in the mid-1500s, it is based on the words of the Talmudic sage Hanina: "*Come, let us go out to meet the Queen Sabbath*" (Talmud *Shabbat* 119a).

Sabbath day, Saturday, is also a time for prayers and for relaxation, a change of pace from the workday. For 35 year old Bluma, "It's my time for renewal and connection to myself and G-d. It's a day I look forward to spending time with my family and friends." There are morning services, followed by a Sabbath lunch, and then afternoon services. The evening service is held after sunset. When worshippers return, they light a single braided candle and recite the *Havdalah*, a prayer said over wine which marks the passage from the holiness of the Sabbath day to the days of the work week.

The Sabbath observance has remained a compelling and constant aspect of Jewish life. Other holidays are important as they mark the seasons in important ways and are connected with significant historical events. But the rhythm of daily Jewish life, most notably in the Orthodox community, revolves around the weekly welcoming into the home, the expansive warmth and light that accompany the Holy Sabbath. It is a time, explains

Rabbi Yoffe, "when families gather together around the dinner table and the world stops."

Challah is a very sweet, golden, eggy bread that is traditionally eaten by Jews on the Sabbath, holidays, and other ceremonial occasions. The loaf is usually braided, but on certain holidays it may be made in other shapes. For example, on Rosh Hashanah, it is traditional to serve round *challah* as the circle symbolizes the cycle of life, the cycle of the years. Jewish law requires that anyone preparing dough for baking bread must first separate a small piece of dough, also called *challah*, bless it and burn it. This is done in memory of the gifts of bread once given to the *Kohen* (Jewish priest). Orthodox women believe that the mitzvah of separating *challah* is very dear to *Hashem* (G-d). One of the reasons is that a person sustains himself with food and the staple of the diet is bread; thus, bread is nourishment for the body and for the soul. When separating the *challah,* one says a prayer that begins:

> *May it be your will, Hashem, that the mitzvah of separating challah be considered as I fulfilled her properly in full detail. And may it be considered as a sacrifice which was sacrificed on the alter and was accepted. And just as previously the challah was given to the Kohen and this was an atonement for one's sins, so too, may this be an atonement for my sins, and I will be like a newborn, clean from all sin, thus enabling me to fulfill the Mitzvah of the Holy Sabbath.*

Sitting at the table drinking tea in Ruthie's* large kitchen, I watch as she takes another loaf of fresh *challah*, this one with poppy seeds, out of her oven. "It's hot," she tells me, "but try it. Here, I will get you some honey my daughter-in-law just sent from Israel."

Ruthie is quite the celebrity on her tree lined Lakewood street which houses both Orthodox and non-Orthodox families. Famous for knitting exquisite baby clothes and crocheting blankets, her greatest notoriety is her baking. She makes eighteen *challah* loaves each *Shabbat* for friends and family – Jews and non-Jews. Knowing that monetary gifts in multiples of $18 are given as *simcha* gifts because the word *chai* (life) is a combination of *chet*, 8 and *yad*, 10, I ask Ruthie if her *challah* loaves represent *chai*. She pats my shoulder: "Yes, that is why." As she carefully transfers more loaves to a large platter, she smiles: "Making *challah* is more than baking bread. It's not only a mitzvah…it's a religious experience!"

At a Lakewood fundraiser in 2008, the hostess invited Devorah Heller, the famous *challah* class instructor to give us pointers on making *challah*. A petite *yiddishe bubbie,* she exudes warmth and vitality as she offers the ladies ongoing comic dialogue and *Yiddishkeit* wisdom while guiding us in preparing the dough. Heller walks around the dining room table with a bag of flour, adding a bit more to some of the bakers' bowls. "The dough should not be sticking to your hands," she warns. Struggling with shaping the dough into braids, I whisper to my friend, Reisa: "I feel like I'm channeling Bubbie Sarah." Heller assures her audience: "If you have any questions when you're doing this at home, just call my *Challah* Hotline. Actually, it's my home number, but you know with technology and blackberries and blueberries, hotline sounds so much more exciting." Encouraging our feeble attempts at trying to perfect the art of braiding the dough, she says, "Where there's a will.....," quietly adding, "there's a relative with a hand out."

It is said in Numbers 15:19-21 that "[*challah*] braids are mystical; that they are from the hair of the Sabbath bride." Indeed, baking a perfect homemade loaf of *challah* is the wish of many young Jewish Orthodox brides. Today almost every traditional Jewish dish can be bought ready to eat, but nothing can ever replace the glorious flavors and perfumes of home cooked Jewish food. Certainly not the pre-Sabbath aroma of loaves of *challah* rising in the oven that fill your heart and table with *Shabbat* spirit and prayer.

Authentic Orthodox life cannot take place without a *mikvah* in the community. The *mikvah*, or ritual bath, is deeply rooted in the spiritual and symbolic act of purification, rejuvenation, and even rebirth. For thousands of years, Jewish marriages and families have been strengthened through the sanctity and holiness inherent in the laws of family purity. Throughout the Jewish diaspora, *mikvahs* were constructed even before *shuls*. Women are required to use the *mikvah* before their wedding day, after childbirth, and following menstruation. *Halakhah*, Jewish law, specifies other uses of immersion in a *mikvah,* including conversion to Judaism, *koshering*, or purification of new pots and dishes, and purification of a body before it is laid to rest. It is law that an Orthodox bride visit the *mikvah* before her wedding ceremony. For the menstruate woman, the *mikvah* is a part of the Divine ordinance of Family Purity to fulfill the laws of *taharat-ha-mischpachah*. According to a rabbinical edict, from the onset of her cycle and for seven days thereafter, she and her husband are forbidden to engage in sexual relations. The Talmud extends that separation for an additional five days following a woman's period. This divides the month into two parts: When sexual relations are forbidden, and when intimate relations are not only permissible, but recognized as essential to physical and mental health. Before resuming sexual intimacy, the woman immerses herself in the *mikvah* and recites a blessing to G-d. Absence, as they say, makes the heart grow fonder.

Forty-one-year-old Judith* says that "when intimacy is resumed, it is with higher appreciation and love, as well as freshness." The *mikvah* is an extremely private and personal ritual. There is no socializing; generally, women go to the *mikvah* alone. Fifty-three-year-old Pearl, who is early postmenopausal, says "I will, with permission, periodically visit the *mikvah*. It is a peaceful and spiritual immersion that is almost mystical, a connection to generations of Jews. I feel renewed and refreshed and, even at my age, like a *kallah* [a new bride]"

Lakewood's first *mikvah* was housed in the Old Shul, the original Congregation Sons of Israel. Today, Lakewood houses approximately ten *mikvahs*; a large central one on Madison Avenue, as well as some smaller ones. Both have separate sections for men and women. Part of the misconception about *mikvahs* is that its purpose is to enhance personal hygiene since immersing oneself in water is typically associated with cleansing.

Indeed, in ancient times, because Jews were often barred from using rivers for bathing, they constructed bathhouses that included *mikvahs*. But the *mikvah* never served as a substitute for bathing; in reality, *halakhah* requires that one must be meticulously clean prior to entering a *mikvah*. It is a fallacy that the *mikvah* waters are not clean; the truth is that they are far more clean than a swimming pool. The water is changed every night. Women who keep the *mikvah* are chaste, and not allowed to go if they have any infections. The water is slightly chlorinated, to be bacteria-free. Before a woman can immerse, she has to bathe and scrub herself to be immaculately clean. It is a medical fact that women who use *mikvahs* have a statistically lower percentage of gynecological problems or diseases.

But the *mikvah* is not the exclusive domain of women. *Midrash* tells us that Adam, after being banished from Eden, sat in a river that flowed from the Garden as a symbol of his repentance and attempt to return to his original perfection. Before the revelation to Moses at Mount Sinai, Jews were commanded to immerse themselves to prepare for coming face to face with

G-d. Today, Orthodox men will visit *mikvahs* on their wedding day, before the High Holy Days, and sometimes even before welcoming in the Sabbath. Men go to the *mikvah* during the day, and women go at night.

Mikvahs have certainly come a long way from the days of Miriam's well in the desert. While the primal *mikvahs* were ocean, spring, rivers, and well waters, modern *mikvahs* are built into the ground and constructed as part of a building. They have evolved from utilitarian baths to well appointed and in many cases, like the one on Madison Avenue, lavish structures that rival European spas, but which still strictly adhere to traditional rules. Each of the pools, which have filtration systems, contains rain water (not tap water) that is siphoned into the pool in accordance with strict regulations. The requisite amount of water in a *mikvah* must be a minimum of forty *seah*—a biblical measure of water, about fifteen gallons. It is a very symbolic number to the Jewish people. It took forty days for Moses to get the Ten Commandments from G-d; The Jews were in the desert for forty years; A fetus is formed in forty days, and pregnancy is forty weeks. The Flood took forty days and forty nights of rainwater to purify the whole world, which had become impure and needed the *mikvah* waters.

Generations of Jewish women have found that the mitzvah of the ritual bath brings them closer to G-d –the source of life, purity, and holiness. Twenty five year old Essie believes that "the *mikvah* is needed more today than ever. We all need our *neshama* (souls) strengthened, because a healthy soul makes for a healthy body." Miriam points out that the *mikvah* "is an age-old way to celebrate and mark events and new beginnings." Shoshana expresses the feelings of many women, including myself, who have experienced the *mitzvah* of *mikvah*: "It's like a rebirth when you emerge from the water totally regenerated. It's just another way Jewish women can express their spirituality."

In Ezekiel 36:25—26, it says *v'zarakti aleichem mayim t'horim ut'hartem* meaning "I will sprinkle clean water upon you, and you shall be clean. I will give you a new heart and put a new spirit in you." We can midrashically, if you will, present the waters of *mikvah* as the waters of Eden, the waters of the womb, Miriam's well, the soft rainwater, or creation. But in the final analysis, the act of immersion allows us to dive down deep and resurface, forever changed and with hope. It literally washes away the past. It has the potential to be an ablution that can open the floodgates of reconnection to Judaism and to the wholeness of the self.

Chapter Thirteen

Orthodox Women and the Dichotomy of Equality and Place

G-d did not create woman from man's head, that he should command her; nor from his feet, that she should be his slave; but from his side that she should be nearest his heart.
Adapted from Talmud

Like many other ethnocentric judgments and distortions of facts about the Orthodox lifestyle, the presumption that the women are marginalized is based on ignorance of Jewish history and law. The perpetuation of the myth by Western feminists that Orthodoxy oppresses and disdains women is, in fact, the very antithesis of women's status and role in traditional Judaism. The ideology of the Feminist movement which, to be sure, fought for and succeeded in gaining social, economic, and political equality for women, was grounded in the elimination of Western patriarchal institutions and achievement of a sense of community with other women, the latter of which has always existed for Orthodox women.

Men and women were both created in the image of G-d; therefore, according to Jewish law, there is no superior or inferior sex; rather, men and women were created, as the Torah teaches, to fulfill a distinct role in His scheme and to contribute to the fulfillment of each other. While a woman is man's equal in intrinsic value, her functions in life are not identical with those of a man.

The terms feminism, inferiority, and superiority thus become irrelevant insofar as they are incompatible with the culture, history, and heritage of

Orthodox Judaism whose basic tenets embrace women's uniqueness and individuality. As author and inspirational speaker, Rebbitzen Esther Jungreis eloquently points out, "Jewish women have never felt the need to battle for emancipation since they never considered themselves enslaved...they understood that no two human beings can be equal...that men are not equal to women and women are not equal to men." Judaism is not an egalitarian religion and, in some sense, Orthodox women are far more liberated than any feminist in terms of the centrality of their place and the reverence accorded them.

Unlike other religions, the corpus of Jewish writings bear eloquent testimony to women's elevated position and accomplishments. King Solomon's poem, "A Woman of Valor," praises a woman for qualities such as wisdom, courage, creativity, business acumen, and the profound insight to recognize how to relate to individuals according to their specific needs. The Torah dispels many of the gross misrepresentations and myths that women were viewed as the inferior sex, and teaches that women are to be held in high esteem and treated with respect and honor. According to traditional Judaism, women are endowed with more *binah*; that is to say, greater intelligence and understanding than men. Which is why Jewish husbands, such as Jacob, consulted their wives, asked them for counsel and guidance, and even quoted their words of wisdom. While other nations of the world vulgarly praised their women as sex objects, Jewish men referred to them as the embodiment of all that is noble and good.

Seven of the 55 prophets were women. Esther was one of the liberators of the Children of Israel, ruining the plans of the evil Haman to destroy all the Jews. Hanna was the great Jewish mother from whom the rabbis learned the manner of prayer. Surely Sarah, Abraham's wife, was not the submissive *balabusta* (mistress of the house), but was in a true partnership with Abraham. In addition to her role as wife and mother, Sarah converted the women while Abraham converted the men. Women in traditional Judaism had greater rights than in most of Western Civilization including the right to buy, own, and sell property and make their own contracts.

When Moses came down from Mount Sinai carrying the stone tablets with the Ten Commandments, he found the Children of Israel worshipping the calf Aaron had fashioned out of gold jewelry offered by the women. But it was the women, too, who refused to engage in such idolatry, choosing to remain faithful to G-d. Moses was instructed by G-d to teach the law to the women first because it was dependent upon them to preserve and pass down Judaism.

The most important role for women, and which most Orthodox women unquestionably accept as a *mitzvah*, is that of High Priestess of the home who preserves Jewish life and guides the children in Torah. Orthodox women are not subservient to their husbands; during the marriage ceremony, it is not the woman who pledges to cherish, honor, and obey; it is the man who promises to serve, honor, and provide for his wife. The Sabbath is personified in legend and literature as a feminine entity; a beautiful bride, a lovely princess, or a gracious queen. The ancient rabbis wrote of greeting the Sabbath as one would a beautiful woman. Sixteenth century Kabbalists expanded this image to include that of a bride; thus, creating a mystical union between G-d, the King, and his Sabbath Queen. Traditional female symbols of home, table, motherhood, and nature are frequently associated with the Sabbath.

That in religious spheres and in social situations, men and women are separated is true. In *shul*, women are shielded by a curtain from behind which they watch the men pray. At weddings, and other celebrations, men and women do not dance with one another and are also in separated sections of the hall. At funerals, they are not permitted to have any physical contact with men. But many of these prohibitions as well as the laws of *tznius*, or modesty, exist because Judaism recognizes that the man is morally weaker than the woman, and thus must insulate himself from distractions and desires.

The charge that the ritual bath, or *mikvah*, is demeaning and primitive, and that it suggests women are unclean is a total fallacy. Ironically, in the 21st century, the *mikvah* is being reclaimed by non-Orthodox women as an affirmation of femininity and fertility, a way to mark new beginnings and strengthen spiritual connections.

To prove that women are viewed with contempt, many detractors will examine, out of context, select phrases from prayers. Men do say a prayer thanking G-d that they were not born women, but more likely as a testimony that women's lives are more difficult. Women have been exempted from certain obligations or *mitzvahs*, not because they are inferior or less spiritual, but because they have a more important and more sacred role in raising children and establishing a *Yiddishkeit* home.

Another misconception is that Orthodox women cannot have a career or work outside the home. In Orthodox households, husbands typically enter *kollel* for a number of years before pursuing a career. Most families struggle financially during the husband's study, and often the wife will temporarily stand in as the primary breadwinner until the husband is able to earn an income. Because of the importance of childrearing within the first few years of marriage, wives must sometimes balance working full time, raising children, and taking care of household chores and duties. For women who are not college-educated, they find employment as office managers in medical or dental offices, as clerical support in businesses, or even information technology if they have the necessary skills.

As discussed in Chapter Eight, many women choose, with their family's blessing, to pursue higher education and their own careers in fields such as education, business, social and health services either within the community or in the secular world. While these unique set of challenges put immense pressure on Orthodox women to fulfill the role of the traditional ideal Jewish wife and find professional fulfillment, devout women manage to intertwine the two worlds to form an identity that accommodates both.

Orthodox women are not shackled in chains and, while divorce among couples is the exception, it does happen for reasons probably similar to those in non-Orthodox homes. While Samuel Heilman estimates that the divorce rate, "although rising, remains far lower than the approximately 30% among other Jews and certainly a great deal less than the rest of America" (163), any incidents of divorce in Orthodox homes, nonetheless remain a concern. When a couple is in crisis, rabbis will intervene with counseling sessions and often recommend professional therapists within the Orthodox community to work with the couples towards reconciliation.

Divorce, like marriage, is governed by Jewish law which seemingly provides the husband with disproportionate power to effect change. Most men, however, recognize their obligation to give a *get* and do so. A *get* is a Jewish document of divorce written by an expert by hand, and at the request of both the husband and wife. "While we pray for successful marriages," says Abbie*, "marriages do fail and divorce is a reality when one or both partners feel the union has fallen apart for whatever reason and cannot be repaired."

Abbie is 38 years old and comes from a divorced non-Orthodox family. A mother of four, she married Zev when she was 18 and lived a model observant life. Two years ago, Abbie announced to Zev that she wanted a divorce and intended to leave the Orthodox community. It has not been easy for Abbie, who had over the years established deep friendships with other *frum* women, who have since severed ties with her. "I was terribly hurt and depressed when my closest friend Tzipi, who was like a sister, told me that she loved me and always would, but could not accept my leaving Orthodoxy. She saw it as a rejection of Torah and G-d." Of even more concern to Abbie is the stigmatizing effect the divorce will inevitably have on her children. "But," she reasons, "I will encourage my sons to make their own decisions and will support them one hundred percent in whatever road they choose, but I could no longer in good conscience stay in a lifestyle that had failed to have meaning to me or which I could not fully embrace."

Some feminists and some outside the realm of Orthodoxy will no doubt continue to criticize women whom they view as choosing to subject themselves to perceived archaic and Patriarchal constructs in their religious and home lives. Ironically, judging this lifestyle as "anti-feminist" is to not only reject the Orthodox values placing women as equal to men but different in their needs and desires and fulfilling a unique role; it is to reject the very set of values and choices that feminists supposedly promote.

Tova* is 59 years old, a retired teacher. She and Joel*, her husband of forty years who still teaches, invited me to their lakefront home to discuss my book and to *schmooze* with some of Tova's friends. Everyone arrives with a home made goodie that I only wish I could create, but I have dutifully brought along various cheeses and bottles of *Pinot Noir* and *Pinot Grigio*. All kosher of course. Tova, despite my protestations the day before, has filled her dining room table with vegetable panini sandwiches, potato salad, noodle pudding, Israeli *couscous*, and fresh fruits.

I am introduced to the guests. Naomi is 76, a mother of six with a carpet handbag overflowing with pictures of her seventeen grandchildren living in Israel. She has been married to Reuven for 48 years. Gittel, a fifth grade teacher, is 51. Freyde is a lively and outspoken woman of 67. An Israeli by birth, she served in the Israeli army, raised her family, and taught history at Ben Gurion University before retiring. She now travels between family in Israel and Lakewood. Twenty year old Miriam* is newly married, a student at Ocean County College who wants to become a speech therapist. She just found out that she is pregnant with her first child. Shira is 29 and has been married eight years. She works at the Chemed Medical Center. Forty two year old Chaya runs a day care center from her home. She and her husband, Dov, have four children. Esther is 34, and the mother of three. Malcha is 44, has a degree in Psychology and works as a guidance counselor in a Bais Ya'akov. Rachel and her husband have been married twenty years and run a jewelry store. She has brought along her youngest daughter, Bluma, who is seven. Rifka* is a 70-year-old widow who works part time in a bakery.

I talk about why I wrote the book and read passages from the introductory chapter. The group listens attentively. They seem excited to be a part of this and treat me like a celebrity. I tell them I will not use their real names if that makes them uncomfortable and I emphasize that my purpose is to create an understanding of what the Orthodox community is about and dispel any myths. Gittel looks up from her needlework: "This is a *mitzvah* you're doing. Education is the only way people can learn respect for each other. We have enough problems in the world. Lakewood shouldn't be one of them." I ask them about the misperception about, and reality of, the role and status of Orthodox women. Do they feel suppressed, choiceless, or like second class citizens? I ask that they complete the sentence "I'm not a feminist but…"

I hear some laughter. Chaya offers her viewpoint: "Men and women each have their special roles and we need both to rear a family and a well balanced society." Esther pipes in: "Like Chaya said, we are equal in every sense, but we each have a part in life."

"Women," asserts Naomi, "are and should be free to choose if they want to go to college, or have a career in addition to raising a family."

"Really," Tova says, "most of us are open minded and believe women can raise a family, have a career, and make decisions about finances, sometimes better than our husbands!" Tova's husband chuckles and nods from the next room. Referring to what Prime Minister Golda Meir once said, Freyde tells us that "to be successful, a woman has to be much better at her job than a man."

Miriam, the youngest and shyest of the group quietly comments: "I'm not sure what a feminist is, but I think that women are equal to men but have different roles. My husband wants me to get a degree and work as a speech therapist. I cannot wait to work with disabled children. When our baby is born, I will stay home for a few months till I can leave her with my mother while I'm in school."

I ask little Bluma what she thinks about all this. She says she is not sure what we are talking about, but announces she wants to be a pediatrician when she grows up. Or a chef.

"Okay," I tell her, "It's always good to have a Plan B."

Shira offers an option: "Blumala, you can be both—a pediatric nutritionist!"

Problem solved. I read excerpts from my newly started chapter on women's place. The group seems to think I got at the essence of the Orthodox view of women as the pivotal center of the domestic sphere, but with choices about what else they can be. Says Freyde: "The great thing is that if we want to devote our lives to taking care of home and family, that's what we do, but if we want more, that's also possible. Like the non-Orthodox world, we have choices."

Gittel summarizes the evening's discussion: "*Hashem* created two genders to enable them to fulfill and complement one another and don't you think it would be counterproductive to force them to conduct themselves identically? Each of us should appreciate our difference and specialness."

I ask the group for their thoughts on the difference, if any, between spirituality and religion, beginning by offering the term religion as more formal and objective, and spirituality as more informal and subjective, or personal. Tova comments that "they go hand in hand, but spirituality is the sense of G-d's presence," to which Rifka adds, "Spirituality also has to do with self-awareness."

Malcha agrees: "The word spiritual refers to a connection to something or someone other than ourself."

"What I think," says Tova, "is that spirituality is something not connected to the earthly or material world. So, the more spiritual you are, the more religious you are and the more you feel closeness to *Hashem* and become less connected to material things."

Esther brings up the point of formality. "Religion has more to do with laws, customs, and institutions but I think spirituality is more about feelings and emotions. But it all works together."

"Good point." notes Rachel, "Spirituality is the essence of true Holiness; it's about how we treat one another because we are created in His image and, through our relationship with *Hashem*, we serve Him on earth by our words and good deeds."

"Exactly." nods Malcha, "It's a partnership with G-d. It's not enough to observe rituals and to pray. It's living every moment with an awareness of G-d and of yourself."

Miriam reminds us that "the prophet Micah teaches us 'What does G-d ask of you? To do justice, to love kindness, and to walk humbly before Him' and that is the core of our Jewish religion and of spirituality when we place G-d before us each day at all times."

Esther comments: "What I cannot understand is when someone tells me that they are not religious, but that they are spiritual –I mean, how does that work?"

"It doesn't."answers Freyde. "Look, ideally, religion or spirituality co-exist. And it is not something outside of ourselves. G-d should exist within us. You observe customs and study Torah; the spirituality comes when you take those teachings, put them into practice every day, and connect them to your soul."

This was an enlightening session with delightful women, and which affirmed that, at the end of the day, we are all human beings created in the image of G-d, each of us trying to fulfill our unique potential. The teachings that Torah offers a woman to grow morally and spiritually while maximizing her individual strengths, enable every woman to be herself with self esteem and joy. And, *Baruch Hashem,* without apologies.

Chapter Fourteen:

The Orthodox Year in Celebration

The Sabbath and holidays are the primary reason for Jewish endurance and glory.
Judah Halevi

Jewish holidays are either based upon agricultural or historical events. Judaism has its own calendar based on the cycle of the moon, not the sun, upon which the secular calendar is based. The Jewish calendar begins in the spring, but the Jewish year number, or the new year, changes in the seventh month. 2010, for example, is the year 5770, calculated based on the biblical date of creation in 3760 BCE. Each cycle is a month and there are 12 months in a year, approximately 29 or 30 days in each month. The lunar year is about 354 days, eleven days shorter than the secular calendar. Where the Gregorian (civil) calendar defines the day as from midnight one night to midnight the following night, the Jewish calendar counts days from sunset of one day until sunset of the next day. *Shabbat*, for example, begins on Friday evening, and is called *Erev Shabbat*. It ends on the following Saturday evening, called *Motsa'ei Shabbat*.

Since, as commanded by Leviticus, Passover must be celebrated in the spring, an adjustment is made each year to the Jewish calendar to keep in line with the Gregorian 365 day calendar. In certain years, an extra (13th) month is added to the calendar, making them leap years. This explains why holidays may not always fall on the same day though they do fall within the same month or two. The names of the Hebrew months are originally *Babylonian: Nissan, Iyyar, Sivan, Tammuz, Av, Elul, Tishrei, Cheshvan, Kislev, Tevet, Shevat, Adar I, Adar II*. While Reform and Conservative Jews celebrate, at the very least, the major holidays of Passover, Rosh Hashana, Yom Kippur, and Chanukah, Orthodox Jews observe all of the festivals during the course of a year as prescribed by Torah, and are meticulous about following each specific holiday's laws and customs.

Rosh Hashana

The cycle of the Jewish holidays commences with the New Year, Rosh Hashana, in the month of *Tishrei* which, on the secular calendar, is September or October. This goes back to the earliest times when the Hebrew year began in autumn with the opening of the economic year and followed in regular succession the harvest seasons of seed-sowing, ripening of the fruits and corn, and the feast of the harvest. The Torah does not use the term "Rosh Hashana," but instead calls this holiday Yom Teruah, The Day of the Sounding of the Shofar.

According to Leviticus 23:23-25, the day was to be celebrated by blowing the primitive wind instrument called the *shofar* or ram's horn, by resting from all work, and by calling a holy assembly, and presenting an offering. The offering is described in Numbers 29:2-6. In Nehemiah 8:2-9 we find Ezra reading the Torah to the assembled people of Israel on this date. Psalms 93-100 are also believed to have been composed for Rosh Hashana. Though decidedly more solemn than the American New Year, Rosh Hashana is a joyous and festive holiday where we pray for a year of life, health, and prosperity. Like the American New Year, it is a time to reflect on the past and make resolutions for the coming year. Rosh Hashana begins the "Ten Days of Awe" (*Yomin Noraim*), or "The High Holy Days" and concludes with Yom Kippur, the Day of Atonement. For thirty days before Rosh Hashana, it is customary to greet one another with the phrase, *L'Shanah Tovah Tikateyvu*, meaning "May you be inscribed in the Book of Life."

Some descriptions depict G-d as sitting upon a throne, while books containing the deeds of all humanity are opened before Him. Within this framework, G-d is sometimes referred to as "The King." During the "Days of Awe" many penitentiary prayers called *selihot* and religious poems called *piyuttim* are added to the regular prayer services and there are special prayer books called the *mahzorhim*. As a child, I looked forward to the Rosh Hashana meal where there would be *ga'le* – mixture of sweet fruits and assorted nuts. We would dip an apple, pomegranate, or piece of *challah* bread into honey to symbolize our wishes that the upcoming year be a sweet one.

As a Reform Jew, it had been decades since I attended Orthodox services, but this year was the exception. On Rosh Hashana, I joined my friend Dini at her *shul* on County Line Road where throngs of people were crushed together like canned herrings. I lost sight of Dini in the mob, but managed to work my way into the *shul* and found a pew in the back of the women's section, overlooking a sea of hats, shawls, and scarves. Some of the women looked at me curiously, recognizing despite my modest attire, that I was not Orthodox. An older woman with salt and pepper hair handed me a prayer book, sat down next to me, and for two hours, patiently guided me through the text written in long forgotten Hebrew. While Orthodox *shuls* conduct their services in Hebrew, in some of the larger *shuls*, such as The Old Congregation Sons of Israel which has a congregation with varying levels of advanced Hebrew skills, page numbers might be called out in English.

The central observance of Rosh Hashana is the sounding of the *shofar*, which proclaims G-d as King of the universe. The haunting soulful cry of the *shofar* is a universal call to repentance, a "wake-up" call of sorts to evaluate our actions and improve our ways and prepare for the upcoming Day of Atonement. Maimonides, in his Laws of Repentance (3:4) implores: "Awake sleepers from your sleep; slumberers arise from your slumber, examine your deeds, return and remember your creator." The *shofar* reminds us of the fragility of life and asks us to consider how we will best use our time on earth.

Rabbi Jonathan Sacks, chief Rabbi of the British Commonwealth, and author of many scholarly books on Judaism, points out other biblical and historical reasons for the sounding of the *shofar*. First, he maintains, it recalls Genesis 22 which tells of G-d's command to Abraham to sacrifice his son Isaac. Second, says Sacks, it reminds us of the Torah given to Moses and the Israelites at Mount Sinai, when "the mountain trembled violently and the "sound of the *shofar* grew louder and louder." Further, the *shofar* was blown as the sound of victory at Jericho, and then in celebration of King David bringing the Ark to Jerusalem. One of the psalms recited on the Sabbath refers to the *shofar* as the herald proclaiming the arrival of the King: "With trumpets and the blast of the *shofar*, shout for joy before the Lord, the King."

Feasting with symbolic food is part of the observance. Like most Orthodox families, the centerpiece of Dini's holiday table is a huge crystal bowl filled with pomegranates, grapes, and dates which are three of the holy fruits in the land of Canaan. The pomegranate, which has been grown in the

Middle East for over 3000 years, is mentioned in the Book of Deuteronomy as well as in other religious texts as a symbol of abundance, knowledge, fertility, and peace. From the Latin *pomun granatus*, it is a "seedy apple" with a distinctive sweet and tangy flavor. It is used in cooking, and the seeds may be eaten raw, dried like raisins, or pressed to produce juice. As guests savor the sweet tangy taste of this biblical fruit, they recite the holiday prayer: "In the coming year, may we be rich and replete with acts inspired by religion and piety as the pomegranate is rich and replete with seeds."

Dini had prepared a traditional Rosh Hashana dinner: salad greens, matzoh ball soup, sweet and sour brisket, and chicken cooked with pomegranate and walnuts. For this holiday, the challah loaf is round instead of the usual braided bread because it is said that the round shape symbolizes a crown. In Jewish thought, Rosh Hashana is the most important judgment-day, on which all the inhabitants of the world pass for judgment before the Creator, as sheep pass for examination before the shepherd. It is written in the Talmud, in the tractate on Rosh Hashana, that three books of account are opened on Rosh Hashana, wherein the fate of the wicked, the righteous, and those of an intermediate class are recorded. The names of the righteous are immediately inscribed in the book of life, and they are sealed "to live." Menachem admits that long services bored him as a child, but "they are so much more introspective to me now as an adult who studies Torah."

Between the first day of Rosh Hashana and Yom Kippur, Orthodox and other observant Jews engage in the practice of *tashlikh*, the symbolic casting away of sins by turning their pockets inside out, throwing either stones or bread crumbs into the moving water to symbolize the cleansing from sin after repentance. This is symbolic of Micah 7:19, *And you will cast all our sins into the depths of the sea*. This year, I joined a gathering at the water's edge of Lake Carasaljo between Route 9 and Hope Chapel Road. There, with a tease of a chill hovering in the air and standing at the water's edge as the blinding sun began to descend, I cast bread crumbs into the water while reciting the penitential prayer, and was surprised at the powerful emotions that came flooding back to me as I remembered the years I would stand at the ocean in Far Rockaway. I guess they don't call it Days of Awe for nothing. A middle aged Hasidic man reminded me that "it symbolizes not an end, but a new beginning. There is no way to undo what we have done, but the holiday season teaches us that if we take the first steps, and express our recognition that we have sinned, and if we perform good deeds and give charity, then Hashem will take care of the rest." His squirming six year old son, Raffie, added "You have to ask *Hashem* to forgive you for bad things you did." I wonder what "bad things" this adorable cherub faced towhead could have done. As if reading my mind, Raffi looked up at me and qualified "I am going to be much nicer to my sisters."

Yom Kippur

Yom Kippur (correctly pronounced Yoam Keepoor), the Jewish Day of Atonement, is the most sacred holiday of the year (The Sabbath is the holiest day), which begins on the ninth day after the first day of Rosh Hashana on the 10th of the Hebrew month of *Tishrei,* or September or October on the secular calendar. Often referred to as the Sabbath of Sabbaths, Yom Kippur is a solemn day of 25 hour fasting and repentance, a time to reconcile ourselves with our Creator and atone for the sins of the past year. It is the day G-d inscribes our names and his judgment before the book is sealed. Yom Kippur atones only for sins between man and G-d, not for sins against another person. For that, and before Yom Kippur, you must first seek reconciliation with that person, righting the wrongs you committed against them if possible. Yet there is a joy infusing the day with confidence that G-d will accept our repentance, forgive our sins, and seal our verdict for a year of life, health, and happiness.

The Talmud specifies restrictions against eating, engaging in marital relations, wearing cosmetics or colognes, and wearing leather shoes which is why you might see Orthodox men and women wearing canvas sneakers to the synagogue. It is customary to wear white on the holiday, which symbolizes purity and calls to mind the promise that our sins shall be made as white as snow (Isiah 1:18). Married men wear a *kittel,* the white robe in which they are married and buried. Men and women immerse themselves in the mikvah before the holiday and give extra charity. Though it is a day of fasting, whenever there is a threat to one's health or life, that restriction can be lifted. Children under the age of nine and women in childbirth (from the time labor begins until three days after birth) are not permitted to fast, even if they want to. Older children and women from the third to the seventh day after childbirth are permitted to fast, but are permitted to break the fast if they feel the need to do so. On *erev,* or the eve of the Day of Atonement, when the congregation has gathered, the Ark is opened and two rabbis or leading members of the community, take from it two Torah scrolls. Then they take their place alongside each of the *hazzan* (cantors) and recite a formula: *In the tribunal of heaven and the tribunal of earth, by permission of G-d, blessed be He—and by permission of this holy congregation, we hold it lawful to pray with transgressors.* The cantor then chants aloud the Aramaic prayer beginning with the word *Kol Nidrei* three times, each time louder than before, and the congregation recites along in an undertone.

The ancient *Kol Nidrei* is named from its opening words "All vows" (*kol nidrei*) and is based on the declaration of the Talmud: He who wishes that his vows and oaths shall have no value, stand up at the beginning of the year and say: 'All vows which I shall make during the year shall be of no value.'" It assumed special significance during the Spanish Inquisition when Jews were forced to convert to Christianity. Probably more famous than the formulaic prayer itself, is the mournful melody traditionally attached to it which has gathered so much attention from the composers of the last century. In the first talking movie, *The Jazz Singer* (1927), Lithuanian born Al Jolson chants *Kol Nidrei* as his father lies on his deathbed, and pop singer Neil Diamond's haunting rendition in the 1980 remake of the film has brought the song into the lives of younger and less observant Jews.

On the day of Yom Kippur, Orthodox services begin early in the morning around 8 or 9 AM and continue until about 3 PM. People then usually go home for an afternoon nap and return around 5 or 6 PM for the afternoon and evening services, which continue until nightfall. In the middle of the day, before the *musaf* service, *Yizkor* memorial prayers are recited, where we ask G-d to remember the souls of our loved ones who have passed away. It is a spiritual time for having that connection that once existed between ourselves and the departed. As the services conclude at nightfall, there are resounding cries of "Hear O Israel…G-d is one," a single blast of the *shofar*, followed by the promise *"Next year in Jerusalem,"* and joy erupts throughout the synagogue as families will now enjoy the festive after-fast meal.

Sukkot

The holiday of Sukkot begins on the fifth day after Yom Kippur, and is a seemingly drastic transition from one of the most solemn holidays in our year to one of the most unreservedly joyous ones. It is often referred to in Jewish literature as *Z'man Simchareinu*, The Season of our Rejoicing. Sukkot is the last of the three pilgrimage festivals following Passover and Shavu'ot.

The holiday has both historical and agricultural significance. It recalls the forty year period during which the children of Israel were wandering in the desert, living in temporary shelters. The Torah tells us that while we wandered the desert, we lived in these simple shacks. We had no possessions. We were protected by G-d from possible harm. Our path was not determined by human intelligence, but by the direction shown by G-d. We lived with the dichotomy of being vulnerable and being protected at the same time. This is symbolized by the *sukkah* itself, temporary, yet a shelter from the elements. Today, observant and Orthodox Jews celebrate the holiday by building temporary outdoor sukkot (booths) in which they live during the seven days of Sukkot, in accordance with the commandment to dwell in temporary shelters as our ancestors did in the wilderness.

"It's a welcomed and spiritual release from the heavy stuff you just went through," explains Aharon, a 31 year old rabbinical student, "Yom Kippur is very intense and after that day comes this joyous liberating holiday." Building and decorating the *sukkah* is great fun for the children who can indulge in fantasies of building a fort. Eight year old Yael tells me "It's like camping out and being on vacation." Her younger brother Mendel interrupts to show me his latest crayon drawings that will decorate the *sukkah*. The walls do not have to be solid and most of those in Lakewood are canvas or aluminum. They must be covered with a material that will not be blown away in heavy winds. The booth can be any size necessary to comfortably accommodate those dwelling and entertaining guests in it. The roof of the *sukkah* must be made of something that grew from the ground and was cut off, such as tree branches, corn stalks, or bamboo reeds.

Another observance during Sukkot involves the Four Species, or the *lulov* and *etrog*. As commanded in Leviticus 23:40, "On the first day, you will take for yourselves a fruit of a beautiful tree, palm branches, twigs of a braided tree and brook willows, and you will rejoice before the Lord your G-d for seven days. The four species are an *etrog* which is similar to a citron or a lemon native to Israel; a palm branch, *lulav* in Hebrew, two willow branches and three myrtle branches. The six branches are bound together and referred to as the *lulav* which is the largest part. The etrog is held separately. Holding all four species, a blessing is recited and all of the species are waved in six different directions (north, south, east, west, up, down) signifying that G-d is everywhere. The four species are also held during processions around the *bimah* (or pedestal) from where the Torah is read. Shmuel, a young BMG student, elaborates on the symbolism. "The *etrog*," he patiently explains, "has a pleasing taste and scent and represents Jews who have achieved knowledge of Torah and performing acts of kindness; the palm branch is tasty but has no scent and represents Jews who know Torah but are lacking in *mitzvahs*. The myrtle leaf is a strong scent but little taste and stands for Jews who perform mitzvahs but have no knowledge of Torah; the willow has neither taste nor scent and symbolizes Jews who have no Torah knowledge and do not perform good deeds." His last comments touch my heart: "We bring all these species together at *Sukkot* to remind us that every one of these four kinds of Jews is important and we must all be united."

Words that are certainly practiced. I was invited to celebrate the first night of Sukkot at the home of Bernie* and Dvorah*. I had only recently been introduced to Dvorah, an accomplished woman and a mother of nine children, some married with children of their own. She runs a successful day school for young boys aged 4-6, and has authored and illustrated a series of popular interactive children's books used in Jewish schools in Lakewood and Brooklyn. I had some reservations about imposing on a family festival, but any initial concerns melted away as soon as I arrived. Much like the safety and protective walls of the *sukkah*, I was immediately embraced by Dvorah's immediate and extended family with an outpouring of warmth and unbridled hospitality.

In the *sukkah*, spiritual energy and Divine light abounded in this most earthly dwelling whose ceiling was the heavens. The holiday meal began with the *Kiddush*, the prayer of praise, and the blessing over the wine. In accordance with tradition, Bernie poured a second cup of wine into the top of the silver wine fountain which, through spouts, distributed wine into each of the two ounce cups surrounding it.

One of the most remarkable customs during *Sukkot* is the *ushpizen*, a prayer welcoming guests which is part of the obligation to feed strangers. These guests, however, are not the earthly ones, but rather the souls of the seven Patriarchs, beginning with Abraham. Like Elijah at Passover, it is the mysterious stranger joining the celebration. Each night, all of the souls are present, but each takes his turn leading the others. Abraham represents love and kindness; Isaac, restraint and personal strength; Jacob, beauty and truth; Moses, eternality through Torah; Aaron, empathy and receptivity for Divine spirituality; Joseph, righteousness; David, Kingdom here on earth. During a delicious dinner of roasted chicken, homemade soup, and *kugel*, there was much exuberant singing and lively discussion about Israel, the myths about the Orthodox, and the divide among Jews. We talked about the New Age Hollywood-ization and misappropriation of the term Kabbalah. When I said "It is pretty disturbing that many people think it's about Madonna, red string, and instant spirituality," little twelve-year-old Yella sitting alongside me turned to her mother and asked, "Ma, who is Madonna?"

Without missing a beat, Dvorah answered: "She's a non-Jewish singer, sweetheart," looking over at me with a smile: "See how sheltered she is?!"

It was nearly 11:00 at night when the guests began to leave. I felt exhilarated and wide awake. I walked down Roselle Court before getting in my car to go home. It was a brisk evening and stars were out in profusion. Amidst the rustling of the leaves in the wind, strains of exuberant singing and hand clapping emanated from Sukkahs and seemed to magically ascend to the heavens.

Simchat Torah

The last two days of Sukkot are called Simchat Torah, Hebrew for "rejoicing in the Law." It is the crowning celebration of a religious cycle that begins with Rosh Hashana on the first day of *Tishrei,* includes Yom Kippur on the tenth, Succot on the fifteenth, Shemini Atzeret on the twenty-second, and finally ends with Simchat Torah on the twenty-third. The first part of the cycle is solemn and serious. It centers around the austere days of Rosh Hashana, the Ten Days of Penitence, and the Day of Atonement. But the second part is joyful; not only because it is the feast on which children parade with the procession of Torah scrolls, but because it symbolizes the deathlessness of the Jewish people. It is also the time when Jews affirm their view of the Torah as a tree of life; that there is no end to the Torah, and that we never complete our learning.

Each week in *shul,* we publicly read a few chapters from Torah, starting with Genesis Ch. 1 and working our way around to Deuteronomy 34. On Simchat Torah, the last portion of Deuteronomy is read by the Bridegroom, and the scroll is immediately rolled back to Genesis and so begins anew, the reading of the Torah; a reminder that the Torah is a never-ending circle. On that first evening, the concluding portions of Dueteronomy are read by an honored member of the congregation called the *Chatan Torah* (Bridegroom of The Torah), and the Torah scrolls are carried or danced around the *shul* seven times. The number seven is symbolic of the seven processions made by the priests around the Temple during biblical times.

The festivities continue the following morning with prayers. Another member of the congregation is honored as the *Chatan Bareisheit* (Bridegroom of Genesis) and reads from that portion of Torah. The scrolls are then carried around the *shul* (sometimes in the street) with spirited singing and dancing. Children follow the processional with toy torahs, paper flags and candles. The next morning, after another processional, the Bridegroom of the Law Beginning reads the opening verses of *Bereshis* (Genesis). An *aliya* is the honor of being called upon to make one set of blessings said before and after each section of the Torah readings. Customarily on Simchat Torah, everyone receives an *aliya,* and it is common to have both individuals and groups of people called up at once.

After the Bridegrooms of the Torah and Genesis do their readings, they are joined on the *bimah* by the male children in the congregation. The honoree holds a prayer shawl aloft forming a canopy, or *chuppah*, over the children. The honoree and children say the blessings and then the congregation blesses all the children by reciting the blessing Jacob gave to his grandchildren. It is in that moment of Simchat Torah, we see the parallel between the unbroken cycle of Torah reading and the never-ending transmission of Torah from generation to generation.

Perhaps because this holiday is more emotional than intellectual, but being a part of this year's Simchat Torah at a small *shul* on 14th Street, I was struck by a penetrating sense of being in the presence of G-d. I watched from the women's section as 50 or so men, covered in their white prayer shawls, exuberantly sang and danced in circles and sub-circles around the men who were honored with taking turns at carrying the scrolls. Some of the men had small children sitting on their shoulders and waving little paper flags. A woman in the *shul,* along with her three daughters, was watching the service. Recognizing me as a 'newbie," Rifka introduced herself and struck up, as many women have done with me over the course of this project, a friendly conversation. "That's my husband carrying the Torah," she said. "I'm a proud wife." As we chatted, I explained how the process of writing a book about Lakewood's Orthodox community had, to my surprise, led me on a spiritual and personal journey through self-examination to self-awareness, and ultimate return to my familial and religious roots but with a more profound understanding of the interconnectedness between Torah, tradition, and truth. Rifka moved closer: "That is because the Torah is the truth we live by," she whispered, "You have found the truth in your *neshama* (soul)." Seeing my eyes well up, she touched my hand and said, "I really hope that you will come here often and pray with us." I promised I would.

Chanukah

Chanukah, the festival which falls in December, commemorates an important historical event when nearly 2000 years ago, Jews in ancient Israel were forbidden from practicing their faith. A monumental battle was won when they rebelled against their foreign rulers. Judah the Maccabee led the revolt. He rededicated the Temple which had once been used for pagan worship. The eternal lamp was relit and though they only had enough oil to last one day, miraculously, the oil lasted for eight days.

The only religious observance related to the holiday is the lighting of candles, though most Orthodox families use oil rather than candles. Those who light candles arrange them in a candalabrium, called a *menorah*, which holds nine candles: one for each night, plus a *shamash* (servant) at a different height. On the first night, one candle is placed at the far right. The *shamash* candle is lit and three *berakhot* (blessings) are recited: *l'hadlik near,* a general prayer over candles; *she-asah nisim,* a prayer thanking G-d for performing miracles for our ancestors at this time and *she-hekhianu,* a general prayer thanking G-d for allowing us to reach this time of year. The first candle is then lit using the *shamash* candle, and the *shamash* candle is placed in its holder. The candles are allowed to burn out on their own after a minimum of 1/2 hour. Each night, another candle is added from right to left (like the Hebrew language). Candles are lit from left to right. Because of the law prohibiting the lighting of a fire on *Shabbat*, Chanukah candles are lit before the *Shabbat* candles on Friday night, and they are lit after *Havdalah* on Saturday night. While the candles burn, children play with *dreidels*, a special spinning top. On each of its four sides is a Hebrew letter standing for the words, *A great miracle happened there.* ["there" referring to Israel.]

It is traditional to eat fried foods on this holiday, because of the significance of oil to the holiday. Among Ashkenazi Jews, this usually includes potato pancakes called *latkes* (pronounced "lot-kuhs" or "lot-keys" depending on where your grandmother comes from). Gift-giving is not a traditional part of the holiday. The only traditional gift of the holiday is *gelt*, small amounts of money, a custom rooted in the Talmud. The Talmud mandates that even a very poor person must light Chanukah lights, even if he can't afford it. A person with no money is required to go 'knocking on doors' until he collects enough to buy at least one candle for each night of Chanukah. The Torah concept of charity — *tzedakah* — requires us to help the recipient in the most dignified manner possible. Therefore, the custom arose to give gifts of money during Chanukah so that someone who needs extra money for Chanukah candles can receive it in the form of Chanukah *gelt*. Children today often receive small mesh bags filled with gold wrapped chocolate representing Chanukah *gelt*." A traditional song of this holiday is *Maoz Tzur*, better known to non-Jews as "Rock of Ages."

Tu Bishvat

Tu Bishvat, or the "Rosh Hashana for Trees," is observed on the fifteenth (tu) of *Sh'vat,* in January, of the secular calendar, which is Israel's spring season. Scholars believe that Tu Bishvat was originally an agricultural festival, marking the emergence of spring. After the destruction of the Temple in 70 A.C.E. this holiday was a way for Jews to symbolically bind themselves to their former homeland by eating foods that could be found in Israel. The festival represents the boundary for trees, between one year and another, since most of the rains of the previous year, in the Land of Israel, have already fallen. A certain percentage of the fruit has reached the stage of "begun to ripen." This is defined as from the time of blossoming until the fruit has reached one third of its full growth. Fruits which have reached this stage are attributed to the previous year. Any new blossoming of fruit after this day is a result of the blessings of the new year. Tu Bishvat has become a tree planting festival in Israel, in which both Israelis and Jews around the world plant trees in honor or in memory of a loved one or friend. Many in Lakewood's Orthodox community sponsor a tree in Israel through The Jewish National Fund.

Purim

Purim falls in late February or March. Ask any little girl in Lakewood who she wants to be at a Purim party, and the answer will most likely be Queen Esther whose story reads like a fairy tale. Purim is one of the most joyous holidays on the Jewish calendar and commemorates a time when the Jews of Persia were saved from extermination. Told in the Biblical Book of Esther, called the *Megillah*, meaning scroll, the heroine is a woman named Esther, who has been raised by her cousin, Mordechai. She was taken to the house of the King of Persia to be a part of his harem. King Ahasuerus loved her more than the other women and, not knowing she was a Jew since Mordechai had told her not to reveal her identity, he made her Queen. The villain is Haman, an arrogant ambitious advisor to the king who hates Mordechai because he refuses to bow before him. Haman decides to destroy the Jewish people since their laws were different and they were a threat to the Persians. The King agreed to issue a decree that the Jews be slaughtered. But having learned that Mordechai had demonstrated loyalty to the king and never rewarded, he told Haman that he was to honor him by leading Mordechai in a royal procession. Mordechai learns of the plot to exterminate his people and asks Esther to intercede with the King which was a dangerous thing to do since anyone who came into the king's presence without being summoned could be put to death. Esther fasted for three days to prepare herself, and then went to see the King who welcomed her. She revealed her Jewish identity and told him of Haman's plot against her people. The Jews were saved and Haman was hanged on the gallows.

On the day before Purim, the thirteenth of *Adar*, Orthodox Jews observe a fast in memory of Esther who asked the Jews of Persia to fast and pray for three days before she risked her life by going to the King to rescind Haman's evil decree. Like all Jewish fast days, eating, drinking, and washing are prohibited. Much of the day is spent in synagogue. *The Megillah of Esther*, is read aloud, first on the eve of Purim at the conclusion of the fast and as with other sacred scrolls, the reading is preceded and followed by a blessing. The reading is chanted with its own melody passed down through oral tradition.

The day of Purim is a joyous and carnival-like celebration. It is a custom for both adults and children to arrive at the *shul* in costume, but it's mostly the children who dress up. Most dress as the lead characters in the Purim story. The synagogue is quiet as they listen again to the *Megillah*, except when the name Haman is recited when *groggers*, or noisemakers, are rattled by the congregation. After the *Megillah* reading, *shuls* hold Purim parades or put on *purimshpiels*, small plays with lots of silly jokes and prizes for the best costumes. The *Megilla* says that Mordechai declared the holiday of Purim as a time "of feasting and gladness and of sending food to one another, as well as donations to the poor." It is considered a special *mitzvah* to send food baskets and packages on this day. The baskets must contain at least two different foods that require two separate blessings. Baskets may be simple or elaborate. There are religious organizations that put packages together for a small fee, or you can put baskets together yourself. They must be hand delivered through a *shaliach*, or representative, usually a small child on the day of Purim. In the late afternoon, family and friends gather for a festive meal, or Purim *seudah*. No specific rituals here; just having fun together is the order of the day. There is a traditional food eaten on Purim: *Hamantaschen,* Yiddish for Haman's pockets, is a small three cornered cake filled with fruits, jams, or poppy seeds. The shape is to replicate the hat Haman is said to have worn.

Pesach

Pesach, or Passover, is the eight day festival in the spring – usually April – which commemorates the story of the Israelite's exodus from Egypt. There is more preparation in the home, in accordance with Jewish law, for this holiday than any other. The home and property must be thoroughly cleaned of all *chametz,* or fermented grain. Shelves, countertops and eating surfaces used year round are cleaned and covered for Passover use, and special dish racks, sink racks and wash basins are used. Cooking surfaces are cleaned and covered and ovens are either kashered by being burnt out, or used with a special insert liner. All cooking and eating utensils must be either set aside exclusively for Passover use, or, in some cases, "made kosher" in consultation with a rabbi, according to the procedures of Jewish law. All of these preparations must be completed by the morning before Passover.

A ritual search for *chametz* is conducted the previous night, and the *chametz* that is found is burned the next morning. The day before Passover is a fast day for Jewish firstborn males, in commemoration of the tenth plague, the slaying of the firstborn male Egyptians, which immediately resulted in the Exodus. In Orthodox congregations, a special celebration called *Siyum* is conducted, following which participating firstborn males are permitted to break their fast.

The first two nights of the eight day holiday are celebrated with lavish meals called Seders during which the history of Passover is read from the *Haggadah*. The story goes back about 3000 years when the Israelites were enslaved by the Egyptians under the rule of the Pharoah Ramses II. Moses, a simple Jewish shepherd, was instructed by G-d to go to the pharaoh and demand the freedom of his people. Moses' plea of *Let my people go* was ignored. Moses warned the Pharaoh that G-d would send severe punishments to the people of Egypt if the Israelites were not freed. Again the Pharaoh ignored Moses' request for freedom. In response, G-d unleashed a series of ten terrible plagues on the people of Egypt. The first nine plagues were: The water of River Nile turned into blood; frogs; lice (vermin); wild beasts (flies); blight (cattle disease); boils; hail; locusts; darkness.

The first nine plagues only served to daunt the Pharaoh's wild spirit, but were unable to make him submit to the will of G-d. The tenth plague was the slaying of the first born son of Egyptian families. So that the Hebrews were not subject to the slayings, G-d ordered them to sacrifice a lamb and mark their doors with the blood of the lamb, as an indication to G-d to 'pass over' their houses while slaying the first born males of the Egyptians so that their first born males were saved from the tenth plague. Pesach means 'passing over' or 'protection' in Hebrew.

This last calamity was a final blow to the Pharaoh and he ordered Israelites to be set free immediately and allow their passage to freedom. Because they were in a hurry, the Israelites could not even wait to let their dough rise and bake bread, but took raw dough instead to bake in the hot desert sun. As Moses led them through the desert, the angry Pharaoh sent his army to chase these ex-slaves and bring them back. But with the grace of G-d, the Israelites managed to reach the Red Sea, where they were trapped by the vast expanse of water. Moses called upon G-d, and suddenly a miracle occurred. The waves of the Red Sea parted and the Israelites were able to cross to the other side. As soon as they all reached the other side the sea closed trapping the Pharaoh's army as the waves closed upon them. As the Israelites watched the waters of the Red Sea sweep away the Pharaoh's army, they realized they were finally free.

While not the only element of Pesach, the beautiful Seder table is definitely the shining star, and setting the table is a most joyous occasion, a chance to use our finest silver and dinnerware reserved for this celebration. The table is covered in the best tablecloth which is often a family heirloom and festival candles and candlesticks are arranged in the center. The *Kiddush* cup is placed in front of the host or leader of the Seder for the ceremonial wine that will be drunk four times during the meal. Wine is placed on the table with glasses for everyone present. There is a special ceremonial goblet filled with wine and left untouched in honor of the prophet Elijah, who, according to tradition, will arrive during the Passover seder as an unknown guest to herald the advent of the Messiah.

During the Seder dinner, biblical verses are read while the door is briefly opened to welcome Elijah. In this way the Seder dinner not only commemorates the historical redemption from Egyptian bondage of the Jewish people, but also calls to mind their future redemption when Elijah and the Messiah shall appear.

There is a special Seder plate containing symbolic foods: An egg to remind Jews of the sacrifices made in biblical times; a lamb shank to symbolize the lamb sacrificed on the first Passover; bitter herbs to reflect the bitter experience of slavery in Egypt; green vegetables to represent spring and a new life; *charoset,* a delicious fruit and nut paste symbolic of the mortar used by Jewish slaves in Egypt to build cities for the Pharoah. A glass of salt water is also placed on the table to symbolize the bitter tears of the enslaved Israelites. There are three matzohs placed on the table in front of the leader in a special three sectioned dish. One of the three pieces of the matzoh is broken in half, wrapped in a napkin, hidden, and later retrieved to be served as the last morsel of food eaten at the end of the lengthy observance of this ancient Jewish feast. This bit of unleavened bread is called the *afikomen* and it symbolizes the Passover lamb. For Jewish children, the *afikomen* is used to hold their attention until the end of the Seder. In some families the children "steal" the matzoh and are paid a ransom in order to get it back to the table. In other families, as was the case with mine as I was growing up, it is intentionally hidden and the children search for it and are rewarded.

During and after the Passover meal, guests sing songs in joyous reminder of having been released from bondage. Passover songs are plentiful, and help create and reinforce the many themes or meanings of Pesach: Physical freedom or redemption; season of rebirth; festival of unleavened bread (*matzah*), and the festival of the paschal offering (lamb)], especially to the children for which they are mostly (but not completely) intended in order to fulfill the Biblical commandment from G-d in Shemot (the Book of Exodus) to "teach and re-teach in every generation" the story of Passover.

The most famous Passover song known universally among Jewish and non Jewish people is *Dayenu*. The words in *Dayenu* list the many ways that G-d sided with the Hebrews. At the end of each mention of G-d's favors, the word *Dayenu* – a Hebrew word that is pronounced "die-ay-new" – is sung, meaning: "It would have been sufficient, or enough." This song is essentially a song of thanks and gratitude to G-d, where its message is saying: "If G-d did a simple favor for us and didn't do anything else, it would have been sufficient," even if granting more favors would have helped the Hebrews to escape slavery sooner, or helped contribute to less suffering. The main point of the song is to recognize and be grateful for even the simplest of favors from another.

Another popular Passover song is *Chad Gadya*, a Hebrew phrase meaning: "one kid," where "kid" in this case means a baby goat. This Passover song inspires a firm and mature faith and belief in the power of G-d by chronologically describing all the empires throughout Jewish history that have occupied the Land of Israel who, one by one, have been destroyed by successive empires.

For Zeva, a 51 year old mother of seven, all holidays have a deeply religious meaning, but "Pesach and Sukkot are my favorites because they bring my family together from NY, NJ and Israel. We talk late into the night about what is happening in our lives and we also recall memories from these holidays over the years. I love seeing my grandchildren shaking the *lulav* and *etrog* as my children did many years ago, and I enjoy hearing the story of the Exodus each year."

Shavuot

Shavuot comes 49 days (seven weeks) after the second day of Passover. The legend of Shavuot is an important key to Judaism and Jewish thought. It celebrates the giving of the Torah by G-d to Moses on Mount Sinai and the beginning of a wheat harvest. Jews in the Orthodox community will stay awake the night of Shavout studying the Torah. This practice is called *Tikkun Leil Shavout,* and it began in the sixteenth century in Safed, Israel, where Jewish mysticism flourished. The Shavuot synagogue service includes readings from The Ten Commandments and The Book of Ruth. Ruth was the great-grandmother of King David. The Book of Ruth tells the story about the relationship, friendship, and love between its three main characters: Naomi; her Moabite daughter-in-law Ruth whose husband has died; and Boaz, Naomi's kinsman who eventually marries Ruth. Naomi and her husband Elimelech and their two sons, move to Moab because of the famine in Canaan. All three men die, leaving Naomi and her two Moabite daughters-in-law without support. Naomi decides to return home and asks her daughters-in-law to remain in their own land, but Ruth insists on accompanying Naomi, telling her: "Your people shall be my people and your G-d, my G-d." Upon their return, Ruth goes to glean leftover grain in the fields and meets the owner of that land; his name was Boaz. Boaz, part of Elimelech's family, liked Ruth and asked her to marry him. Boaz and Ruth had a son named Obed, who became the father of Jesse, father of David.

Simple as is its story, The Book of Ruth is remarkably rich in examples of faith, patience, industry, and kindness, and in indications of the care which G-d takes of those who put their trust in Him. The saga of Ruth is particularly relevant to Shavout because Ruth voluntarily accepts the Torah and Judaism as the Israelites did at the foot of Mount Sinai. When the Jewish people were brought to Mount Sinai to receive the Torah, they were told that the other nations were asked first if they desired to receive the Torah. They politely asked what was in the Torah. When the reply came that there were various acts that were forbidden and on their transgression they would be punished if they were to accept the Torah, they kindly refused the Torah. When the Jewish people were asked if they would like to receive the Torah, they simply replied, "We will do what is in it and we will learn it." After the reply of the Jewish people, a voice came out of heaven, booming, "Who revealed to my children the secrets that only the angels know?" Tradition tells us that the angels gave two crowns to the Jewish people, one for saying that they will do and, the second, for saying that they will learn. Dovid, a BMG Kollel student, elaborates:

> *Without this unconditional commitment to G-d and the Torah, the Jews would have quickly changed their minds. For this they received the "crown" which is above intelligence. The second crown was the crown of intelligence, to be used for understanding the teachings of the Torah. This is the mistake that the other nations made. They wanted to make their commitment to the Torah based on their own intellectual understanding of the goodness. But the angels knew the secret; an unswerving decision based on total devotion to G-d. This is the secret of the specialness of Shavout. We, too, can re-commit and dedicate ourselves on this very day that the Torah was given. We can be a part of that great nation, who abandoned themselves for their greatest yearning, to become close to G-d.*

Chapter Fifteen

Yom HaShoah: Remembering the Unforgettable

In any free society where terrible wrongs exist, some are guilty—all are responsible.
Abraham Joshua Heschel

I don't believe in accidents. There are only encounters in history. There are no accidents.
Elie Wiesel

Shoah is the Hebrew word for Holocaust. For non-Orthodox Jews, Yom HaShoah, also known as Holocaust Remembrance Day, occurs on the 27th of *Nissan* (March-April). For Orthodox Jews, Yom HaShoah is observed as part of Tisha B'Av, meaning the ninth of *Av* which occurs on the ninth day in the Jewish month of *Av* (July-August). According to the sages, many terrible events happened on this day. Tisha B'Av primarily commemorates the destruction of the first and second Temples, both of which were destroyed on the ninth of Av (the first by the Babylonians in 586 BCE; the second by the Romans in 70 CE). Although this holiday is primarily meant to commemorate the destruction of the Temple, it is appropriate to consider on this day the many other tragedies of the Jewish people, many of which occurred on this day, most notably the expulsion of the Jews from Spain in 1492. Tisha B'Av is the culmination of a three week period of increasing mourning, beginning with the fast of the 17th of *Tammuz*, which commemorates the first breach in the walls of Jerusalem, before the First Temple was destroyed. During this three week period, weddings and other parties are not permitted, and people refrain from cutting their hair. From the first to the ninth of *Av*, it is customary to refrain from eating meat or drinking wine (except on the Sabbath) and from wearing new clothing. The restrictions on Tisha B'Av are similar to those on Yom Kippur: to refrain from eating and drinking, even water; washing, bathing, shaving or wearing cosmetics; wearing leather shoes; engaging in sexual relations; and studying Torah. Work in the ordinary sense of the word, rather than in the Sabbath sense, is also restricted. People who are ill need not fast on this day. Many of the traditional mourning practices are observed: people refrain from smiles, laughter and idle conversation, and sit on low stools. In synagogue, the Book of Lamentations is read and mourning prayers are recited. The ark, the cabinet where the Torah is kept, is draped in black.

World War I – which began the downward slide to the Holocaust – began on Tisha B'av. The Holocaust refers to the period from January 30, 1933 when Adolph Hitler became chancellor of Germany to May 8, 1945 when the war in Europe ended. During this time, Jews in Europe were subjected to progressively harsh persecution that ultimately led to the murder – the genocide – of 6 million Jews, 1.5 million being children – and the destruction of 5000 Jewish communities. What Hitler called "The Final Solution" was his deliberate and systematic attempt to annihilate the entire Jewish population of Europe. Others killed were gypsies, homosexuals, mentally and physically disabled, Jehova's Witnesses, and righteous Christians who helped their Jewish neighbors.

Tisha B'Av is a day to memorialize those who died in the *Shoah*. Why do Jews insist on remembering, some might say obsessively, the sufferings of their people? Why do they retell the story, each Passover around the Seder table, about the Israelites' exodus from Egypt where they were slaves to the Promised Land? Why do those who bore witness to the most organized mass killing of a targeted group ever witnessed by modern history command us all to *Zachor*, to remember and to "Never Forget"? Clearly, remembering the Holocaust can serve to heighten awareness of human beings' capacity for humanity and for evil and somehow prevent the destructive whirlwinds of hatred and violence in our own time. The Nazi assault on humanity was perpetrated by human beings against other human beings – ordinary people who, through mass persuasion and social structural constraints, were led into committing genocide. Hitler made that a possibility for anyone, and neither the Jews nor any other group on earth can feel safe from that crime in the future. The legacy of the victims, the historical and human significance of those who have suffered, is found in George Santayana's admonition that those who forget the past are condemned to repeat it.

Throughout history, and as discussed in Chapter 1, observant Jews have always been easy targets for abuse and persecution simply because of their visibility and tangible difference in dress and customs. In Hellenistic Palestine, in Moorish Spain, in Weimar Germany, the so called "golden ages" of pluralism and tolerance, all gave way to vile conquerors; and with each pogrom, inquisition, expulsion, their identity was defined solely by their Otherness.

The Nazi genocide was fueled by hatred and intolerance. Today, there is a rehashing of the ancient canard about Jewish control, vilifying Jews and Israel as agents of imperialism, and adopting anti-Semitic stereotypes about Jewish financial influence. Venezuelan President Hugo Chavez repeatedly compares Israel to Hitler and the Nazis, and he has accused Israel of engaging in genocide against Arabs. Iranian President Mahmoud Amadinajab repeatedly denies the Holocaust, and refers to the Jews as vermin. Add to that list Hezbollah's Secretary General, Hassan Nasrallah and Syrian President Bashar al-Assad.

Since I began this book, the climate of local, national, and global anti-Semitism has escalated at an alarming rate. The Bernard Madoff Ponzi scheme that continues, at the time of this writing, to rock Wall Street and the global marketplace, is feeding into and regenerating anti-Semitic stereotypes about Jews and money on mainstream and extremist websites. Madoff is neither Orthodox, nor is he typical of Jewish business ethics.

As the war between between Gaza and Israel escalates, incendiary news clips and worldwide protests reveal something far more insidious than a bias against the Jewish state. In France, a car rams into a French synagogue. In Belgium, a Chabad menorah is vandalized and Jewish shops are covered with swastikas. At a protest rally in Austria, there are signs "Clean the earth of deadly Zionists," In the Netherlands, demonstrators chant "Gas the Jews." In 2008 in Mumbai, India, terrorists attack Americans, Brits, and Jews. Among the 140 killed were Brooklyn born Rabbi Gavriel Holtzberg and his wife Rivkah. The young outreach couple was targeted in the Chabad House they ran since 2003. In the United States, in Florida, a woman in a burkha yells "Go back to the ovens."

On college campuses across America, a handful of extremist liberal professors, many of whom are Jewish, use the banner of academic freedom to indoctrinate students and push their agendas of hatred towards Israel, the only democracy in the Middle East. In 2009, three Monmouth County synagogues are forced to evacuate hundreds of congregants after receiving a bomb threat. In Jackson, N.J., which borders on Lakewood, a young Hasidic boy is the victim of a hate crime by neighborhood youth. If we have learned anything from the lessons of the massacre of six million Jews in World War II, it should be to identify early warning signs to prevent its recurrence. Is it that farfetched that given the climate where Islamic extremists and governments foster intolerant attitudes and behaviors towards Jews of all denominations – but particularly those in Orthodox communities who can be easily targeted as Other – that excoriations, bans, and perhaps another Holocaust cannot happen?

Despite their seemingly isolated lifestyle, Lakewood's Orthodox are, in fact, very aware of world events as they pertain to Israel and to the future of Judaism, and to the vulnerability of Orthodox enclaves to acts of terror. Looking back at their Eastern European history, they know how extreme prejudice and intolerance of "the other," hate-based policies, disregard for individuality and difference, inter-ethnic and inter-cultural conflict, and cultural exclusivity allow for a society where all morality and laws go by the wayside. They know the Holocaust happened because individuals and the world stood silently by and let the hatred and mass killings happen. They did nothing. They know the Holocaust happened because governments and people made choices which allowed it to happen. It has been said that when one person suffers, all must be concerned with his or her suffering. Holocaust survivors carry a heavy burden, the burden of remembering, and a painful duty of passing on those memories so the world will learn and so that the Holocaust never happens again. As I tell my students, listening to their stories make all of us witnesses who must make sure the world never forgets.

Rose Korcarz Laiter is an Adjunct Professor of History at Ocean County College in Toms River, New Jersey. She has lectured extensively about the Holocaust and her own experiences, and graciously and bravely shared her ordeal with the audience at this year's *Yom ha Shaoh* event at the college. She fights back tears several times as she remembers her horrific ordeal and the murder of her family and neighbors. Her devoted husband Morris, sitting in the audience, breaks down as he sees his wife reliving the pain. Rose was four years old when the Holocaust began and ten years old when the war ended, "which is why," she says, "everything still lingers in my mind and my nightmares."

Laiter was raised by her bubbie (grandma) while her father earned a living running the family grocery store and working as a master tailor making custom made suits. Her mother was a businesswoman who had attended the University of Warsaw. Laiter's childhood in Poland came to an abrupt end when the Nazis invaded Poland. Within days, Nazi soldiers marched up to every house in her village, pointing their bayonets, and herded the villagers in threes and fours to the train station where they were packed into crowded unsanitary cattle cars headed to Warsaw where the nightmare began.

Laiter had the audience spellbound as she held out her arms: "Out of the ashes of the Holocaust I've emerged. My bubbie was killed in the gas chamber and my heart breaks when I think of that," she recalled, as her eyes welled up. "I have known hunger and pain. For those of us who survived and have come to America, it was, I believe, for a reason and greater purpose. That is why I stand before you today and look out at your beautiful young faces, and do my small part to make sure that the world does not forget. My purpose on earth is to teach people about the Holocaust and to tell you all how blessed I feel to live in the greatest country in the world, where I have gotten an education and where I can live freely as a Jew."

Long time Lakewood resident, Helina Sininsky, was born in a small village in Linize, Czechoslovakia, to a wealthy Satmar family. Her father, a successful businessman, after hearing rumors of what was happening in neighboring villages and across Eastern Europe, managed to purchase tickets for his family to go to America, but his wife refused to cross the ocean alone with her six young children. Helina vividly remembers the Friday morning in April of 1944 when Hungarian soldiers deported her, her parents, and her five younger siblings to the Carpathian Mountains before they were all put in a cattle car, with ninety people and one pail of water, bound for Auschwitz. She is still haunted by the memory of an SS soldier forcibly separating her from her family and pulling her grandfather, a respected Satmar Rabbi, by his long beard for selection.

"The conditions were horrific and dehumanizing," Sininsky whispers, "and five people had to use the outhouse at one time and eat from one plate. We were given soup which was warm water and grass, and one slice of bread each day. When I asked when I would see my family, a Gestapo woman told me, 'Look up at the smoke in the sky. That is your family burning.'" Sininsky was transferred to Dachau and then Alach. In April of 1945, when the Americans liberated Europe, fifteen-year-old Helina began a long solo journey back home in hopes of finding her immediate family, especially her father whom she had heard was still alive. Helina believes that her ability to endure that difficult journey, during which she met others returning to her village, was due to her newfound sense of invincibility, the exhilaration of being free and the realization that nothing in the world could happen to her worse than what she experienced and witnessed in the camps. But when she reached her village, she learned that her father had died the same day he had been liberated. Helina remembered that, before the Jewish families had been rounded up, her father had given their Christian neighbors his *shtreimel* for safekeeping. She was able to retrieve the hat from the new family who lived there and later gave it to her father's brother, a rabbi in America.

Helina, too, eventually came to America, where she was taken in by relatives in Brooklyn. At that point, she shares, "I had to make a decision. Here I was, all of 16. I knew I was no longer a "Satmar princess" in my little shtetl, and that I could either be an American teenager and fit in with my cousins, or hold on to my religious observances. So I became one of them," quietly adding, "and I even cut myself off from the other refugees because I was so happy to be an American."

Helina soon moved out on her own, worked hard, attended school, and eventually met her husband, Gary. They moved to Lakewood where her father-in-law, Yankel, owned a kosher meat market which the young couple eventually would take over. Gary was among those who brought Rabbi Levovitz to Lakewood and the Sininskys were active members of The Old Shul for many years. Ten years ago, her daughter, Gwen, served as president of Bezalel Day School.

Today, as she approaches 80, this accomplished and feisty woman evaluates her life, which has not been an easy one but one she speaks about with no self-pity. As a survivor, she speaks at schools because she knows it's important that this generation knows about the Nazi genocide. Her beloved husband, Gary, passed away several years ago, and in 2008, she lost her son, Mark, a lawyer and judge in Lakewood, to cancer. But when they were all still together, her family wanted to visit her homeland; reluctantly, she agreed so that her grandchildren would know their roots. In Poland, she even took them to the camp, pointing out the barrack she lived in. "It was worth reliving the pain," she tells me, "when my grandchildren told me that night in our hotel room, 'We know this was very hard for you, momom, but we are better people and richer than we were yesterday for having been here.'"

Helina still works for the township of Lakewood. "If you can come back from Hell," she reasons, "you can come out a shining star. I came from Eastern Europe, from the camps, and here I am working for the government in the greatest country in the world. I am proud of my achievements." Certainly, what she holds most dear are her children and grandchildren. "At my seventieth birthday," she says, holding back tears, "My young grandson Josh, an entrepreneur, told the guests: 'I'll bet my grandma told you that my heroes are Bill Gates and Donald Trump, but truthfully, my momom is my hero.'" She reaches across the table, touches my hand, and laughs, "Then Josh told everyone that his momom travelled all over the world on her own. And here she is today where she will only drive from her house to ShopRite and to work!"

Lakewood's Jean Wechsler's story is another one of courage and the spirit of the human heart to endure what few of us can imagine. A child during the Nazi Holocaust, she speaks to schools and organizations about her family's experiences in hiding and of the small acts of kindness by non-Jews that saved her family from extermination in the gas chambers of the concentration camps. "My mother's tenacity and stubbornness kept her seven children alive when they ran from their village of ruined homes and slaughtered people and animals." The life of Wechsler's mother, Esther Kornwitz Parnes, is documented in Avraham Azrieli's book, *One Step Ahead: How a Mother of Seven Escaped Hitler's Claws*.

The survivors who bore witness will eventually diminish. There will be those who say the Holocaust never happened. There are those today who say it never happened. Hearing first hand accounts of those who survived, makes all of us witnesses who must take a stand against indifference, against prejudice, against injustice. When students in my Jewish and Holocaust Literature course read and hear survivor memoirs, many for the first time, they are left visibly shaken. These are stories that document the culmination of the human capacity for inhumanity, but they are also stories that stand as testimony to the indestructibility of the human spirit in the face of evil, and which have a remarkable absence of self-pity. I feel compelled to tell them about the episodes of kindness and caring, of the Righteous Gentiles, like the farmer, who risked their own lives to help their fellow man. But I want them to understand that these are but courageous exceptions to the whole story – and that they must never forget that in the twentieth century, our lifetime, six million innocent men, women, and children were massacred at the hands of the Nazis while the world stood by.

Chapter Sixteen

Chaim's Story: A Survivor Speaks

All I can do is tell the story; and this must be sufficient.
Eli Wiesel, The Gates of the Forest

To the Jews who left the ashes of their homeland after the Holocaust, coming to America, many to Lakewood, which was already established as a haven for Eastern European Jews, represented religious freedom and the opportunity to start over, to work hard, and to make a new and better life for themselves and their families. Chaim Melcer, an Orthodox Jew, is one of the survivors who has called Lakewood home since 1954. Born in 1930 in the small village of Sobibor in Eastern Poland, Chaim was the eldest of four children born to David and Fayga Melcer. He is also the only one of the Melcer children to survive the Nazi Holocaust. Chaim remembers his village where Jews were the minority. "It wasn't a problem," he says, "because we all were equally poor." "When I was ten years old," Chaim recalls, "my father would give me ten potatoes to deliver to a poor man who lived five or six miles away." Life was hard for the Melcer family who owned a modest three room home on a four acre farm. David Melcer worked in the field from early morning tending to cattle and harvesting vegetables such as corn, potatoes, and beans. A deeply religious man who had an impressive library of Jewish texts, he instilled in his children a respect for, and love of, Torah and the laws of Judaism. "My family's moral fiber came from these books of G-d," explains Chaim. "We found direction and hope in these scriptures."

Fayga took care of the house and children, baking, cooking meals, and keeping Sabbath and holidays. Chaim's life was not unusual for a young Jewish boy. He went to the tiny community school about a mile and a half from his house where he learned reading, writing, and arithmetic. The secular school day was from 7 in the morning till 1:00, after which he would come home and eat lunch with the entire family before going to Hebrew school until 5:00. "We then sat down to dinner with the entire family eating and conversing. Family time was key in our home, along with Torah."

In the modest Melcer home, *Shabbat* was a much awaited celebration. "We waited all week for Friday and would take our baths in a large wooden barrel filled with well water. We would then put on our finest clothes and go to pray at the synagogue. We'd come home to a sumptuous dinner. Mama would have spent most of Friday baking *challah* and wonderful desserts, and preparing meats and fish. Sometimes, not often, we would have wine."

Nine year old Chaim's life and innocence forever changed on September 1, 1939. That was when Germany began its attack on Poland; two weeks later, 100 German troops invaded Sobibor. "I asked my grandpa what was happening," he recalls. "He said he didn't know and when I told him that maybe we should move away, grandpa said 'Why run away from the Germans? They are good people.'" But when the Germans began beating the Jews and ripping out their beards, the elder Melcer admitted that "these are not the same Germans who treated the people well in WWI." The Germans seized properties and valuables, and herded nine Jewish families into three houses. Over the next few days, the German troops gutted the synagogues and set the religious items and sacred books on fire. What Chaim remembers most about those days was that the Rabbi was ordered to take out the Torah scroll and unroll it on the ground. "The Germans forced the Jews to jump up and down on this Holy document, destroying it."

The SS prohibited Jews from going to schools and from praying, though they did so in secrecy even though they were unable to organize a proper minyan of ten Jewish men. "The Germans enjoyed degrading and beating us," Chaim recalls. David and Fayga worked for the Germans, cleaning offices. The children worked on the farms and were given a pound of bread each week as compensation which Chaim would sneak to his mother. "We lived one day at a time; we had almost nothing to eat except for some bread and a potato here and there. A lot of people lost faith and hope and died. I remember walking five or six miles when I was eleven years old to bring ten potatoes to a poor man." Barely surviving the winter of 1942, the family's spirits were lifted thinking that the New Year would see an improvement in their lives. But in April, a train arrived carrying more German soldiers who unloaded lumber, bricks, and spools of barbed wire. Over the next week, they chose 125 men for labor on a secret construction project. A few months later, Chaim and his neighbors realized the horrible unimaginable truth: " I learned that this fortress built by Jews was the Sobibor Death Camp. The Jewish people were forced to build their own tool of destruction." But what followed was even more horrific. The initial "test victims" forced through the death machine were gassed in the chambers they built and burned in the ovens. 1300 Jewish people were murdered that day.

Months passed. German and Polish prisoners from other towns arrived by trains to the Death Camp where they would be contained in barracks behind barbed wire fences until they were systematically executed by poisonous gasses. Multiple bodies would then be thrown into the large ovens to destroy any evidence of innocent people who had been killed for no reason other than that they were Jews. "We would hear the screaming and shooting and smell the burning." And as for his non-Jewish neighbors, "they followed along with the Nazis and all we could do was try to survive." In October of 1942, The German SS ordered all of the Jews of Sobibor to pack their bags and go to the center of town, where they were then marched over eight kilometers through wet mucky woods to the village of Wlodova. Over 10,000 Jews were pushed by rifle butts and kicked into locked cattle cars where the air was thick with the horrendous smell of human waste, and death and disease. It was on that fated train that Chaim made a courageous life altering decision which would take him on a journey through Hell and back, a journey no human being, certainly no child, should ever have to go through.

In the confinement of that death car, "among the groans and prayers for life," the prisoners knew they were headed for their final destination. Chaim heard some men talking about escaping from the train. "I could not believe my ears. I thought they were crazy." But then two of the men put their plan into action, "smashing and ripping at the bars… with superhuman ferocity…and with the power and fury of G-d." Suddenly, a breeze of fresh air from the cool night wafted through the car. After seeing the two men, hands mangled, bodies bleeding, jump through the small opening, Chaim made his way to the portal to freedom…My mother handed me her earrings and wedding band. I took one glance back at my family. That moment, that second, has been the most vibrant memory of my family… My father pushed me up… I didn't think I'd make it, but I believed it was better than dying in the gas chambers… In a hypnotic state of mind, I placed my two shaking feet over the edge of the train and jumped." Freedom.

Realizing he had a chance at life, Chaim says "I found hope and a revitalized desire to live. Let them kill me when I'm running. I am going to fight! I am going to give life the best chance I can." For the next year, Chaim swam through bone chilling waters, crept through the woods by day, sometimes taken in at night by kind farm families who risked their own life feeding and hiding the young Jewish boy from the Germans. At one point as he was walking through the labyrinth of trees, he came across other escapees. "It was a wonderful moment. We all cheered and ran around in excitement." We had a serious conversation about how to live though and survive another day." They also discussed the situation all over Poland, how the Germans were rounding up all the Jewish people and sending them to slave labor camps. Chaim found out from his friends that in Wlodova, that on the other side of town from where the working ghettos housed 1500 prisoners living in hellish conditions, there was still a non-working ghetto, a holding camp which housed mothers, children, the elderly, and some young men and fathers. Chaim made his way to the ghetto where to his surprise, he met his father. "It was a miracle," Chaim remembers. His father showed him the house he lived in and a hidden basement "where you run if there's ever a roundup."

The next morning, David Melcer shared with his son a dream he had the previous night about Chaim's grandmother who had been dead for a decade. In the dream, David's mother told him: I could only make arrangements for you and Chaim to get out." She predicted "You and Chaim will be the only people to survive from your town. You will live safely and be saved."

Soon after this, there was the fifth ghetto roundup in Wlodova. Germans came into the ghetto "like the psychopathic murderers they were with trucks and machine guns. Everyone knew what was going on." Chaim, his father, and three other men ran to a drainage pipe under the street staying there until they stopped hearing the screams of the Jews who the Germans had rounded up and executed, and some of whom forced to dig their own graves. Of all the inhumane acts the Germans inflicted on the Jews, Chaim painfully recalls that day and seeing a three year old boy wandering around in shock. "A German soldier threw him into a grave with others who had been shot, filling in the grave with this little boy in it. I heard that little child ask, 'Why are you putting sand in my eyes?'"

The roundups continued for several days. Chaim asked his father to go into the woods with him. His father did not think it was a good idea, so Chaim decided to go it alone. One night he stayed with a farmer who allowed him to stay in his barn before deciding it was putting his own life in danger. He then went to the market to join a group of escapes who knew all the news and "the underground" – the secret basements that connected buildings and shops. Hearing that the Germans left the ghetto, Chaim returned to find his father who had also miraculously survived the German massacres. Chaim spent the winter and following year through Easter of 1943 in the ghetto in one room that housed eight families, leaving occasionally to hunt for food and trade some goods.

In April, there was another roundup in the ghetto. German soldiers charged the ghetto in rows of ten, rifles in hand, shooting and beating people. Chaim and his father, along with the other residents, managed to reach the basement but were discovered by the Germans who ordered the prisoners to strip naked and line up against a wall. "The German soldiers formed a firing squad and the officer screamed 'Prepare to fire.' I snapped. I made a dash for freedom as I felt a burning sensation in my left ear and a wet warmth flowing down the side of my face onto my neck." Chaim jumped through the window into the house, and up to the attic where there was another hidden compartment. He could hear the German soldiers rampaging the house, "but they did not do a very good job, thank G-d." From his vantage point, Chaim was able to see the sunlight through a loose roof board. He saw a soldier rip a crying baby from its mother's arms. As the mother cried and begged for her baby, the soldier kicked her away and another soldier held her. She was forced to watch the officer swing the baby upside down, and then throw the infant head first into a wall."

After days of hiding, Chaim was able to get to another secret basement where he found his father, by then weak and emaciated. This time, there were no arguments. He took his father into the woods with him, carrying him through the rain and darkness towards the village. Setting his father in a large deep hole he had dug, Chaim went out in search of food which he was able to find discarded at a nearby farmhouse. Chaim returned to his starving father with the remains of soup, potted meat, and potatoes.

Life in the woods those next few months was not easy. There was the never ending threat of German soldiers who worked in concert with local farmers offering goods in exchange for information on Jews. To make matters worse, heavy rains filled the living hole with mud, the cold and wetness took a toll on their health, and they were "always struggling for the next crumb of bread."

Through July of 1944, life on the run consisted of daily survival, kindness of strangers, and occasional meetings with other fellow escapees. Late in November of 1943, while sleeping on a hayloft in a farmhouse, he found a hole that someone had obviously been living in. He decided to crawl into the hole which reeked of decay. When he asked in Hebrew, "Is anyone here?" a muffled "Yes" came from deep inside the hole. It was a husband and wife, Lazer and Ester Melcer, Chaim's third cousins who were living there for some time after their two children were killed by the Nazis. One day the farmer told Chaim that Ester was pregnant and keeping the family safe was getting too risky. He asked that Chaim take his cousins to the group living in the woods where survival chances were much better. Chaim thanked the farmer for his sympathy and kindness and asked him to hold his mother's earrings and wedding band "in case I survive and ever come back." The farmer told him he would do that and wished him luck. In May of 1944, Ester, with the help of a woman in the group who was a nurse, gave birth to a beautiful baby boy and the entire group took care of them both.

In July of 1944, amid clear blue skies, life in the woods ended. The Ukrainians had joined forces with the Germans, fighting together against the Russians and Chaim's group was situated right in the middle of the battle. To find out what was going on, Chaim crossed a swamp, crawled on his belly and listened to the troops talk about how the Russians now owned the land. Passing himself off as the son of a farmer, he spoke with a Russian soldier who gave him some food. When he asked if there were any Jews in the army, he was told that the unit's Major was in fact Jewish and where he might be found. When he located the Major and told him that he was also a Jew, the Major fainted. "Imagine! This man who had seen it all; murders, rapes, and pillages had fainted from the words of a small Jewish boy who was hunted by the Germans." The Major informed Chaim that the Germans were being defeated, words which the young boy happily ran back to repeat to his group who celebrated with loaves of bread and water the Russians had given him.

That was the day Chaim and his father began their journey home to Sobibor. But the old village had changed and Chaim realized "it would never feel like home again." Many of the houses were totally destroyed. A Polish couple now living in the home of Chaim's aunt, took in the father and son not quite believing anyone could have lived through those years. True to his father's dream years earlier, Chaim and his father were the only ones in the family who survived.

But life in the village was still neither healthy nor safe for Jews who were regarded as "undesirables." There was animosity and the Poles were not kind to the Jews and did not want them in their village. Too, the survivors were haunted by nightmarish memories of what they had witnessed in their old home.

Chaim remembers seeing a funeral procession in town and asked the priest who had died. "A little girl," replied the priest. I said, "One little girl has died and you are all crying? You are all praying and walking with a cross? You are praying to G-d? How long ago was it that you said 'Find them and catch them and kill them'?" The priest was stunned by the words of this young man, but Chaim wanted to teach them all a lesson. "I wanted to teach them humanely, maturely, and intelligently that what they had done and were still doing to the Jewish people was wrong.

I was talking with all of my mind, all the years of death, destruction, hiding, starving, and running were now pouring out. I finally had the chance to say all I ever wanted to and never could without fearing for my life." Chaim then turned to the villagers, demanding "How long ago was it that my neighbor's kid could have gone to the crematorium? How long ago was it that you were applauding when a group of 350 Jews, including my innocent baby sister, were driven out of the village. That was not so long ago. What could have changed your minds so quickly and absolutely?"

The people were left shaken, "These seemingly violent and cruel people were rendered powerless, motionless, and lifeless by my words and I declared with all my might and pride that before the war I was a Jew! During the war I was a Jew! Now, after the war I am still a Jew! And I am going to continue to live my life as a proud Jew which G-d has made me and has let me live to see this great day."

A group of men, including Chaim began to organize the escape of the Jews from Poland which was a severe crime punishable by death. After much planning and bribing, the first refugees were smuggled out. Word quickly spread to other survivors. Meeting in secret restricted areas by night, hundreds of refugees, among whom were Chaim and David Melcer, were transported by large trucks 40 miles from Poland to Berlin, all eventually finding freedom in America and Israel. In August of 1951, Chaim and David Melcer boarded a ship headed to America. After ten days of rough seas, the ship docked in Manhattan.

Three weeks later, the Melcers moved to Englishtown, NJ where Chaim decided to earn a living the only way he knew how; working the land. He and his father started a small chicken farm. Three years later, a citizen of the United States, which Chaim says "is the best country in the world," he met a woman who would become his wife. Chaim and Rita married in Lakewood and together ran a successful farming business. The proud parents of four sons and a daughter, the Melcers have since sold their farms and become involved in real estate. David Melcer died in 1979 at age 81. The family of the baby that Chaim helped deliver so many years before in the woods, immigrated to Israel. The farmer who hid that family and other families received a deserved award for their courage and righteousness.

I feel so privileged to know many survivors. My questions to them are always the same. As a young child who lost family, friends, and your own innocence, who witnessed the unspeakable, how did you sustain belief in G-d? As an observant Jew, an adult, who confronted human evil face to face, how have you kept your faith?

Chaim and I sit in his office in the Bathgate Complex in Lakewood's Industrial Park. At age 80, he is everyone's fantasy *Yiddishe Zeide* (Jewish grandpa). Still sprite and very active in real estate, he excuses himself several times to answer the phone to talk business. With his sense of humour and aphoristic wit, Chaim is one of the wisest and most humble men I have ever met. I tell him how much I have heard about him and how honored I am that we have finally met. You think I'm smart?" he asks with a twinkle in his eye, "You can live to 100 and die a fool." But I know better. I ask him about the state of Judaism today. "Ah, Jews. Jews are their own worst enemy who need to see that the worst animal can be the human being."

As Chaim puts out coffee and cuts a fresh cheese Danish for us, I delicately approach the question of faith. "I never gave up, but I never believed; I thought it was all a made up story. But I was a child and the more I look back, I knew there was a higher power pulling the strings or I would not have been one of the 10,000 who survived near death. My father and grandfather were strong believers. For me to give up my faith and my legacy would be to disrespect them and the millions who were killed."

As I am about to leave, Chaim hands me three loaves of fresh bakery bread: "Here, please take these home to your family." For a brief moment I am puzzled, but then I understand the profound meaning of this kind gesture. For survivors, bread is the symbol of life; it is fulfilling and nourishing and was the main staple in the ghettos and camps; it was traded, savored, and treasured. Bread also holds religious significance; it was seen as *manna* from heaven which was sent by G-d. Chaim cannot and will not forget: "You cannot appreciate today if you weren't here yesterday," he tells me, "*Zai Gezunt* (Be well)."

Chapter Seventeen

Living with Diversity: Lakewood's Ethnic and Racial Mosaic

What is hateful to you, do not do to your neighbor.
The Talmud

If you want to make peace, you don't talk to your friends. You talk to your enemies.
Moshe Dayan

Today, Lakewood is comprised of several ethnic groups – Jews, Latinos, and blacks. Kosher markets and Hasidic-run stores coexist with the Mexican bodegas and African-Mexican markets peppering the city's main business district on Clifton Avenue between Route 88 West and County Line Road. Day laborers line up at street corners at early dawn, seemingly oblivious to Orthodox men hurrying off to morning prayer services. Later in the day, on Second Street, strains of Latin music harmonize with Hebrew songs emanating from Torah Treasures across the street where, on any given day, dark-hatted men in long coats crowd into the tiny store to browse the shelves lined with leather bound Talmudic and scholarly texts. A few blocks East, gang graffiti decorates storefronts bearing the initials L.M. (La Mugre) and M.S. 13.

But this multi-ethnic town is far from a heterogeneous melting pot. Despite living side by side, Orthodox Jews, African Americans, and Latinos occupy separate and distinct cultural worlds which could have the potential for fueling a climate of mutual suspicion and hostility. It is precisely the climate that sparked the rioting in Brooklyn's Hassidic Crown Heights neighborhood in 1991, when a Jewish driver tragically and accidently killed a young black child and anti-Semitic violence erupted for days. Over the past few decades, proportionately increasing with the town's growth, there have been isolated incidents of bias and hate crimes against the Orthodox population, many of the victims rabbis and students. Bias crimes can take many forms. In 2006, a 20-year-old Orthodox woman was abducted from a parking lot and raped after leaving a gym where she had been working out. Police apprehended the suspect who is still behind bars. In 2007, a man wielding an aluminum baseball bat attacked an Orthodox rabbi walking to synagogue, critically injuring the 53-year-old man.

In 2006, an anti-Semitic internet group of some 75 students at nearby Georgian Court College was immediately disbanded after it was brought to the attention of college administrators by the Jewish Community Relations Committee of the Jewish Federation of Ocean County. The college appropriately reacted with disciplinary action and by mandating sensitivity training classes about the culture, religion, and traditions of the Orthodox community. The college also co-sponsored a standing-room only lecture at the historic Strand Theatre by Nobel Peace prize winner Elie Wiesel, noted proponent of peace and reconciliation who pioneered single-author Holocaust literature based on eyewitness accounts.

According to recently released statistics by the Anti-Defamation League, New Jersey leads the country in anti-Semitic incidents, with the highest numbers occurring in Monmouth, Middlesex and Ocean Counties. Of the 43 incidents reported state-wide, Ocean County had 28, most of them in the once sleepy town of Lakewood. To be sure, before the Orthodox influx and like any inner city, Lakewood had its share of crime, gang-violence, inter and intra-ethnic assaults and homicides. But the township's demographic shift resulting from an exponential growth of the Orthodox population over the past decades added another dimension to existing tensions by establishing a new physical and political stronghold, and stretching already compromised town resources.

There have been allegations that town officials give preferential treatment to the Orthodox majority population. The Attorney General's office has looked into charges that the Lakewood school district's administration and funding of special education programs discriminates against black and Hispanic children by favoring Orthodox students. The US

Department of Housing and Development (HUD) has investigated complaints that Jewish landlords are predisposed to showing preferential treatment to Orthodox tenants at a housing complex that receives local grants.

Adding to the bubbling tension is the charge that members of the Orthodox community hold positions on planning boards, school boards, and the local housing authority. The Orthodox community argues that although they send their children to private schools, they are Lakewood citizens who still pay property and school taxes and, thus, should have proportionate representation on local boards. On a Sunday morning over coffee in Bagel Nosh, Clifton Avenue's popular Orthodox hangout, I asked Lakewood psychotherapist Lauren Roth about the popular myth that the Orthodox do not pay taxes. "Of course we pay taxes," laughs Roth, "just like any other American citizen and Jerseyite. It's the law. In fact, we pay public school taxes and our children attend private schools. We believe that we are obligated to do our share to contribute to the overall good of the community."

Other sources of skepticism and hostility are directed towards the *Vaad*. First is the perceived political power wielded by this Orthodox governing board, a twelve member council of Rabbinical and community leaders who endorse and, by virtue of sheer numbers, impact legislation and election results. Too, is the criticism of the leniency of the *Vaad's* tribunal panel, *Batei Din*; specifically, that there has been a reluctance, on the part of the tribunal, to turn suspected sex criminals and pedophiles over to the authorities, mainly because the tightly knit religious community with roots in Eastern Europe has historically been wary of outside law enforcement and their perceived lack of sensitivity to religious differences. But recent high profile media coverage and the Internet, as well as the concerns of child advocacy groups, therapists, and social workers, and the victims themselves speaking out about child molestation in Lakewood and other Orthodox communities (where, it should be pointed out that sexual crimes are no more prevalent than in other communities), religious leaders, parents, and victims agree that communal sanctions and required therapy are no longer sufficient.

As of late 2009, the community has begun to cultivate a positive relationship with the Prosecutor's Office, discussing mechanisms and processes to report molestation and prosecute perpetrators to the full extent of the law. Penina Glick* a school psychologist, welcomes this breakthrough: "Parents, educators, and religious leaders have to be trained to detect warning signs in children and to also recognize traits of child molesters." Explains Glick: "Torah mandates that if someone poses a danger to society, he must be prosecuted. It's *dinah d'malchusa dinah*, the law of the land, and it is the law of any free and democratic society."

The June, 2009 issue of *The Jewish State* addressed the staggering numbers of anti-Semitic acts in New Jersey. Referring specifically to the New Jersey public schools, Etzion Neuer, regional director of the ADL's New Jersey region, admits that "there are ingrained stereotypes that children are acting out on," but he warns that "We need to avoid the attitude of 'oh well, it's always going to be around.'" To combat such incidents, Neuer encourages vigilance as well as anti-bias and diversity programs in schools, but reminds people that it is up to the parents to reinforce those values in the home. Senator Robert Singer, who has also served as Lakewood's mayor, pointed out that "When a community is growing by leaps and bounds as we are, there is a certain amount of displacement of certain people…[and]… people tend to misguide their anger." Indeed, as Singer asserts, acrimonious sentiments and distrust seem inevitable whenever a locale experiences significant demographic changes that precipitate residents seeing their familiar world being increasingly populated by "Other," in this case, Orthodox Jews who establish their own enclave.

The fact is that the de facto self-segregation is not intended as such; rather, it is the by-product of lifestyle practices intended to preserve tradition and religious standards. One might argue that few other demographic groups move into communities en masse with the intent to create and patronize their own schools, places of worship, eateries and stores. And, as discussed in Chapter 7, in which they fulfill the *mitzvah* of kindness and service to the entire community.

In a case several years ago that grabbed national headlines, an Orthodox man assaulted a young black high school student who was taking a short cut across private property and whom the older man perceived as a threat. There were allegations of racial epithets. The NAACP charged town officials with leniency in handling the case against the Orthodox man. The community responded, calling the head of the NAACP anti-Semitic, arguing that the victim in question had initiated the confrontation. As reported in an article in the *Ocean County Observer* in 2007, the entire Lakewood community was warned by the Township Committee that unless the various ethnic groups in Lakewood learned tolerance and respect, the "simmering hatred may soon boil over into the streets." U.S. Rep. John Adler (D-3) cautioned that hate and anti-Semitism will not be tolerated in his state and that those who commit such horrific acts will be "tracked down and held accountable for their actions."

Thanks to the cohesive efforts of community and religious leaders in concert with the Lakewood police force, that tragic scenario did not happen. Robert Lawson has been Lakewood's Chief of Police since 2006, bringing to that office three decades of decorated service as a police officer. Lawson has had phenomenal success in fostering community relations and lowering incidents of criminal activity. "Bias crimes," he tells me, "erode the very fabric of the community. The Lakewood police take these situations seriously and investigate them thoroughly." And when it comes to punishing those who commit a bias crime, Lawson admits he takes "a conservative approach," immediately and formally reporting incidents to the Department of Criminal Justice. "For a long time," he recalls, "there were teens from other towns who would come to Lakewood on *Shabbos* just to throw eggs at the Orthodox and make a sport out of grabbing their *shtreimel* hats. We were able to apprehend them and prosecute them to the full extent of the law." Says Lawson: "I wanted to send a clear message that no one comes to *my* town and attacks *my* citizens."

One of the proactive measures that Lawson spearheaded was the installation of surveillance cameras at key areas, including the streets surrounding Beth Medrash Govoha and the Clifton Avenue business district, where there was a spiking number of criminal assaults, robberies, gang activity, and vandalism. Beth Medrash Govoha is a susceptible crime area because the students often walk the streets after late night Torah study. With funding from Homeland Security, there are plans to install more cameras throughout Lakewood. Monitoring neighborhoods prone to crime will enable quicker identification, assessment and response to incidents; hopefully preventing them.

In 2008, Lawson was one of fifteen delegates, including senior law enforcement officials, FBI, and homeland security personnel to be invited to Israel. Sponsored by the Anti-Defamation League, the weeklong visit included a first- hand look at counter-terrorism tactics and strategies, meetings with the highest levels of Israel's police and security forces, and visits to the bordering Syria and Lebanon. The seminars included a broad range of topics including preventing and responding to terrorist attacks, bomb disposal, intercepting suicide bombers, working with the media, increasing public awareness and, equally important, understanding the need for opening lines of communication and sharing of information. Lawson did some sightseeing as well. He visited Nazareth, The Dead Sea, Masada, The Holocaust Museum at Yad Vashem, and the Golan Heights. Commenting on his visit to the famous security wall, Lawson said "While it was uncomfortable and strange to go about my day as an unarmed civilian when I am so used to being armed, I got used to it quickly, especially when surrounded by police and soldiers at all times."

Aware of the vulnerability of Lakewood in a post 9-11 world, Lawson has developed and sustained mutually respectful professional relationships, many of which have evolved into personal friendships, with leaders of the three groups that make up Lakewood's ethnic mosaic. One of these friendships is with Rabbi Aaron Kotler. Lawson has been vigilant in working closely with BMG to ensure the safety of students, including the installation of special shatter resistant glass windows and heavy decorative concrete devices in front of the entrance to prevent cars from penetrating the building.

Chief Lawson and Rabbi Kotler also collaborated to alleviate long held community feelings that some Orthodox landlords do not rent to non-Jews, and that those who do fail to vet their tenants carefully enough, which results in increasing burglaries and assaults from renters with criminal records. More than a dozen leading rabbis signed and circulated a letter in Hebrew, censuring Jewish landlords for leasing to and enabling "people not of the same values." To correct the record that the Orthodox rental practices are biased, Rabbi Kotler points to the history of Lakewood as proof that there is no discrimination, and that Jews do rent to a large population of non-Jews. "The outcry in our community," the rabbi made clear, "was not about renting to non-Jews; it was about the impact on daily life from criminals and gangs."

The Lakewood police department has worked with Orthodox first response emergency teams, including coordinating their certification by the Office of Emergency Management. They were also instrumental in working with the community to establish the Lakewood Citizen's Security Watch (LCSW) comprised of blacks, Latinos, and Jews who drive in pairs to patrol the streets. Equipped with IDs and uniform vests, they look out for, and alert the police to, any suspicious activity. Chief Lawson was adamant, for legal and safety reasons, that the LCSW volunteers neither confront nor intervene in any suspicious activity. Since its inception, the LCSW has contributed to the apprehension and arrest of burglars and other perpetrators.

To foster trust and understanding among the three groups that comprise Lakewood's ethnic mosaic, a grassroots group, Let's Talk, was formed in 2005. The committee, currently being regrouped, includes a cross cultural representation of residents and religious and civic leaders. From matters of crime, housing, homelessness, school bussing, traffic, cultural conflicts, to community and police relations, the group works as a collaborative team, engaging in open dialogue to air issues and foster a sense of community with a common purpose. The Ocean County Prosecutor's Office and the Ocean County Human Relations Commission have developed sensitivity training programs for teachers, civic leaders, and the police department, as well as educational programs, such as *Stopping the Hate* to teach tolerance and respect.

But divisiveness in Lakewood is not limited to inter-cultural conflicts. In my conversations over the past two years with Jews of all denominations, in Lakewood as well as the surrounding towns of Jackson, Howell, and Toms River, probably the most unsettling comments to me were those from non-Orthodox Jews. Disturbingly similar to the Woodenton scenario, they denigrate the Orthodox whom they insist are fanatical. The common allegations are that the Orthodox are "taking over," "hopelessly isolated," and that they delegitimize and "despise the non-Orthodox."

Not only are these claims without merit; they are insidious and polarizing statements that foster the same atmosphere of hatred of one Jew for another that many sages say caused the destruction of the Temples in Jerusalem and led to the dispersion of the Jews. Have we already forgotten that the Nazis did not care whether their Jewish victims were secular, Orthodox, Conservative, Reform, Reconstructionist, or Zionists? They only saw Jews. The idea that Orthodox Jews do not view the non-Orthodox as Jewish has been repeated so often it has become a false fact. Yet no Orthodox organization or leader has ever suggested that *Halakhak* status as a Jew is a function of one's level of belief or observance. Until the last 200 years, Jews maintained a remarkable degree of unity despite their dispersion over the globe without a land of their own. This unity was possible by their common law.

In 2006, Lakewood businessman Ben Heinemann and Reisa Sweet, a retired teacher who now develops anti-bias educational workshops for schools and teachers, worked in tandem with the Jewish Federation's Community Relations Council, to launch Schmooze, a program that encourages dialogue between Jews of diverse backgrounds and varying levels of religious commitment to promote unity and understanding. Meetings are held several times a year at the Strand Theatre.

It is speculated that as the population of Lakewood continues to grow – and those projected numbers are staggering – so will divisions and hostilities. Not if Chief Lawson has anything to say about it. "Considering the size and diversity of the township, he argues, "both serious and minor crimes are on a downswing and impressively low in comparison to other cities." For centuries, "in the best of times and worst of times," as Dickens said, Lakewood has been able to sustain and reinvent itself against all odds. Chief Robert Lawson is confident that this historic town with its rich and vibrant history will continue to thrive as a home to people of all beliefs and backgrounds who can enjoy a fruitful and safe life: "We have our problems as do other major cities where there are different ethnic cohorts, but despite isolated bias incidents, people here really do get along very well. They care about their neighbors and reach out to them in times of need. Lakewood's a wonderful family oriented community and, slowly but surely, its residents are recognizing that everyone must respect each other's differences and live together in peace."

Most of the Lakewood community agrees that life has gotten a lot better in their hometown. And they attribute the improving climate to outreach programs and to the work of the police department. "Having residents, police, and town leaders talking openly and resolving problems early is helping to avoid potentially explosive situations," says Rosa, a Latino shop owner in Lakewood. "It's creating a much needed sense of neighborhood. And as they say, respect begets respect. The truth is that most people, no matter what color they are or what higher power they believe in, just want to be happy and make a good life for their family. You just have to live and let live."

CHAPTER EIGHTEEN

And Speaking of Melting Pots, or, Eat Something, Mamala

Worries go down easier with soup
Jewish Proverb

For generations of Jewish cooking – going back to Sarah, Rebecca, and Rachel – the master chef has always been the mistress, *balabusta,* of her particular tent: mom and grandma. Jewish cuisine, though decidedly ethnic, never gets monotonous; it is thoroughly international in flavor, truly a melting pot. Since the kettles of the Hebrews, Jewish cooking has simmered in every country of the world since the Diaspora. It has tasted the spices of Italy, the herbs of the Slavic countries, the tender lamb of Israel, and the potatoes of Ireland. My father used to tell me that he could still recall, as a young boy on the Lower East Side, the cooking aromas wafting out from beneath apartment doors in the hallways of tenement houses on his way home from school.

Food has always been important to the Jewish family. Not just in and of itself, but as a gift from G-d. It plays a symbolic role throughout the year at religious holidays, life cycle events, festivals, and *simchas* (joyous celebrations). During mourning, it is customary to have chick peas or lentils. Rosh Hashana is celebrated with dipping bread in sweet honey in hopes of a sweet new year. On *Shabbat*, since cooking is prohibited, cholent is the ideal meal because it takes 8-12 hours to cook and combines beans, meat, potatoes, onions, and whatever else each chef adds to make it the traditional family favorite. *Hamantaschen*, named after the evil Haman and shaped in the form of his three cornered hat, is the delicious Purim pastry filled with fruits and nuts. On Shavout, we eat dairy dishes such as blintzes, because after the Jews witnessed the revelation at Sinai, they were too hungry to take time to slaughter an animal and prepare it ritually. Sukkot is a time to enjoy fruits and vegetables. Chicken soup, of course, is the elixir for anything from the common cold to a broken heart. In the twelfth century, Jewish scholar and physician Moses Maimonides wrote that chicken soup "has virtue in rectifying corrupted humours" and is particularly effective for convalescence and asthma.

Observant Jews begin and end each meal with a blessing for the miracle of food which should not be taken for granted. So, here is a sampling of a few traditional foods from Lakewood's families (and Bubbie Sarah's) to yours. And, as any *Yiddishe* mama will tell you, "Enjoy, enjoy."

Mother's Stuffed Cabbage

Ingredients: Large head of cabbage
2 tablespoons fat
2 onions sliced
3 cups canned tomatoes
3 teaspoons salt
½ teaspoon pepper
beef bones
1 pound of ground beef
3 tablespoons uncooked rice
4 tablespoons grated onions
1 egg
3 tablespoons of cold water,
3 tablespoons of honey
¼ cup of lemon juice
¼ cup of seedless raisins.

Preparation: Pour boiling water over the cabbage to cover and let soak for 15 minutes. Remove 12 leaves carefully. If leaves are small, use 18. Heat the fat in a deep heavy saucepan.
Lightly brown the onions. Add tomatoes, half of the salt and pepper, and all the bones. Cook over low heat for 30 minutes. Mix together the beef, rice, grated onion, egg, and water. Place some of the meat mixture on each cabbage leaf. Tuck in the sides and roll up carefully. Add to the sauce.

Cover and cook over a low heat 1 ½ hours.
Add the honey, lemon juice, and raisins.
Cook ½ hour longer.

Malchie's Flanken Soup

Ingredients: 3 pounds plate flank
beef bones
3 ½ quarts water
1 onion
1 tablespoon salt
soup greens
1 bay leaf
¼ teaspoon peppercorns.

Preparation: Combine the beef, bones, and water in a deep saucepan.
Bring to boil and skim.
Add the onion, salt, soup greens, bay leaf, and peppercorns.
Cover loosely and cook over low heat 2 hours or until meat is tender. Remove beef and strain the soup.
Makes about 2 ½ quarts of soup.
Serve the beef with horseradish.

Alana's Noodle Kugel

Ingredients: 3 eggs
4 tablespoons brown sugar
¼ teaspoon nutmeg
4 cups cooked broad noodles
½ cup seedless white raisins
½ cup sliced blanched almonds
1 tablespoon lemon juice
4 tablespoons chicken fat
2 tablespoons bread crumbs.

Preparation: Beat the eggs and brown sugar until fluffy.
Add nutmeg, noodles, raisins, almonds, lemon juice, and fat.
Turn into a well-greased ring mold or baking dish. Sprinkle with bread crumbs.
Bake in 375 degree oven 50 minutes or until browned.
Can be served as side dish or as a dessert with fruit sauce.

Gittel's Sweet Potato and Prune Tzimmes

A tzimmus means fuss or excitement. But tzimmes dishes are easy to prepare and are usually served as a main course in place of green vegetables. It is almost any combination of meat or vegetables or fruits.

Ingredients:
  1 ½ pounds of prunes
  3 cups boiling water
  2 tablespoons fat
  3 pounds brisket
  2 onions, diced
  1 ½ teaspoons salt
  ¼ teaspoon pepper
  3 sweet potatoes, peeled and quartered
  ½ cup honey
  2 cloves
  ½ teaspoon cinnamon.

Preparation:
  Wash prunes and let soak in boiling water ½ hour.
  Melt fat in Dutch oven.
  Cut the beef in 6 or 8 pieces and brown with the onions.
  Sprinkle with the salt and pepper.
  Cover and cook over low heat one hour.
  Add the undrained prunes, sweet potatoes, honey, cloves, and cinnamon.
  Replace cover loosely and cook over low heat two hours.

The Rebbitzen's Traditional Cholent (meat)

Ingredients:
  3 lbs. red Bliss potatoes
  1/2 lb. dried beans (lima, navy, great northern, or a mix)
  1-1/2 lbs. lean flanken, cut in cubes
  1/8-1/4 cup vegetable oil
  3 onions
  2 tbsp. flour
  1 tsp. salt, pepper to taste
  2-3 cloves garlic, crushed
  1/4 tsp. paprika
  1 small can tomato paste (optional)
  4 quarts water

Preparation: Place the meat, water, salt, onions and garlic in a large Dutch Oven. Bring to a boil. Skim the foam off the top and add the beans and other ingredients except the potatoes.
Cook for one hour (on top of stove) adjusting seasoning and adding water if necessary.
Add the cut potatoes and cook another one to two hours.
Cover and place in an oven set at 180 degrees.
This can be kept in the oven at 180 degrees overnight. Or place on a blech and keep covered.
Check again in the morning and serve at *Shabbat* lunch.
Refrigerate after serving.
You may add different spices such as chili powder or cumin, or use chicken or turkey pieces instead of meat.

Leah's Chicken Giblet Fricassee

Ingredients:
2 pounds mixed giblets
4 tablespoons chicken fat
1 cup diced onions
2 tablespoons flour
4 cups boiling water
3 tablespoons salt
½ teaspoon pepper
½ teaspoon garlic powder
¾ pound ground beef,
2 tablespoons cold water
¾ cup raw rice.

Preparation: Buy necks, gizzards, livers and wings.
Wash thoroughly. Heat chicken fat in saucepan and brown the onions in it. Add giblets and let them brown for 5 minutes. Sprinkle with flour and add boiling water, 2 tablespoons salt, ¼ teaspoon pepper and ¼ teaspoon garlic powder. Cover and cook over low heat one hour.
Mix beef, cold water, and remaining salt, pepper, and garlic powder together. Shape into balls and add to the giblets with the rice. Cook 20 minutes.

Nana Rose's Hanukah Potato Latkes

Ingredients:
4 medium Idaho potatoes
6 tablespoons cooking oil
2 tablespoons matzoh meal
3 eggs beaten
2 tablespoons Kosher salt
1 teaspoon coarse black pepper.

Preparation:
Fill large bowl with cold water.
Peel potatoes, immediately placing each one in water to prevent browning.
Heat oil in large skillet.
Cut potatoes into quarters and grate, (or use a post-mom food processor) to make thin strips.
Transfer to large bowl.
Add eggs, matzoh meal, pepper and salt. Mix.
Drop as many spoonfuls of mixture into the hot pan without crowding as they expand and can become soggy.
Use back of spoon to pat down and flatten each latke.
Fry 3-4 minutes on each side until golden brown and the edges are crispy.
Blot with paper towel.
Serve with sour cream or apple sauce.

Bubbie Sarah's Quick** Chicken Soup

Ingredients:
Celery and carrots cut up
1 onion chopped
2 cloves garlic minced
olive oil
7 cups chicken stock, chicken pieces (preferably breasts) cooked and cut into bite sized pieces
package of noodles
salt, pepper, rosemary to taste.

Preparation:
Heat oil and sauté carrots, celery, onion and garlic (do not burn).
Add seasonings.
Add chicken stock and simmer for 15 minutes.

Add cooked chicken and cook another 15 minutes.
Add noodles.

**So maybe it's not the traditional "Jewish Penicillin" that required the whole chicken and simmered all day on the stove, but Bubbie was not one to cook for hours and, like most Yiddishe mamas, wouldn't commit to specific measurements. "A pinch of salt, a pinch of pepper." But... in a pinch, when you're under the covers sneezing and sniffling, it sure smells and tastes good!

Afterword

In everyone's life, at some time, our inner fire goes out. It is then burst into flame by an encounter with another human being. We should all be thankful for those people who rekindle the human spirit.
Albert Schweitzer

Light is a powerful pervasive force throughout the history and customs of Judaism. From G-d's first utterance in Genesis, *Let there be light* has become the overarching definitive metaphor for G-d's presence and Jewish understanding of all reality, the path to Divine light and to the best in ourselves. Amid darkness, we kindle the *Shabbat* and *Havdalah* candles and pray for a *shalom bayit*, a peaceful home. The menorah lights symbolize freedom and independence, as well as a spiritual light that enables us to overcome obstacles. Theodore Herzl once said that the task of each of us is to kindle light against darkness. In the Book of Isaiah, we are told that *Israel will be the light unto nations*. The concept of *Tikkun Olam*, of repairing the world, refers to the energy of G-d's light shattering the vessel that contained it and scattering countless shards of sparks that spread throughout the universe. Too, most of the major trends in Jewish history, such as the eighteenth century Haskalah movement, were enlightenments, which opened up eyes to new knowledge and understanding.

There is a powerful passage that appears near the end of Deuteronomy when Moses presents the Children of Israel with his farewell speech: "And not until this day has G-d given you the heart to understand, the eyes to see, and the ears to hear. I led you through the wilderness for forty years." At the end of forty years, as we know, Moses presented the Israelites with the Torah. Today, many of us float aimlessly through our own desert, a secular world of materialism, consumerism, and superficiality.

Afterword

My travels through the Orthodox world have taken me on a personal path towards enlightenment; not only about Orthodoxy, but about myself. Remember Bekkah, who initially questioned the possibility of this book? After reading the manuscript, she asked me: "So? What? You're becoming *Frum*?" Bekkah was never one to mince words. "Of course not," I curtly reply, "but I have been drawn back to Judaism and to Israel in a new and infinitely more spiritual way."

Growing up, I outwardly followed the dictates of custom and prayer, never really experiencing internal joy or religious intimacy with G-d. When you greet an Orthodox woman on the street and inquire as to how she is, she will inevitably reply, "*Baruch Hashem* (Thank G-d), very well." The Orthodox are acutely conscious of, and inspired by, G-d's Holy presence and of the G-dliness that permeates our world in the everyday, making all good things possible.

Admittedly, it has been many years since I regularly observed *Shabbat*. Tonight, eighteen minutes before the sun sets, I carefully place Bubbie Sarah's silver candlesticks and Zeide's silver goblet on my mother's white *Shabbat* tablecloth. I feel an inner light and powerful connection of my past with the present; of timelessness and eternity. I think of my mother and Bubbie, and all those women before them, welcoming the Sabbath into their homes. And as I kindle each candle, the darkness of the day's problems recedes, exiled by the peaceful glow of the flames, a gift from heaven that illuminates the world. All that is good, all that is Holy is symbolized - indeed realized - in those flickering lights. I feel spiritually replenished, at one with my family, my history, my faith, and my G-d.

The Proverbs tell us that a *mitzvah*, a good deed, is flame; the Torah, light. Over the past year, I have been re-reading the *Torah Chumush* narrative on a deeper and more profound level than before. Not just as a history book, an arcane text of the ancient world; but engaging with it more creatively and personally. Like the warm shimmering glow of the *Shabbat* candles, we too can be a light in the darkness by actively engaging with the true essence of Judaism, which is the essence of ourselves; each of us unique in how we live as a Jew, but ultimately as one soul radiating into many bodies, each ray shining forth on a unique mission.

CHAI TIMES TWO PLUS FIVE: A TEACHING GUIDE FOR TOLERANCE AND UNDERSTANDING

Education merely concerned with the transmission of information is doomed to failure. It must serve the greater and more noble purpose of cultivating the student's moral character.
Rabbi Menachem Schneerson

The following discussion prompts and projects can be used as educational tools for promoting understanding, tolerance, and respect for other cultural, religious and ethnic groups.

Identify one (or two, three, etc.) major religions represented in the United States and research the history and fundamental beliefs of these religions.

What myths and misperceptions do people hold about other ethnic or religious groups and what can be done to debunk them?

Read the Ten Commandments from the *Bible*. Debate and discuss the importance today of the moral and ethical code of behavior.

Do you think that human beings are innately wired to act kindly? Or is kindness a quality that needs to be taught (nature versus nurture)?

Three qualities define the Torah-observant Jews. They are compassion, modesty, and performing acts of kindness. Which of these need more attention in our lives today?

Why is the importance of community stressed in Judaism to the extent that it is? How important is community in your own life?

What are some obstacles you might face turning an enemy into a friend?

What would you consider some of the strengths and weaknesses of your upbringing? If the influence of home environment exerts such a strong influence on the rest of our lives, how can a person rise above the weaknesses he or she experienced in his earlier years?

We all know people who are perfectly content living a single lifestyle. Why do the rabbis put strong emphasis on sharing a life with a spouse? What emphasis do you put on it?

The Talmudic rabbis stress self-reliance as a virtue. How can we help to make others self-reliant?

What are some ways we can teach our cultural values to our children and grandchildren so that they are interested in and prepared to pass down the same values to their children and grandchildren?

The Talmud suggests that many people follow ritualistic details of their culture, yet may have a shallow understanding of the religious, intellectual, or historical basis for such rituals. Discuss examples from your own experiences.

The Nazi regime used political propaganda to rally support for Hitler's Third Reich. How is such propaganda used in today's society?

Research the political, economic, and social climate and conditions in pre-Nazi Germany and how it led to growing anti-Semitism. What were the stages that led to the annihilation of six million Jews?

What is hate speech? Research Adolf Hitler's hate speech. What words and arguments did he use to inflame anti-Semitism? Are there any political figures today who engage in hate speech against Jews or any other ethnic or religious group? What is being done, if anything, to stop it?

What symptoms of intolerance towards a specific group have you observed or experienced? Describe the circumstances and how you felt.

What do you think is the most serious abuse of human rights in the world today? What, if anything, is being done to end it?

Research and discuss the prevalence of and reason for hate and extremist speech on the Internet. What can be done to stop it?

Define the term "freedom of Speech" as it is explained in the US Constitution. Is it used to allow and excuse extremist speech? How do you relate it to hate speech that is prevalent on the Internet? Should anyone be able to say what they want about another ethnic, national, or religious group?

What similarities and differences do the religions of Christianity and Judaism share? The religions of Judaism and Islam?

Tradition is a part of the Jewish religion and culture. What traditions are associated with your ethnic or religious identity? Are they important to you and why?

How do people with dual cultural identities (Jewish-American, Irish-American, Italian-American, Hispanic-American) assimilate into American society while maintaining their heritage ? Is this as important to second and third generation Americans as it was for the immigrant generation?

Research problems that immigrants who came to America in the late 19th and early 20th century experienced in terms of acceptance, assimilation, and discrimination. How did they cope with the problems of living in a new land?

Write about a particular custom of your ethnic, religious, or national background. What is its significance? Is it important to you? Why or why not? What do you think is the importance of traditions in our life?

Research the issue of separation of church and state in terms of religious education in public schools. Should prayer be required? Should the words, "under G-d" be left out of the Pledge of Allegiance? Why or why not?

Should members of religious groups who attend public schools be allowed to engage in prayer and other required rituals in the school?

Jewish holidays are generally associated with historical or religious events. What other cultures have such holidays?

Consider your particular faith's tolerance towards other religions and share your feelings about the responsibility of one religion to others.

Anti-Semitism is a unique form of hatred that has endured for centuries and that is still very much alive. It has been studied by historians, sociologists, psychologists, economists, and theologians. How does each group explain it? How would you attempt to explain it? Will it ever be eliminated?

Is it possible to be an American and also maintain your ancestral heritage and religious beliefs? Do they conflict? What is the conflict of the Orthodox? Is assimilation good or bad?

Research the meanings and significance of dating and marriage customs in another culture.

Research ethnic foods and dietary laws from another culture and their importance to that culture.

Research the cultural importance of music to Judaism or another ethnic group.

What is the importance of one's cultural or national language? Should English be the only accepted language in public schools in America?

Respond to the following statement: "It's not too late to do something about the atrocities today."

Research incidents of hate crimes today. What are the similarities among the groups of individuals who commit these crimes? Who do they target? How are they similar to or different from the Nazis? What kind of actions can we take to counter these crimes? How do you answer revisionists who deny that the Holocaust ever happened?

Examine and discuss one or more of the Talmudic sayings quoted in this book and apply it to your own life.

How does treating animals well foster respect for all living creatures?

Martin Buber, the Israeli philosopher, maintains that the way to approach the Divine is through "becoming human." What does he mean by this and are there other ways?

What is your position on inter-faith dating and marriages? What are some pros and cons?

Research and conduct interviews with your or other families within your ancestral heritage. What contributions has that group made to America?

Discuss the following statement by Professor Yehuda Bauer: *Events happen because they are possible. If they were possible once, they are possible again. In that sense the Holocaust is not unique, but a warning for the future.*

From: *Is the Holocaust Unique:*

Perspectives on Comparative Genocide in The Holocaust

Historical Perspective, *1978*

A Bissell Glossary (A Little Glossary)

Aliya(h): Literally means " ascent" used to describe the honor of being called up to the bimah to read a portion from Torah. It also is generally translated as "immigration," moving from the Diaspora to settle in the Land of Israel.

Amidah: From the Heb. "standing," refers to the central prayer of Jewish service, recited while standing in silent devotion.

Ashkenazi Jews: Jews who lived in France, Germany, Eastern Europe.

Balabusta: Literally, the mistress of the house.

Bar Mitzvah: Upon reaching the age of thirteen, a boy becomes a "son of the commandment," usually accompanied by a religious ceremony and celebration.

Bat Mitzvah: Upon reaching the age of twelve, a girl becomes a "daughter of the commandment"

Bashert: Destined to be. "Leah and Ari are a perfect couple; they are bashert."

Beit/Batei Din: Jewish court of law. In ancient times, the beit din was made up of rabbis who arbitrated disputes between Jews. Today, a beit din rules on religious and ethical matters.

Bentsch: To recite a blessing; usually refers to the blessing after meals.

Blech: Aluminum sheet placed over gas or electric fire to warm food since Torah prohibits lighting a fire on the Sabbath.

Brucha: Prayer or blessing.

Bubbie, Bubbeh, or Bubbe: Grandmother.

Challah: A piece of dough that is removed and burned before forming the dough into loaves. In contemporary times, refers to the Shabbos bread itself.

Chaver: Study partner in a yeshiva.

Chazzan: Cantor in the synagogue.

Cheder: Hebrew elementary school.

Chuppah: Canopy under which a couple is wed.

Chumash/Humash: The Bible or Pentateuch; Five Books of Moses.

Daven: To pray.
Devekut: Uninterrupted devotion to G-d.
Diaspora: Sixth century term originally meaning the expulsion of Jews from Palestine; through the ages, term was used to mean Jews forced to leave their homeland. Today, it also refers to those who reside outside of the State of Israel.
Eretz Yisrael: Land of Israel; the Promised Land.
Gemara: Part of Talmud containing 300 years of rabbinical legal and ethical commentaries on *Mishna*. Together with *Mishna*, comprises the Talmud.
Get: Jewish document of divorce.
Halakhah: The religious laws that Jews are obligated to follow.
Havdalah: Cermony marking the end of the Sabbath on Saturday evening.
Hashem: G-d.
Hesed (chesed): Kindness.
Heder (cheder): Traditional elementary school teaching Judaism and the Hebrew language.
Hasdism (Chasidism): Orthodox sect founded in 18th century Europe by the Ba'al Shem Tov.
Haskalah: The Jewish Enlightenment movement of the 18th century.
Hebrew: The language of the Torah and in which prayers are recited. Modern Hebrew is the official language of Israel.
Kaballah: Jewish mystical and spiritual traditions.
Kaddish: Ancient prayer said by Jewish mourners.
Kasher: To make kosher.
Kashrut: Dietary laws; foods that adhere to laws of kashrut are deemed kosher.
Ketubah: Marriage contract detailing a husband's obligations to his wife.
Kiddush: Prayer recited over wine or grape juice.
Kippah: head covering worn by religious Jewish men.
Kosher: Food prepared according to Jewish dietary laws.
Ladino: Judeo-Spanish language of the Sephardic Jews.
Messiah: Moshiach (Heb. for "anointed") is the messianic king who will usher in the Messianic Age by ending the world's evil and commencing years of justice and peace.
Mezuzah: Passages from scripture enclosed in a case which is affixed to doorposts of Jewish homes and of rooms in the house.
Midrash/Medrash: Record of oral traditions interpreting the Torah.

Minchah: Afternoon service.

Minyan: Literally means "number" and refers to the quorum necessary for congregational worship and other religious ceremonies. Traditionally composed of 10 adult males, 13 years of age or older.

Mishna: Oral Torah. Section of Talmud that contains rabbinical commentaries handed down, beginning with Moses, from generation to generation.

Mitzvah (pl. mitzvot): commandments; commonly used to mean a good deed.

Mohel: Religious person trained in performing ritual circumcision.

Neshama: The soul; the aspect of an individual that is spiritual and immortal.

Oral Torah: Known also as Oral Law, refers to Jewish teachings and elucidations about the written Torah handed down by word of mouth through the second century CE.

Parsha/Parashah: Weekly portion of the Torah reading.

Patriarchs: Abraham, Isaac, and Jacob.

Phylacteries: See Tefillin.

Rabbi: Heb. For "Master." Authoritative ordained teacher in Judaism; legal and spiritual leader.

Rav: A title of reverence for a great rabbi.

Rebbe: Teacher of religious studies, usually associated with Hasidic sects.

Rosh Yeshiva: Dean or head of a yeshiva.

Schmooze: To talk casually and in a friendly way.

Kaballah: Jewish mystical and spiritual traditions.

Sefer: Book.

Sefer Torah: The actual parchment Torah scroll.

Shabbat: The Sabbath, a day of rest, prayer, and study.

Shabbos: Yiddish pronunciation of *Shabbat*.

Shacharis: The morning service.

Shalom Bay'it: A peaceful home.

Sheitel: Wig worn by married Orthodox women.

Shema: Daily prayer expressing faith in G-d.

Shidduch: Matchmaking.

Shadchen: Marriage broker.

Shtiebel: Small shul, usually in a home.

Shuckle: To sway back and forth during prayer.

Shul: Orthodox term for house of worship.

Siddur: A prayer book.
Simcha: Joyous occasion.
Sofer: A scribe.
Tallis/Tallit: Prayer shawl.
Talmud: 63 volume collection of Jewish Oral Law interpreting the Torah; consists of *Mishna* and *Gemara*.
Talmud Torah: Afternoon Hebrew school
Tanach: Acronym of Torah.
Tefillin: Also called Phylacteries. Pair of small black leather boxes that contain pieces of parchment on which passages from Torah are inscribed.
Tikkun Olam: The philosophy of making the world better through making ourselves better. To perfect the world under G-d's sovereignty.
Torah: Collective sacred texts of Judaism. Also refers to the Five Books of Moses.
Tzadik: Righteous person.
Tzedakah: Donating money for charity.
Tznius: Codes of modesty, usually referring to women's dress and behavior.
Upsherin: Ritual where a three year old boy receives his first haircut.
Written Torah: The Hebrew Bible.
Yiddish: International vernacular of Ashkenazi Jews. It is a hybrid of Old German, Hebrew, and Slavic languages and uses Hebrew script.
Yiddishkeit, Yiddishkayt: Jewishness or a Jewish way of life.
Yeshiva: Jewish school or seminary of higher learning where students study Torah, Talmud, and other religious texts.
Yeshiva Bochur: Young male yeshiva student.
Yeshiva Gedola: Advanced yeshiva.
Zeide: Grandfather.
Zionism: Worldwide political movement established by Theodor Herzl that worked toward the establishment of a Jewish Homeland.

Sources Consulted and Suggested Readings

_____. **The Art Scroll Weekday Minchah Maariv.** Rabbi Nosson Scherman, trans. Brooklyn, NY: Mesorah Publications Ltd., 1986.

_____.**Chumash: The Torah, Haftoras, and Five Megillos with Commentary Anthologized from Rabbinic Writings.** Rabbi Nosson Scherman, trans. Brooklyn, NY: Mesorah Publications, Ltd., 2002.

_____. **The NCSY Bencher: A Book of Prayer and Song.** NY: National Conference of Synagogue Youth (Orthodox Union), 1993.

_____. **Ohel Women's Siddur: Korban Minchah.** Dovid Weinberger, ed. Brooklyn, NY: Mesorah Publications, Ltd, 2003.

_____. **The Tanakh: The Hebrew Bible.** Philadelphia: Jewish Publication Society, 1982.

_____. **The Torah: The Five Books of Moses.** Standard Edition. Philadelphia: Jewish Publication Society of America, 1992.

_____. **JPS Torah Commentary Series: Five Volumes.** Philadelphia: Jewish Publication Society of America, 1986.

_____. **Zohar: Annotated and Explained.** Tr. Daniel C. Matt. VT: Skylight Paths Publishing.2007.

Afterlife. Encyclopaedia Judaica. Ed. Michael Berenbaum and Fred Skolnik. Vol. 1. 2nd ed. Detroit: Macmillan Reference USA, 2007. 441-442

Abrahams, Israel, ed. **Hebrew Ethical Wills. Bi Lingual Edition: Hebrew and English.** Philadelphia: Jewish Publication Society of America, 2006.

Adams, Abigail and John. **Letters of John and Abigail Adams.** F. Shuffleton, ed. NY: Penguin Group, 2003.

Ben-Sasson, H., ed. **A History of the Jewish People.** MA: Harvard University Press, 1969.

Bunim, Amos. **Fire in his Soul! Irving Bunim 1901-1980: The Man and His Impact on American Orthodox Jewry. Israel:** Feldheim Publishers, 1989.

Cardoza, Nathan T. **The Written and Oral Torah: A Comprehensive Introduction.** NY: Rowan and Littlefield, 2004.

Chametsky, Jules, Fletcher, J. Flanzbaum, K. Hellerstein, eds. **Jewish American Literature.** NY: W.W. Norton & Company, 2001.

Cohon, Beryl David. **Judaism in Theory and Practice.** FL: Bloch Publishing Co., 1948.

Dershowitz, Rabbi Yitzchok. **The Legacy of Maran Rav Aharon Kotler.** Israel: Feldheim Publishers, 2005.

Dimont, Max J. **Jews, God, and History.** NY: Penguin Group, 2004.

Diner, Hasia. **The Jews of the United States 1654-2000.** CA: University Cal. Press, 2006.

Donin, Hayim Halevy. **To Be a Jew: A Guide to Jewish Observation.** Israel: Basic Books, 1991.

Dubrovsky, Gertrude Wishnick. **The Land Was Theirs: Jewish Farmers in the Garden State.** Alabama: University of Alabama Pr., 1992.

Dwork, Deborah and Jobert Jan van Pelt. **Holocaust: A History.** NY: W.W. Norton and Company, Inc., 2001

Feitman, Yaakov. "It Takes a Kollel: How Higher Learning is Transforming American Jewry". **Jewish Action Online: Magazine of the Orthodox Union.** Winter, 2002.

Gilbert, Martin. **The Holocaust: A History of the Jews of Europe during the Second World War.** NY: Henry Holt and Company LLC, 1985.

Heilman, Samuel C. **Sliding to the Right: The Contest for the Future of American Jewish Orthodoxy.** LA: Univ. California Pr., 2006.

Helmreich, William D. **The World of the Yeshiva: An Intimate Portrait of Orthodox Jewry.** New Haven: Yale University Press, 2005.

Hertzberg, Arthur. **The Jews in America: Four Centuries of an Uneasy Encounter.** NY: Columbia University Press, 1998.

Heschel, Abraham Joshua. **Maimonides.** NY: Barnes and Noble, 2009. Reprint of 1935 ed. published by Erich Reiss Verlay, Germany.

Hoffman, Norbert, Joseph Sievers and Philip Cunningham. **The Catholic Church and the Jewish People: Recent Reflections from Rome.** NY: Fordham University Press, 2007.

Holtz, Barry W., ed. **Back to the Sources: Reading the Classic Jewish Texts.** NY: Simon and Schuster, 2006.

Howe, Irving. **World of Our Fathers: The Journey of the Eastern European Jews to America and the Life They Found and Made.** NY: NYU Press, 2005.

Jacobson, Simon. **Towards a Meaningful Life: The Wisdom of Rebbe Menachem Mendel Schneerson.** NY: Harpur Collins, 2004.

Jungreis, Esther. **Women's Lib: A Jewish View.** NY: Hineni Publications, 1973.

Kohut, Alexander, Max Cohen, and Barnett Elzas. **Ethics of the Fathers.** Jerusalem: Koren Publishers, 1920.

Kozelnik, Scott M. **Images of America: Lakewood, N.J.** SC: Arcadia Publishing, 2000.

Lazarus, Emma. **Selected Poems of Emma Lazarus.** J. Hollander, ed. NY: Library of America, 2005.

Levine, Maurice. **Diary of Maurice Levine, 1901-1910.** Courtesy of the Goldstein and Teitelbaum Families. Unpublished.

Maimanides, Moses. **A Guide for Today's Perplexed.** Tr. Kenneth Seeskin. NY: Behrman House , Inc., 1991.

Melcer, Chaim. **Chaim's Journal: The Story of a Survivor.** Narrated by Chaim Melcer to Jason Weiner. Courtesy of Chaim Melcer. Lakewood, NJ, 2000. Unpublished.

Mintz, Jerome R. **Hasidic People: A Place in the New World.** MA: Harvard University Press, 1994.

Nachmanides. **A Maimonides Reader.** A Letter for the Ages: Iggeres Haramban: The Rambam's Ethical Letter with and Anthology of Contemporary Rabbinic Expositions. Avroham Feuer, ed. Brooklyn, NY: Mesorah Publications, Ltd., 1989.Neusner, Jacob. **Talmud: What it is and What it Says.** NY: Rowan and Littlefield Publishers, Inc., 2006.

Peters, Madison C.,ed., **The Wisdom of the Talmud.** Mineola, NY: Dover Publications Inc., 2001.

Raphael, Simcha Paull. **Jewish Views of the Afterlife,** Second Edition. MD: Rowman and Littlefield Publishing Group, 2009.

Roth, Cecil. **World History of the Jewish People.** Israel: Jewish History Publications, 1961 8 vols.

Roth, Philip. "Eli the Fanatic." **Goodbye Columbus and Five Short Stories.** NY: Random House, 1903.

Sacks, Jonathan. **To Heal a Fractured World: The Ethics of Responsibility.** NY: Knopf Doubleday, 2007.

Scholem, Gershon. **Major Trends in Jewish Mysticism.** NY: Schocken Books, 1995.

Seidman, Brian. **Jews and Reincarnation.** Washington Jewish Week, (August 10, 2000).

Scholem, Gershon. **On the Mystical Shape of the Godhead.** Tr. Joachim Neugrosschel, NY: Schocken Books, 1995.

Strassfeld, Michael. **Embracing Judaism as a Spiritual Practice: A Book of Life.** VT: Jewish Lights, 2006.

Telushkin, Rabbi Joseph. **Jewish Literacy: The Most Important Things to Know about the Jewish Religion its People, and its History.** NY: Harpur Collins Pub., 2008.

Vernon, Leonard and Allen Meyers. **Images of America: Jewish South Jersey.** SC: Arcadia Publishing, 2007.

Weissman-Joselit, Jenna. **Wonders of America: Reinventing Jewish Culture 1880-1930.** NY: Hill and Wang, 1994.

Wigoder, Geoffrey, Shmuel Himelstein et al., eds. **The New Encyclopedia of Judaism.** NY: NYU Press, 2002.

Winkler, Gershon. **The Soul of the Matter: A Jewish-Kabbalistic Perspective on the Human Soul Before, During and After Life.** Brooklyn, NY: Judaica Press, 1981.

Winkler, Gershon. **The Soul of the Matter: A Jewish-Kabbalistic Perspective on the Human Soul Before, During, and After Life.** Brooklyn, NY: Judaica Press, 1981.

Wyman, David S. **The Abandonment of the Jews: America and the Holocaust, 1941-1945.** NY: New Press, 2007.

Zinkin, Sarah. "A History of the Congregation Sons of Israel, Lakewood, NJ." **Congregation Sons of Israel, Lakewood, NJ 75th Anniversary. 1982 Souvenir Commemorative Program.** Unpublished.

Personal Interviews

William Goldstein. December 28, 29, 2009. Telephone.

Rabbi Aaron Kotler. June 10, 2009. Lakewood, N.J.

Robert Lawson, Chief of Lakewood Police. August 27, 2009. Lakewood, N.J.

Rabbi Pesach Levovitz. December 13, 2009. Lakewood, N.J.

Chaim Melcer. December 4, 2009. Lakewood, N.J.

Lauren Roth. August 5, 2009. Lakewood, N.J.

Helina Sininsky. February 5, 2009 and January 7, 2010. Lakewood, N.J.

Rabbi Baruch B. Yoffe. January 12, 19, 26, 27, 2010. Lakewood, N.J